BREAD
upon the
Waters

ISBN: 978-1-943929-99-3

Cover and layout design: Kristi Yoder

Second printing: January 2018

Printed in the USA

Published by:
TGS International
P.O. Box 355
Berlin, Ohio 44610 USA
Phone: 330.893.4828
Fax: 330.893.2305
www.tgsinternational.com

TGS001614

BREAD
upon the
Waters

Elizabeth Wagler

Table of Contents

Author's Preface

Everyone likes to read about the exploits of heroes. In reality, few of us are called to be Pauls or Peters. The majority of Christ's followers live out their lives in unrecognized obscurity.

The name of Gertel Wagner never appeared in any international publication, but all those who came in contact with her were blessed by her warmth and hospitality. She poured out her life as a loving mother, faithful in the daily grind of thankless tasks. She often prayed something similar to the Serenity Prayer—for grace to accept circumstances she could not change and for strength to do what she could to bring blessing to those around her. Even when her workload seemed overwhelming, she learned to share food with the hungry and the stranger.

Gertel's trials seemed insurmountable at times, yet she found a way to push through each one with God's help. Few people beyond her family ever knew what all she went through. Simply because of this, her story deserves to be told as a testimony to God's grace and a call to faithfulness in unseen service and generous dispersal of the blessings God has given His children.

Acknowledgments

❧ All praise to God, the great Enabler.

❧ Thanks to the Wagner family: Miss Gertie herself, who reached into her memory to tell me this story; Matt and Glenda Matute, who befriended and encouraged me; Sandra, who presided over the cooking pots and answered questions; Ken and Rosie Kratzer, who acted as liaison between me and the family in Belize.

❧ Thanks to Julie Glick for starting this project and giving me an outline to work with.

❧ Thanks to my husband Glen for encouraging me to write the story and driving me, many times, the three hours to Miss Gertie's house.

❧ Thanks to the editors at TGS for toiling behind the scenes to transform this story into a book.

1

A Summons

The elderly woman's head and shoulders rose jerkily into view as she climbed the flight of wooden stairs leading up to the house on stilts. Inside the house, seven-year-old Gertel[1] stopped sweeping with her grass broom. She straightened to watch her Hispanic neighbor ascend the last of the steps.

Señora Ramona reached the landing and paused in the open doorway, her keen black eyes focusing on the three little girls: Gertel with her broom and her two younger sisters, Marlene and Myrtle, who sat on the floor, their legs spread wide, rubbing the kernels from dry corn cobs. *"Buenos!"*[2] she greeted them.

"Come in," invited Gertel's mother. Muriel Morris was a slender Creole woman with a perpetually worried frown.

"Looks like everybody's busy here." Señora Ramona beamed an approving smile at the girls and maneuvered herself past the canvas mailbag hanging on a nail near the door. Gertel's father, Charles Morris, served as the village postmaster and always kept the mailbag in its place.

Señora Ramona lowered herself onto the stool Muriel pushed toward her, wiping her face with a yellow cloth. "Sure is hot today," she said. "Feels like we should have a good thunderstorm one of these days."

"It will come. It always does." Muriel sat down and pulled the baby, Charles, Jr., onto her lap. She was grateful for the break.

"I saw the boatman coming up here with a message for you this morning." Señora Ramona looked at Muriel, open curiosity in her wrinkled brown face. Even without telephones or radios, there were few secrets

---

[1] Gurt-EL.

[2] BOOEH-nohs. Short for *Buenos dias*, a greeting in Spanish.

in a small village in British Honduras[3] in the 1930s.

Muriel raised her eyebrows and nodded significantly toward the girls. She waved her arm at them. "You git," she ordered.

Marlene and Myrtle jumped to their feet, glad for the chance to stop working. Corn kernels bounced from their skirts and rolled across the floor. Gertel bent to sweep the scattered kernels into a pile.

Muriel pointed her chin at her oldest daughter. "You too. Leave it." Her tone was sharp and impatient.

The girls knew that when a friend came to visit their mother, the visitor was *her* company, not theirs. They were expected to disappear. Children did not participate in adult conversations, nor were they allowed to listen in on them.

Reluctantly Gertel propped the broom in its corner and clumped slowly down the steps to the yard. She rounded the corner of the house and padded across the grass to where her little sisters were untying the goat. "What you gonna do with her?" she asked.

"Gonna take her to play under the plantain. She likes to eat rotten plantain," explained Myrtle.

"Well, watch her and don't let her get away. There she goes! Run!" she shouted as the frisky animal took off, her frayed rope trailing behind her. Gertel spoke loudly enough for her mother to hear if she was listening. She wanted Mom to think she was under the plantain with the other girls.

When she was sure her sisters were occupied with the goat, she circled around through the standing dry corn and approached the house from the other side. On tiptoe she stealthily made her way to a spot under the house just beneath the open window. There she could hear Mom and Señora Ramona talking. They were speaking Spanish, but that didn't bother Gertel. She knew Spanish because her dad was Hispanic. He had come here to British Honduras from Honduras. Many people in her village of Santa Rosa spoke Spanish, although the most common

---

[3] British Honduras was renamed Belize in 1973.

language was English Creole.

She hunkered down on her heels, tucked her skirt around her legs, wrapped her arms around her knees, and held very still. She hardly dared to breathe. She had to know what message the boatman had brought to her mom.

About twice a week, a riverboat chugged up the river on its way to San Ignacio, a few miles upstream near the western border between British Honduras and Guatemala. Since San Ignacio was the end of the line, a day later the boat would pass again on its way back to Belize City. If there were supplies to unload for the small shop in the village or passengers to let off, the boat would pull over to the side and stop next to their little beach. That morning a riverboat had blown its whistle and tied up on the rocks beside the beach. From her vantage point in the yard, on the hill above the riverbank, Gertel had watched a crew member come puffing up the path to their house. "Message for you, Mrs. Morris," he had called out as he clambered up the stairs.

Gertel had moved closer but, hard as she tried, had been unable to hear the exchange between the messenger and her mom. When the man had gone, her mom had looked hard at Gertel, who was standing expectantly at the bottom of the stairs.

"Is Grandma coming?" she had asked. Grandma Liza lived in Belize City, far away at the other end of the river.

"Yes, she's coming," Mom answered, frowning slightly as she continued to study Gertel. "She said she'll be on the next boat. She could be here this week, depending on the river." Mom heaved a tired sigh. "So much to do," she muttered.

"What you gotta do, Mom? Grandma's skinny. She don't eat much."

"But she's . . ." Mom looked again at Gertel, almost kindly. Then she clamped her mouth shut, descended the stairs, and disappeared into the small thatched kitchen that stood to one side of the stairs.

Mom had seemed troubled. Was Grandma coming to take them to school? There had been talk of that. Gertel had never been to school. When she had begged to attend the little school in the village, Mom had told her that when she was older she might send her to live with Grandma so she could go to a good school in Belize City. Could this be why Grandma was coming?

So Gertel sat under the open window, still as a coiled snake, and listened.

"My mother is coming to visit," Mom confided to Señora Ramona. "She is on the way now and could be here in a few days. She says she wants to take Gertel and Marlene back to Belize City with her to send them to school."

Under the house, Gertel felt as though a scorpion had stung her. She almost squeaked, but she held her breath and listened hard.

"It is time they went to school, especially Gertel. She is old enough," Señora Ramona agreed. "But why send them all the way to Belize City? Why can't they go to school right here in Santa Rosa? I know the school is not very big, but they could at least learn something."

Gertel could almost hear her mother shaking her head. "This is a Roman Catholic school. My mother is loyal to the Anglican Church. She was not happy with me for marrying a Catholic, and she does not want my children to grow up Catholic. She wants to make sure they get a good education and are confirmed in the Anglican Church."

"I keep forgetting you are not Catholic," replied Señora Ramona. "I see you at worship here, so I forget."

"I need to worship somewhere, and this is the only church here, so I go—but I am not Catholic."

"Are you going to let them go?"

"Yes. It's time they go to school."

"I'll miss that Gertel girl," said Señora Ramona with a sigh. "She's such a cheerful little thing."

"She's cheerful enough," Mom admitted, "but she can be sassy too."

Under the house, Gertel felt her insides tumble. She nearly stopped breathing altogether. Go to Belize City, that faraway, mysterious place? Live with her grandma, who was so ladylike? Learn to read? Oh, it was too much! She felt as though her insides would burst with nervousness and excitement.

"What will your husband say?" asked Señora Ramona upstairs.

"He will say I should do as I like," answered Mom. "He will not be home for another month. By that time the girls will be gone."

Their father drove a Caterpillar tractor for the lumber company that cut mahogany logs way up the river. He had to travel far into the virgin forest where the biggest trees stood, sometimes even across the border into Guatemala. He stayed away for months at a time, so they saw him only occasionally.

Just then Gertel heard Myrtle wailing. The sound was headed for the house. Those girls! They were always fighting about something. She jumped to her feet, remembering that she was supposed to be with them. It was her job to keep them happy. When the younger girls quarreled and fussed, her mom would say, "Gertel, what's wrong with those girls? Did you do something to them?" As the oldest, she was responsible for what any of them did.

Myrtle ran toward Gertel, howling. "Marlene hit me. She's mean," she tattled.

Marlene was right behind her. "She let go of the rope. She let the goat go." She gave Myrtle another shove for good measure, and Myrtle hit her back.

"Where is Chocho now?" asked Gertel, positioning herself between the two little roosters who kept trying to assail each other.

"She ran down to the river, and it's all Myrtle's fault," said Marlene, aiming a kick at Myrtle behind Gertel's back.

"Then let's go get her," said Gertel. All three of them ran down the trail to the river to look for the tricky goat, and the quarrel was soon forgotten.

When Gertel was washing the dishes that evening, she felt her mom's eyes on her. "Your dress is too short. Grandma won't like that."

Gertel couldn't help it. The question just popped out. "Are we going to Belize City with Grandma? Am I really going to school?"

Mom whirled to glare at her. "You were listening!" She raised the big spoon she had been using to stir the boiling corn and took a threatening step toward Gertel. "How many times have I told you not to listen when I visit with my friends? You little sneak! I'll lash you, I will."

But Gertel was quicker. At the first syllable, she had dropped her dish-cloth and scooted around to the far side of the table. Mom advanced with her spoon, but she had the baby in her other arm. When the corn in the kettle suddenly started to boil over, she had to run quickly to stir it down. In that moment Gertel escaped outside, where she stayed until bedtime.

By then, Mom seemed to accept that Gertel knew about the plans for the girls to go to school in Belize City, and she chose to forget just how Gertel had learned of them.

2

The River

Rub, rub, rub. Gertel scrubbed the small shirt against the rock, working the soap into a lather. She and her mother were knee deep in the river, doing the laundry. The little girls played at the water's edge, and baby Charles slept in a feed sack hammock dangling from a tree branch. Overhead, big, fluffy clouds floated in a deep blue sky. From between the clouds, the sun beat down, roasting their backs. Gertel worked fast, knowing that as soon as she was done with her small pile of laundry, she could throw herself into the water and cool off.

She loved the river. The path down the hill from the village ended at a wide, sandy beach. The water was shallow here, just right for washing and bathing. When they finished washing, the girls helped Mom drape the clothes over the low bushes along the edge of the beach. Then Mom picked up the baby and headed up the path to boil cassava for their lunch.

Gertel splashed back into the river and threw herself flat out into the water. The coolness felt so good on her hot skin. She hated to feel sticky and sweaty and was glad the river was close enough that she could bathe many times a day if she felt hot or dirty. She swam like a frog, kicking both legs at the same time, her knees together and her arms reaching straight out in front of her. She floated face down, her eyes open wide so she could watch the fish darting through the water. She liked looking for surprises on the sandy bottom. Sometimes she saw a turtle, and often there were snails on the sand under the water. People said there were alligators in the river, but she had never seen one.

The river was wide here. Huge trees trailed their branches over the low banks, making the water under them appear dark green. The water was clear, clean enough to drink. Close to the banks, the water flowed lazily. But the girls were warned not to venture out too far into the middle of the river, where the current ran swiftly as though in a hurry to get somewhere.

Gertel gazed at the river whenever she could. Every morning she would run to the open doorway of their house and stand at the top of the stairs looking down the hill to the river that sparkled and glinted between the trees. Sometimes the rising sun turned the water pink and orange. She would stand there with her hands clasped behind her back, leaning against the doorframe until the rosy shades turned to sparkling crystal.

When she had to watch her little brother, she would often carry him down to the riverbank and sit on a rock under the trees and just watch the water flowing on and on. Where did all the water come from? Where did it go? What did it see as it hurried on? Did it ever stop? Why did it never turn around and go back to where it came from?

She stood in the river now and tossed a small stick into the current. She watched the river carry it away, away, until it was out of sight. Now, in just a few days, the river was going to carry her, little Gertel Morris, away on its back. She shivered at the thought. She thought about how, once she was on that river, she would not be able to stop it. She would just have to keep going. Even if she changed her mind and decided she didn't want to go, she couldn't stop it. Like a stick floating on the surface of the water, she was at the mercy of the unceasing river. She would have to go wherever it took her.

After a rain, the river became angry. The water was chocolate brown, and sometimes it rose up to the top of the bank and even tried to climb the hill. The swirling waters carried trees and sticks and pieces of lumber along with it. Then people feared the river. But it usually settled down and cleaned itself up after a few days.

Sometimes big log booms would come floating down the river. Huge logs, tied together into rafts, glided by like silent ships on their way to the dock in Belize City where the river emptied into the Caribbean Sea. Gertel had never seen the sea. She wondered if it was clear like the river.

The river was their highway—their connection to the rest of the world. Riverboats chugged up and down the waterway, carrying passengers, freight, and mail to the villages scattered along its shores. Gertel's father traveled on a riverboat to go to work upriver in the jungle where the big mahogany trees grew. Any day now the riverboat from downstream would bring Grandma to their dock, and then it would carry her and Marlene away.

"Let's catch some fish, Gertel," begged Marlene from the shallow water. Gertel swished back to shore and ran to the hollow place in a nearby tree where they kept their fishing lines. She pulled out a stick with fishing line wound around it for each of them. Little hooks dangled from the end of the fishing line. Carefully she unwound the lines and handed one to her sister.

"What'll we put on for bait?" asked Marlene.

"Run up to the house and ask Mom for some corn," suggested Gertel.

She was surprised when Marlene scooted off up the hill without a fuss. Usually she didn't want to do what Gertel told her to. *She must really want to go fishing today,* Gertel concluded.

Soon she was back with a handful of cooked corn. Gertel fixed a kernel on each hook. The girls waded out into the water. "You stay right here," she ordered Marlene. She went out a little deeper and dropped her hook into the water. Soon there was a jerk on the line, and she pulled in a little shiny fish about five inches long. Marlene caught two fish before she tired of the sport, and Gertel caught three more.

Gertel wound up the fish lines, put them back in their hidey-hole, and picked up the calabash[4] with the six little fish in it. They sure would be good, fried with their cassava. She followed her sisters up the hill.

"We caught fish," reported Marlene, as though she had caught most of them. "Can you fry them for us?"

Mom gave the fish a quick glance. "They're too little to clean. If you want them, you will have to clean them yourself."

---

[4] A gourd commonly dried and used as a container.

Gertel cleaned the fish. This was how it was. When there was work to do, the younger girls ran off to play and she ended up doing it all. She didn't really mind. She'd almost rather be working than being in the middle of the other girls' frequent squabbles.

That night when the girls were alone in their bed, Marlene confided in Gertel. "I don't want to go to school," she whimpered.

"Doesn't matter whether you want to go or not. If Grandma says she is going to take us, we go," Gertel told her unsympathetically. She, on the other hand, thrilled at the idea of going. She wanted to learn to read and do sums. She wanted to leave the village where all she ever did was wash clothes and sweep floors and help make tortillas and try to keep her sisters from squabbling. She had the vague feeling that, for some reason, her mom liked her sisters better than her. She always seemed to take the brunt of her mom's disapproval. Certainly living with Grandma would be better than living at home.

On Saturday afternoon she helped Mom prepare the church for the Sunday service. Since her father served as village chairman, it was their family's job to take care of the little wooden building that served as church and school. On most Sundays a few worshipers came to pray and say the rosary, but every few weeks the priest would come from San Ignacio to hear confessions, conduct Mass, and serve communion.

They swept the floor and dusted off the school benches. Her mother arranged a freshly washed white cloth on the table and set a new candle in the carved wooden holder. She made sure there was incense in the censer. The incense was a lump of hardened resin from a tree in the jungle. Gertel thought it stank, but she liked to watch the thin column of smoke rising into the air. It reminded her of prayers going up to God.

Remembering what Ramona had said, Gertel asked, "Is the Anglican church different from this one?"

"Yes," said Mom.

"How different?"

"We don't say the rosary and we don't pray to Mary."

Gertel had watched and listened as her Catholic neighbors knelt and fingered the rosary beads. "Hail Mary, full of grace . . ." She could say the rosary herself in Spanish or English just from hearing others say it so often.

"I worship here cuz it's the only church here, but I'm not a Catholic," Mom said with a defiant set to her chin. "I was married in St. Mary's Anglican Church in Belize City. According to custom, we should have been married here in your father's village. The priest who comes here to give communion scolded me once for not getting married in my husband's church, but I told him, 'I was married in front of the altar in the Anglican church. If we had been married here, you would not have let us stand at the front; you would have made us stand in the back because I am not a Catholic, and then I would not have felt like I was married.' He didn't say any more about it because it was true. Maybe someday there will be an Anglican church here. There is one in San Ignacio where you were baptized, but that is too far away to go all the time."

Gertel didn't know anything about it. She liked to go to church with her mom. They sat on a bench and the priest read out the prayers, some of them in a language she did not understand, but they sounded like holy words. At times the congregants responded in unison. She had even learned some of the strange phrases by memory. She thought it would be fun to have a rosary and count the beads and pray. Sometimes the girls played church with an old string of beads they had found down by the river. She wondered what the Anglican service would be like. She would soon find out—when Grandma came.

3

Grandma

Gertel heard the dull *thrump-thrump* of the motor before the long, hollow sound of the boat whistle echoed from the river. She lurched out of the hammock slung between two palm trees and raced for the house, shouting, "Mom! Mom, the boat!" They had been waiting for days. Surely Grandma would be on this boat.

Mom dropped her broom, scooped up the baby, and took Myrtle by the hand. "Come, girls," she called. "Let's go see Grandma." Gertel and Marlene hurried down the path after Mom to meet their grandmother.

And there she was. On the rocks beside the boat landing, surrounded by numerous bags and boxes, stood a tall, straight figure in a long, full-skirted green dress and a wide-brimmed white hat. She did not look as though she had just stepped off a boat. She looked as though she were going to a party.

"Ma!" called Mom as she hurried to meet the new arrival.

Grandma Liza waited until they were close enough that she did not have to shout. "Hello," she said in a quiet, controlled voice. Gertel and Marlene tried to hide behind their mother's skirts.

Grandma leaned down and held out her hand to Gertel. "Hello, Gertel," she said. Mom's firm hand guided Gertel out from behind her so she could whisper hello and shake hands with Grandma. Grandma greeted Marlene and Myrtle too. Then she straightened her shoulders and adjusted her high collar. "The trip took ten and a half days," she reported.

"Da boat get stuck?" blurted Gertel in wonder.

Grandma pulled her eyebrows together and frowned at Gertel. "Speak English," she commanded. "Creole is not a language."

Gertel hung her head, ashamed. Her mother had warned her that

Grandma spoke correct English. She did not approve of the butchered English Creole that was spoken in most of British Honduras.

Gertel remembered what else her mother had told her about Grandma. Grandma had been born in Jamaica, an island out in the Caribbean Sea. Her mother was a black Jamaican woman, but her father was an Englishman. When her mother died, her father had brought her by boat to British Honduras to live with an aunt. On the journey from Jamaica, her father died and was buried at sea. Grandma had been raised by her British aunt in Belize City. When the little orphan girl had first arrived, she spoke nothing but the Creole tongue she had learned in Jamaica. She was sent to an Anglican school run by the British people in Belize City. There, the children teased her about her funny way of speaking. She had learned to speak proper British English, and that was all she ever spoke now. She did not allow her children or grandchildren to speak anything else to her.

Lugging her grandma's small bag, Gertel trailed after the adults and wondered if she was going to like living with Grandma after all. She was so strict.

Up at the house, Grandma sat on a chair, her back straight, and visited while Mom patted out tortillas for supper. Gertel stood by the door, her hands clasped behind her back, listening to the clipped, distinct words that Grandma used. They were not hard to understand, but Gertel didn't know if she could ever learn to speak that way. She would just have to keep her mouth shut around Grandma until she learned good English.

Grandma looked over at Gertel, standing in the doorway with her hands clasped behind her back, and chuckled quietly. "She still stands like that," she said to Mom.

"Just like an iguana." Mom laughed too. "She was born that way."

Gertel had heard the story before, but she enjoyed hearing Mom repeat it.

"I'll never forget it," Mom recalled now. "The evening before that child was born, her daddy came home with a trussed[5] iguana. You know how they tie their legs up behind their backs so they can't crawl away. It was already dark, and I had gone to bed, so he just laid that iguana down on my pile of firewood under the *comal*.[6] When I got up in the morning, the kitchen was still dark. I reached under the *comal* for a stick to start the fire and I laid hold of that iguana's tail. I screamed loud enough to wake the dead, and I dropped it like a hot coal! I thought it was a snake. I was so frightened I shook like a leaf for an hour. I was mighty mad at my husband for playing such a trick."

"And that night your baby girl was born with her hands behind her back like a trussed iguana," finished Grandma, laughing quietly. "I remember how surprised I was to see a baby appear like that."

"And she still likes to stand like that," Mom said as she nodded at Gertel standing in her familiar pose against the doorframe.

Gertel didn't know what to think about the iguana story. She stood like that because it felt right. Maybe it was because she liked to be busy, and if she had nothing else to do with her hands, they could hang onto each other behind her back. She smiled to herself, hung her head, and rubbed her bare toe in an arc along the floor.

"I never did like iguana," Grandma went on. "Grandpa likes it. When we were first married, he wanted me to cook it, but I told him if he wants iguana, he will have to cook it himself. Too much like a snake for me. One time he brought an iguana home and asked if he could take my cooking pot to his brother's place so they could cook it for him. I let him take it. The next time I started to cook rice in that pot, it smelled like iguana. I took that pot, rice and all, and threw it out the door. I couldn't stand the smell. I told him he is never to lend my pots to anyone again."

The girls enjoyed listening to Mom and Grandma tell stories of the olden days. Mom and Grandma looked alike. They were both slim with

---

[5] Tied up with rope, string, or a cord.
[6] (koh-MAHL) A large, flat disc of metal or clay on which tortillas are baked.

fine, wavy hair and creamy brown skin, unlike Gertel. She was dark and had short, frizzy hair like her dad. Marlene had pretty hair like Mom and Grandma. Maybe that was why Mom seemed to like her better.

Even though Grandma was strict, Gertel could sense her love. She felt that Grandma would be fair. Perhaps she would not always be displeased with her as Mom was. Gertel decided she wanted to go live with her in that faraway, storybook Belize City.

The next few days were busy ones spent washing and packing the girls' few dresses, shoes, and hair ribbons into a satchel, as well as preparing food for the journey down the river. Grandma did not expect the trip to take very long this time because it had rained and the river was higher. On the way up there had been many low spots and exposed rocks that the crew had had to winch the boat over, but now they would be going downriver with the current. Grandma hoped it would take only two or three days.

While Mom and Grandma made johnnycakes[7] and powder buns[8] and fried chicken to take along, Gertel wandered across the path that led through the community pasture. White egrets flew up from around the cows where they were picking ticks from the animals' hides. *No cows or egrets in Belize City,* she thought. She turned down a narrow path that led to a small thatched hut surrounded by red and white hibiscus bushes. *"Buenos!"* she called.

"Come in," answered a voice in Spanish. As Gertel entered the dim hut, Señora Ramona stood up, brushing the masa[9] crumbs from her colorfully woven wraparound skirt. She welcomed Gertel with a hug and an endearment: "So my little *chica*[10] has come to say goodbye." She chased a chicken off a low stool for Gertel to sit on. "Are you happy? Do you want to go to Belize City?" she asked, pulling her dark eyebrows together and staring hard at Gertel.

---

[7] Johnnycakes are sometimes called "journey cakes"; they are similar to baking powder biscuits.
[8] Same as a johnnycake, only sweeter.
[9] Flour made of dried corn.
[10] (CHEE-kuh) An endearing term for a young girl.

"It doesn't matter if I want to go or not, I have to go," said Gertel, watching Señora Ramona pat out tortillas and lay them on the *comal*. "But, yes, I think I want to go," she added.

"Well, don't forget your old friend," warned Señora Ramona.

"I won't."

"And don't forget your Spanish," added Señora Ramona, shaking her finger at Gertel. "When you come back, I don't want you to forget how to talk to me."

Gertel couldn't imagine that she would forget how to speak Spanish any more than she would forget how to count, but she said nothing. Señora Ramona gave her several tortillas to carry home, and she wandered back across the field, stopping to watch a heron circle and land in the river. No river in Belize City. But there was the sea. She wondered if she would go swimming in the sea. Grandma said the sea was salty. What would it be like to swim in salty water? You surely couldn't drink it. Ugh! Although they collected rain water in a barrel for drinking, the girls often drank water straight out of the river because it was so clear. Grandma scolded them; she did not drink river water.

"When will the boat come?" Gertel asked Grandma that evening while they were eating their rice and beans.

"Children should not speak unless they are spoken to," Grandma reminded her sternly. "That is one of my rules, and you might as well learn it now." Gertel gulped and looked down at her plate. How could she ever remember all of Grandma's strict rules?

4

Riverboat Journey

At last the day of departure arrived. The boatmen helped Grandma step from the rocks into the boat and take a seat on the bench along the side of the long, narrow, flat-bottomed craft. Gertel and Marlene scrambled in after her. Their bags were loaded onto the barge that was pulled behind the boat, except for the basket that held their food; that sat on the floor at Grandma's feet. Mom handed over two long-necked gourds filled with drinking water, and Grandma quickly tied them with string to one of the poles that held up the roof of the boat. She dropped the gourds over the side of the boat so the river would keep the water cool inside the gourds. With a blast of the whistle, the motor sputtered to life, and the boat slowly pushed out from shore.

"Goodbye!" they called as they waved at Mom, Myrtle, and baby Charles, standing alone on the rocks. The girls were too excited about riding in the boat to be sad. Away they went, out into the middle of the wide river. Soon they were rushing along at what seemed to them a fast rate. The trees on the riverbank became a green blur as the current aided the motor in carrying the boat downstream. Gertel stood up to look behind and watch the barge following them. One crewman stood amid the bundles and parcels with a long pole in his hand, ready to push the barge away from the bank or any floating logs that might get in its way. The captain sat on a stool near the back of the boat, his hand on the tiller of the motor. One corner was blocked off with boards; that was the kitchen where a cook prepared food for the crew and the passengers. Two more crewmen, also holding long poles, held their positions, one on the front by the big winch and one on the side.

Two other passengers traveled with them. One was a farmer traveling to Belize City to sell a load of corn. The other, a Hispanic man from across the border, was going to visit his aunt at a village down the river.

"Look at the iguana in that tree!" Marlene cried, pointing to a large orange reptile spread full length on a big branch that hung over the river.

"And see the morning glories?" Gertel pointed to a purple-pink curtain of flowers that cascaded over the trees on the other side. Oh, there was so much to see! The girls twisted and turned on their wooden seat so they wouldn't miss anything.

"Sit still, girls," complained Grandma. "Next you'll be in the river." Gertel thought it would be fun to jump into the river, but right here in the middle it might be too deep.

Soon they stopped at a cluster of houses nestled close to the riverbank under some spreading mango trees. A man loaded several bunches of plantain onto the barge and climbed into the boat. An hour later there was a "halloo" from the far bank, and the boat pulled over to take on two lumbermen returning from their stint in the jungle.

Sometimes the river flowed beside pastures where white hump-backed cattle grazed in knee-deep grass. At other times they crept alongside jungle so thick with tangled vines, it was like a dark wall on either side of the river.

"What do you think is hiding in the jungle?" whispered Gertel to Marlene. "Lions? Tigers? Bears?"

Marlene shuddered and moved closer to her sister.

"There are no lions or bears in British Honduras," said Grandma, who had overheard them. Her fingers kept right on working the crochet hook while she sat primly on the rough wooden seat. "There are jaguars, which some people call tigers, and tapirs, and plenty of snakes."

The girls felt safer when they saw some men chopping through the jungle close to the riverbank. Their machetes swung rhythmically back and forth as the high grass and smaller trees fell in swaths on either side of them.

At noon Grandma opened her basket, handed them each a piece of chicken, and told them to help themselves to the johnnycakes. Gertel leaned over the side of the boat as she nibbled on her cake. Some large crumbs flaked off and dropped into the water. She watched them float to the back of the boat. She dropped some more crumbs on purpose and was delighted when a school of small fish swirled to the surface and nibbled at the crumbs. Marlene, seeing her, joined the game. The girls had fun dropping crumbs and watching the fish come up for them.

"Stop wasting food," snapped Grandma. "I didn't make that food for the fish to eat." But she didn't sound too cross. "I suppose the fish have to eat too," she added, and her mouth turned up a bit at the corners. "The good Lord has blessed us with plenty of food to eat. We should always be willing to share with those less fortunate. If we feed the fish, someday the fish might be food for somebody—so go ahead and drop your crumbs." She chuckled softly at her little joke.

As the afternoon sun beat down, the travelers were grateful for the roof over their heads. The breeze across the water kept them from feeling too hot, and the girls leaned over and dangled their hands in the water to cool off.

A river boat on the Belize River like the one Gertel and her sister traveled on.

Before dark, the boat pulled into a landing with high, steep banks. Two small boys scrambled down the narrow path from the top, toting a bulging sack. "Oranges!" they called out. They dragged their sack to the boat and passed out oranges to the passengers. The cook had made rice and beans for everyone, and the oranges were a welcome treat. Grandma sliced their oranges in half, and the cook let them sprinkle some red pepper on the surface before they sucked the juice out of them.

"Why did the boy bring us oranges?" asked Marlene.

"He is sharing," Grandma explained. "Most people here are glad to share their abundance with others. His pa likely has a good crop of oranges, and he knew the boat passengers would enjoy them. I hope you girls are always generous. The Good Book says, 'Freely ye have received, freely give.' "

The girls were allowed to bathe in the river, and they splashed and played happily in the clear water. After pulling clean dresses over their heads, they climbed back into the boat. For the adult passengers, the crew had tied hammocks across the boat from the roof supports. Grandma made beds for the girls on the floor of the boat under her hammock. As darkness fell and the cicadas started to vocalize, the crew unrolled tarps that were tied to the edge of the roof. These would keep the mosquitoes out. Everybody was all snug and secure on the little riverboat.

The familiar nighttime jungle chorus swelled around them: the humming of insects, the intermittent cries of nighthawks, and the faraway roaring of howler monkeys. The gentle rocking of the water lulled the girls to sleep.

Their journey continued the next day. Gertel was surprised at how winding the river was. She always thought the river flowed straight east to Belize City. "Oh my, no!" exclaimed Grandma. "It twists and turns and loops back on itself. Right now we are moving north. The river empties into the sea north of the city."

Before noon, they came to a place where rocks stuck out of the water. The captain steered the boat closer to the bank where the water rushed through a narrow rock-free channel. He shut off the motor, and the crew members used their poles to keep the boat from brushing the rocks on either side. All at once the boat stopped with a jerk. They were stuck. The men worked hard with their poles to move the boat, but it would not budge.

"Okay, men. We'll have to winch 'er," called the captain, maneuvering around the people and bundles to reach the big wooden spool, wound with heavy steel cable, which was mounted on the front of the boat.

One of the men jumped off into the water, carrying the hook at the end of the cable. He scrambled over the rocks while the cable unwound behind him. Once at the shore he pushed his way along the edge of the jungle to a large cabbage bark tree ahead. There he wrapped the cable around the tree and fastened it with the hook. Then he waved an arm in signal.

"Everybody out," called the captain. "Get all the weight off we can." The girls were glad for a chance to get into the water. They struggled around and over the rocks to the shore from where they could watch the action.

On the boat, a crewman began to wind the big handle of the winch. The other men used their poles to push against the rocks. The male passengers helped by pushing the boat from behind. Slowly the boat began to move, and soon it was floating again. The passengers waded up to the boat and climbed in.

"That was fun," said Marlene.

"Humph!" grunted Grandma, trying to arrange her wet skirt so it would dry quickly. "Not if you have to do it half a dozen times a day."

The hot sun made the girls sleepy. They leaned against Grandma, one on each side, and closed their eyes. When they awoke, they were still chugging down the river, rounding one bend after another.

"Look at the monkeys," called Marlene, pointing. In the trees, hanging out over the river, were dozens of black howler monkeys. The girls were used to hearing the howlers roar at night, but they had never been so close to them before. Here the channel ran close to the bank, so their boat floated right under the branches where the monkeys perched. The girls held their hands over their heads. They were afraid one of the animals might drop on top of them. The monkeys' beady, black eyes stared down at the girls. Reaching out with their long, hairy arms, the monkeys swung from branch to branch. One little baby rode on his mother's back. Another one threw some nuts down on the boat roof as they passed by. They acted so much like little people.

At one village a girl carrying a dressed chicken came down to the boat landing. Seeing a girl her own age, she shyly handed the chicken to Gertel.

Gertel looked at Grandma doubtfully. "Take it to the cook," Grandma instructed. Turning to the girl, she said, "Thank you very much."

Gertel scrambled over the bags and bundles to the back of the boat and stood on the bench to hand the chicken over the low wall to the cook. He grinned, took it from her, and said, "Dat go good witt our rice and beans."

Gertel stood and watched him expertly chop the chicken into pieces and fry it in a pan of lard. Here at the back of the boat the vibration from the motor rattled the bench so much her teeth chattered. She soon returned to her seat.

"The river is bigger now," Gertel pointed out to Grandma.

"Yes, see there? Another river has just emptied into this one. All along the way, other rivers and creeks join this one. All the water runs into the sea."

This was a wonder. If all the water ran into the sea, where did it go then? She dared not ask Grandma too many questions, but she was learning that even if Grandma was strict, she was also kind.

During the afternoon a black cloud rolled over the sun, and they saw the tops of the cohune palm trees swaying in the breeze. Then raindrops began to pelt the roof of the boat, and a spear of lightning shot from the cloud, followed by a rumble of thunder that was louder than the boat motor. The captain shut off the motor and threw out the anchor. While their small vessel rode the waves caused by the wind, the rain dumped down, lightning lit up the sky, and thunder crashed. The girls were used to thunderstorms. Squalls were almost daily fare during the rainy season, but it was a little scarier to be out in a boat on the water during a storm. They were glad when the rumbles moved off to the west and the sun came out from behind the cloud.

That night they tied up at a place where the houses were close enough to the river that they could see the glow of cooking fires from open doorways. The girls romped about on a narrow sandbar and splashed in the water before settling down for the night in the bottom of the boat. Tomorrow, Grandma told them, they would arrive in Belize City.

5

Belize City

The next morning at one of the many villages they passed, a small boy handed out warm corn tortillas to the passengers, now numbering a dozen. All the passengers seemed to be headed to the city to buy or sell or visit.

Small trees grew in the water, so it was hard to tell where the river ended and the bank began. The water appeared to spread out into the surrounding forest. In some places spindly trees grew masses of roots like curved claws reaching down into the water. "Mangrove swamps," said Grandma. "The sea is just over there." She pointed with her crochet hook.

The girls knelt on their bench and peered through the thick mangroves, but they couldn't see the sea.

"What is that?" squeaked Marlene, pointing to an enormous wooden structure ahead that towered above the river.

"That is the Haulover Bridge," explained a male passenger. "We are leaving the river now and entering Haulover Creek. The river empties into the sea just over there, but this creek flows on down into the center of Belize City."

The girls stared in fascination as they drew nearer to what looked like a huge wooden spider web. The only bridge they had ever seen was a big log lying across the creek near their home. A horse pulling a wagon was trotting across the bridge just as they passed under it, and the girls ducked instinctively. Gertel didn't know what held the thing up. Maybe it would crash onto her head. It took only a moment to slip under the bridge. When she turned around, the horse and wagon were just reaching the end of it. She didn't know if she would ever want to ride across the Haulover Bridge.

The waterway was narrow now. Other boats maneuvered around them on the river: dugout canoes and small boats with no roofs. Gertel feared they would crash into each other.

Some of the banks had been built up with rocks. The water was not as clear as it was out in their western district of Cayo. Gertel could no longer see the fish that had swirled around the boat along the way from her village.

More houses appeared along the banks. They were made of wood and built on poles like their house at home. Some were painted bright blue or green or pink, but most were just gray weathered boards. They rose from muddy, cluttered yards. Only a few tufts of grass and scattered trees grew around them. The houses became closer together as they neared the center of town. The water grew dirtier and dirtier. The shallow sides of the creek were strewn with rusty tin cans, broken boards, scraps of cloth, and food garbage. And the smell! The city stank. It smelled like their outhouse on a hot, sultry day. Gertel clamped her fingers over her nose.

At last they reached the landing site at the Swing Bridge. This bridge was not as high as the Haulover, and Grandma explained that it was a bridge that could move out of the way if a tall vessel needed to pass through. How could a bridge move? Such strange things they had in the city.

At the landing, several burros[11] hitched to two-wheeled carts were waiting to carry goods or passengers. A hubbub of voices rose as the cab men shouted, the passengers greeted waiting friends, and little boys darted in and out, watching the activity. Grandma directed the loading of their luggage onto one of the carts and gave instructions to the cab man to deliver it to her house on Euphrates Avenue. "We can walk," she told another driver who offered to give them a ride. "It is not far."

Grasping a little girl firmly by each hand, Grandma marched away from the water, between high brick buildings. Here there were no dirt

[11] Small donkeys.

paths or grassy meadows or green trees, only brick and cement and cob-blestone. They turned a corner and walked alongside a canal. The canal was even dirtier and smellier than the creek. Straight sides ended in water that looked like tea, with all kinds of rubbish floating on the sur-face. *No wonder Grandma didn't want to hear about drinking water from the river,* thought Gertel. This water was not like their clear, clean river.

The girls' heads swung from side to side as they trotted to keep up with Grandma. So many houses, so many children playing in the streets and under the houses, so many dogs sniffing at the garbage, and so many corners. Gertel began to wonder if what her uncle had told her was true. When he heard she was going to Belize City, he had teased her by saying, "Ha! In Belize City the houses move around. The streets move around. You'll get lost for sure."

She didn't really believe the houses were moving around, but they all looked alike. And they had turned so many corners it seemed they might soon arrive right back at the Swing Bridge where they had come from. How would she ever find her way around in this place?

"This is it," announced Grandma, leading the way up a flight of wooden steps into a small house. Gertel caught a glimpse of bright red flowered curtains and a checkered tablecloth before Grandma opened a door into a tiny bedroom where the one bed took up most of the space.

"This is where you'll sleep. You will share the room with Lolette."

Mom had told them that their cousin Lolette already lived with Grandma. Lolette's mother was Grandma's oldest daughter. As was often done, she had given her first child to her mother to raise. Older ladies needed someone to fetch and carry for them after their own children had left home. Lolette had lived with her grandma since she was a toddler.

Lolette came soon after they arrived. She was just a few months older than Gertel and was delighted to have two cousins to play with. "You can share my bed," she invited generously. She showed the girls where to hang their extra dresses and made room on the single shelf for their underclothes. Her many little braids swung back and forth as she sat on the bed, bouncing up and down in excitement.

"Where is Grandpa?" asked Marlene.

"He's working. He'll be home tonight."

"Who cooked for Grandpa when Grandma was gone?" asked Gertel.

Lolette looked at her in surprise and then rolled over on the bed in a fit of giggles. "Why, Grandpa *is* a cook. That's what he does all day. He is a stevedore.[12] He works at the dock, cooking for the dock workers. He can cook just as well as Grandma. And sometimes they ask him to go onto a big ship in the harbor and cook for the sailors. They like to eat rice and beans."

"I like to eat rice and beans too," said Marlene.

"Let's go see if Grandma has food ready for us," said Lolette. She led the way into the little kitchen attached to the back of the house by a short veranda.

"You girls go on and sit down at the table. I'll bring your food, and you can sit up and eat like civilized people," said Grandma. "I want you girls to learn good manners."

She made them bow their heads while she recited a blessing, and then the girls happily dug into their large bowls of rice and beans. There was nothing better, they agreed.

That night the little girls from the country watched, fascinated, as a man carrying a ladder and a can of gas walked down the street. High on a pole near their house hung a gas lantern. The man stopped by their pole and propped his ladder against it. Then quick as a cat, he was up the ladder and had lifted the globe off the lamp. He pulled a rag out of his back pocket and wiped the glass, then filled the lamp from his can and lit it with a match. A circle of golden light lit up the street beneath the lamp on a pole.

"Who puts them out in the morning?" asked Marlene.

"The same man," answered Lolette. "He comes back around 6:00 and blows them all out."

"You mean he has to climb the ladder and do it?"

---

[12] Someone whose job is loading and unloading ships.

"Yup."

"What a lot of work!" Gertel marveled.

Lolette shrugged. "It's his job."

The girls stood in a row at the edge of their yard and watched as the lamplighter moved down the street and repeated his act at the next pole. All about them, little pinpricks of light glimmered through the darkness. Lights on poles! What wonders would they see next? The poles were far apart and the light so feeble that they left a large, dark expanse between them. Gertel thought that if she had to go down the street after dark, she would run as fast she could from one puddle of light to the next.

Before they crawled into bed that night, Gertel asked Lolette where the outhouse was.

"It's in the back yard," she answered. "But we don't go outside after dark. Here." She reached under the bed. "You use this if you have to go at night." She pulled out a white enamel bucket with a lid.

Gertel stared at it in horror. "You mean you go in *that?*"

"Sure."

"Uh-uh." Gertel shook her head. No way was she going to sit on a bucket in the bedroom.

"That's all right. I don't like to use it either," said Lolette, pushing the offending bucket back under the bed. "If you use it, you have to empty it in the morning."

Empty it? Gertel shuddered. She would wait.

To her dismay, she discovered the next morning that the only thing inside the little wooden outhouse was another white bucket.

"Why don't you dig a hole for an outhouse?" she asked Grandpa, who was chopping firewood beside the kitchen.

He stopped chopping and looked at her from under bushy gray eyebrows. "Well, now," he answered, "the land here is so low that if you tried to dig a hole, it would fill up with water real quick. You can't dig a hole here in the city. That's why they built the canals—to carry the waste out to the sea."

"You mean . . ."

He nodded his head soberly. "That's right. We all empy our buckets into the canal early in the morning so no one can see us. Don't know why we try to hide, because everyone does it."

Gertel shook her head. No wonder the canals stank—they were full of sewage. She wondered if she would ever smell fresh air again. She knew for certain she would never swim in those canals.

Early every morning Grandma walked to the market and bought fresh meat and vegetables for the day. The girls soon learned that Grandma cooked some strange things. She often put carrots or cabbage in her chicken stew. They were used to eating river fish, but Grandma sometimes cooked seafood like lobster and conch and shrimp.

One day she set a bowl full of yellowish-green mash in front of them.

"What is this?" Gertel asked Lolette, sniffing at the food suspiciously.

"It's split peas. It's not so bad."

Gertel sniffed again. She didn't like the smell. She was sure the taste would be worse. Marlene was stirring her food around with her spoon too, but none of it was going into her mouth.

Gertel looked around. Grandma was out in the kitchen. She snatched up her bowl, carried it to the little front porch and, leaning over the railing, scraped the obnoxious mess onto the ground. The skinny yellow dog that slept under the house rushed out and lapped up the food in a minute. He wagged his tail and looked up expectantly. Marlene appeared beside Gertel and dumped her split peas over the railing. The dog gobbled it up before returning to his hollow under the house. The girls went inside and filled up on bread.

Grandma always made plenty of food. She always had extra johnny-cakes or powder buns that she would hand out to the many children who ran in and out of the yard at will. More than once Gertel noticed Grandma handing a dish of food to a poorly dressed man who walked along the street picking up empty bottles. Gertel thought about the people who had shared food with them on their journey down the river. Grandma was doing the same thing here in the city.

After that, whenever Grandma fed them something new that they were sure they wouldn't like, they fed it to the dog. Since Grandma always ate in the kitchen, she never found out. The dog started to get fat.

The time had nearly come for school to begin. One day Grandma took all three girls shopping. She bought new writing slates for Gertel and Marlene, new black shoes and white socks for all of them, and bright hair ribbons to match the dresses that a seamstress had made for them. Gertel had never had so many new things in her life.

"Now we need to get hats," said Grandma. "You can't go to church without a hat. It isn't respectful." She led them downtown and into a store. A row of girl-sized straw hats lined a shelf in the dark, crowded shop. Gertel picked up a sunny yellow hat with a blue ribbon. It fit her just right, but it was too small for Marlene. Marlene had big feet and a big head. Grandma thought both girls should have the same kind of hat, and there were no bigger yellow hats.

Marlene insisted that she wanted a white hat. Grandma found a white hat with a green ribbon that fit Marlene's big head. The white hat she chose for Gertel slid down and rested on her ears, but she knew better than to argue. She really preferred the yellow hat, but she would just have to wear this oversized white one.

6

School

O n the first day of school, the girls woke up early and slipped into the new light blue dresses Grandma had laid out for them. Gertel's dress felt funny around her legs. When she bent over to see what was wrong, the hem brushed her ankles.

"This dress is too long," Marlene complained, leaning over to watch her own hem descend toward the floor.

"Stand up straight," ordered Grandma, coming to inspect their appearance. She bent down and checked the length of the hem. "An inch or two below your knees," she reported, nodding in satisfaction. "Just right. The school code says you have to have your knees covered."

"But I won't be able to run fast in this long dress," wailed Marlene.

Grandma got that lecture look on her face. "The Good Book says that women should dress modestly. That means to cover your body. There will be no short skirts or low necklines or dresses without sleeves in this house."

Gertel said nothing. She might as well get used to it. There was no sense in making a fuss. Grandma had given them the dresses. They should be grateful.

When they had eaten, Grandma hurried Gertel across the street to Miss Hazel's[13] house. Miss Hazel combed and French-braided Gertel's kinky hair into corn rows[14] from the front to the back of her head. Marlene and Lolette had smoother hair that Grandma herself could braid.

Grandpa had made each of them a slender wooden box with metal

[13] In Creole culture, any lady, married or unmarried, is addressed as "Miss," usually followed by her first name.
[14] Narrow rows of French braids.

hinges and a handle. In the new boxes they carefully arranged their slates, slate pencils, and a felt cloth for cleaning the slates. Then they closed the little brass clasp. Dressed in their new clothes and shoes and swinging their new boxes, the three girls set off down Euphrates Avenue. "I went to school last year, so I know what to do," Lolette stated imperiously. "I'll show you where to go."

On they walked, along streets lined with boxy houses, beside the smelly canal, around corners, and between the big brick buildings of downtown. They crossed the Swing Bridge, but the walls were so high Gertel couldn't even see the water flowing beneath them. They turned left and then right and there it was: St. Mary's School. The school consisted of two long buildings, one on either side of a brick church adorned with a cross and topped by a square steeple.

The school buildings stood like stark yellow concrete boxes, two stories high, punctuated with rectangular black holes for windows. Children swarmed over the dirt yard, running, jumping, shouting, laughing, skipping, kicking, or just standing. All the activity made Gertel think of an anthill. She felt shy and alone in that throng of children.

A bell clanged mechanically, bringing all the activity to a halt. The children ran to form lines in front of the classroom doors. "You will be in Infant One. That is your room. Go stand in that line," Lolette said, giving them a push in the right direction. They knew they would complete Infant One and Infant Two before starting Standard One, which would be their third year of school.

Taking Marlene by the hand, Gertel swallowed hard and stepped into line behind a fidgeting little boy. A large, very black lady in a white blouse and dark blue skirt stood at the head of the line. "Inspection!" she called in a loud, no-nonsense voice. She leaned over the first girl in line, who spread out her hands, palms down, so the teacher could see if her nails were clean. The teacher inspected her face and hair, and the little girl spread her lips in a grimace so the teacher could see that she had brushed her teeth. With a nod of approval, she moved to the next child in line.

Gertel furtively checked her own fingernails. Good, they were still clean.

When the teacher reached the little boy in front of her, she took one look at his fingernails and then pulled a wooden ruler from her pocket. She gave his knuckles a sharp slap and pointed to the spigot across the yard. "Go wash your hands!" she ordered.

Gertel held out her trembling hands. The teacher loomed over her, running her fingers efficiently over Gertel's. "Good," she pronounced. Gertel breathed a sigh of relief. *I'm gonna wash my hands every morning!* she promised herself as she followed the line into the classroom.

Once inside, the teacher, who introduced herself as Miss Stuart, arranged the children in alphabetical order and then had them stand while she read from the Bible. Gertel was too busy scanning the room to remember what she read that day. Two pupils shared each wooden desk. Gertel's deskmate was a very dark-skinned girl named Maribelle. Gertel, who had always felt dark beside her sisters and Lolette, felt light-skinned beside Maribelle. A big blackboard stood on a wooden stand beside the teacher's desk. The teacher had written numbers and letters on the board. Some calendar pictures adorned the walls between the three windows. A shelf across the back held a few books.

Miss Stuart closed the Bible and asked the children to shut their eyes, bow their heads, and repeat the Lord's Prayer with her. Gertel had learned the Lord's Prayer long ago. She helped say it, but not many others did.

"Now we will sing our national anthem," announced the teacher. "Our country, British Honduras, is a colony of Great Britain, so we sing 'God Save the King.' You must all stand at attention. Stand up very straight with your arms at your sides like this, your head up, and your eyes straight ahead. This is to show respect to King George VI." She pointed to a picture hanging beneath the Union Jack, the British flag, in the center of the front wall. Gertel thought the face in the picture looked very much like Mr. Smith, the principal of their school.

Gertel had never heard of King George. She wondered where he lived. Mr. Smith was a white man from England. Gertel had seen him talking to her teacher before school.

Some time passed before the teacher was satisfied that everyone was standing at attention. Then they sang:

God save our gracious King,
Long live our noble King,
God save the King.
Send him victorious,
Happy and glorious,
Long to reign over us.
God save the King.

That first day they copied numbers from the blackboard onto their slates. Then they printed the ABCs. The teacher helped each student write his or her own name. Gertel could already do this. They learned a poem about a girl named Mary who had a little lamb that followed her to school. Gertel thought that was rather silly. She should have tied that lamb up properly at home before she went off to school. But it would be funny to have a lamb or a goat like Chocho in the classroom.

The teacher spoke English, just like Grandma. When one little boy asked, "Wha da ma slate pencil gone?" the teacher scolded him.

"In school you will speak English," she said. "Mr. Smith, our principal, says Creole is not a language. He will not allow anyone in his school to speak Creole. Say, 'Where is my slate pencil?' "

When the noon bell rang, Lolette found her cousins and led them to the lunch line. Some women handed out platefuls of rice and beans and fish in exchange for a penny. "If we had another penny, we could buy a piece of banana bread," said Lolette. "But Grandma gives us only one penny a day."

On the way home the girls chattered about their day. Gertel spoke animatedly about the interesting things she had seen and heard, but Marlene did not have a lot to say.

When they reached home, Lolette led them straight into the kitchen where Grandma was mixing powder buns. "Good afternoon, Grandma," she said. "We're home."

Grandma looked up. "Hello, Lolette." She looked hard at Gertel. "Gertel?"

Gertel didn't know what she was expected to say. "You have to say 'Good afternoon' to her," whispered Lolette behind her hand.

Gertel quickly said, "Good afternoon, Grandma."

"That's better," said Grandma with a slight smile. "How did you like school?"

"I no like school," blurted Marlene. "I no know dat king song, and I can't write me name. And dat lee boy behine me, he done poke me in de back."

"Marlene." Grandma's tone was severe. "I did not address you. I was speaking to Gertel. You will not speak unless you are spoken to. And I will not tolerate Creole in my house. I don't know what is wrong with your mother. She knows English and yet she allowed you girls to grow up speaking Creole and Spanish."

Gertel resolved again to keep her mouth shut until she learned proper English. As for school, she knew she would like it. If she kept all the rules and learned everything the teacher taught her, she would get along all right.

In the days that followed, the girls became familiar with the route to school. They learned to sing "God Save the King" and to say their ABCs. They had lessons in adding numbers and sounding out the letters of the alphabet. At recess they played tag or skipped with the other girls in their class. Every evening they walked home and greeted Grandma before they changed their school clothes.

On September 10 they took part in a parade. Miss Stuart explained to them that the tenth was an important day for British Honduras. On that day, in 1798, the British defeated the Spanish in the Battle of St. George's Caye.[15] From that time on the land belonged to the British.

---

[15] (KEE) An island that forms on top of a coral reef.

"That is why we speak English today and are loyal to the British King," she said. "If the Spanish had won the battle, we might all be speaking Spanish. British Honduras is the only English-speaking country in Central America, all because the English fought to keep this land for themselves."

None of it made much sense to Gertel or to her classmates. Many of them did speak Spanish, though; for some of them, it was a lot easier than the proper English they learned in school. But though the holiday meant little to them, they all looked forward to the parade and celebration on St. George's Caye Day.

That day the whole school marched in time to the music from a band in front of the government buildings while crowds lined the streets to watch them. Other schools marched too, so their teachers had drilled them for days ahead of time. They stood four abreast, at attention, just as they did when they sang "God Save the King." One of the older boys carried the Union Jack on a tall pole in front of the formation. Miss Foreman, an upper-grade teacher, stood beside their lines and shouted out, "One, two, three, *march!* Hup, two, three, four; hup, two, three, four." They had to lift their knees high and march in exact time. Over and over they practiced under the blazing sun until their legs ached with weariness.

Once while they were waiting for another class to get into line, Gertel swung her arms behind her back and clutched her hands together in her comfortable, familiar pose. "You there, in Infant One!" shouted Miss Foreman. "Stand at attention."

Gertel jerked her hands against her sides.

On the day of the parade, Miss Foreman marched beside the columns of St. Mary's, cheering them on. "Come on, St. Mary's. You can do it! Show them your stuff! Hup, two, three, four." Gertel noticed that she carried a little book in her pocket, and if her eagle eye caught anyone out of step or misbehaving, she jotted down a name in her book. The next day a number of children got scolded or punished for disgracing the school.

On the tenth they also stood and listened to boring speeches delivered by sober men with whiskers and dress suits. After the speeches, they all trooped back to school, where each child received a paper bag of goodies—candy, peanuts or popcorn, a cupcake, and a whole bottle of lemonade. Gertel's lemonade was grape flavored. Some of the others had orange or lime, but all of it was fizzy and bit their tongues when they sipped it. What a celebration St. George's Caye Day had been—grander than Christmas!

7

St. Mary's Church

The bell in the steeple of St. Mary's Anglican Church peeled out its call to worship at 6:00 on Sunday mornings. Grandma laid out their green-checked dresses on the bed while the girls bathed in the little washhouse in the yard.

"I don't want to wear this dress," Marlene whined on the fourth Sunday morning. "I get tired of wearing the same dress to church every Sunday."

Grandma arranged her face into its "I will tolerate no nonsense" look. "You will wear what I choose. I buy your clothes; I decide what you wear. Little girls should not question their elders. It is not respectful." Dutifully the girls donned the green-checked dresses.

The three girls, in their white Sunday hats, followed Grandma along the streets to church, trying to avoid the worst of the mud and debris to keep their shoes and socks clean. The church stood between the two school buildings, which looked stark and abandoned today with their closed windows and bare yards.

It was cool and dim inside the church. Uncle Albert had told them the church was built using bricks brought as ballast[16] on ships from England. The ships unloaded the bricks on the docks and filled up their holds with squared-off timbers from the mahogany logs that had been floated down the river past their home village.

Gertel enjoyed watching people: the ladies in their lovely, pastel dresses and the men in white dress suits with gold watch chains across their chests. The ladies' wide-brimmed, flower-bedecked hats, colorful as a

---

[16] Any heavy material carried on ships to make them more stable.

cloud of butterflies, bobbed above the pews. No lady would enter the church without a hat.

The priest appeared, dressed in rich, black robes, the traditional vestments of the Anglican Church. To Gertel, his robes looked luxurious, with their gold braid trimmings glittering in the lamplight. He stood behind the carved pulpit and read solemnly from a small book, words that sounded holy and grand. The worshipers held their own prayer books and responded with more fine-sounding phrases. A choir accompanied by a small organ led the singing while the congregation sang along, reading the words out of their little books.

Then the confirmed members filed up to the front, one bench at a time, and knelt at the railing that stretched across the front of the platform. The priest moved along the line and handed a wafer to each communicant before returning along the row, offering each person a tiny sip of wine from the goblet he carried. Gertel, who was usually hot and thirsty by this time, thought she might drink the whole cupful if she had a chance. This, Grandma had explained, was called communion. *It is almost like a Catholic Mass,* Gertel thought, *except that only the priest got to drink the wine at the Catholic service.* She looked forward to the time when she would be old enough to take communion.

Grandma expected the girls to sit up straight, listen to the sermon, and refrain from fidgeting. She always quizzed them later to see if they had learned anything.

One Sunday when they were seated in their bench, a lady with a sleeveless dress slid into the seat in front of them. The girls heard Grandma's audible "Humph!" When they glanced up at her, she had drawn her lips into a straight line and was shaking her head at the woman's back. A lady with a sleeveless dress in church? Shocking!

When the people on the bench in front of them filed to the front to receive communion, the sleeveless lady went too and knelt with the others. But when the priest reached her, he stooped, whispered to her, and passed by without giving her a wafer. The lady got up, looking very ashamed, and returned to her seat. Gertel sneaked a look at Grandma.

She nodded in agreement. The priest would not serve communion to a lady dressed immodestly.

After church they hurried home, changed their dresses, and ate the food Grandma served them. They were not allowed to work or play noisy games on Sundays. It was a day of rest. "Thou shalt do no servile work therein," Grandma often quoted. After lunch, she sent them into their bedroom to rest. Rest? How could lively little girls rest in the middle of the day? The girls dreaded this part of Sunday. Grandma sat in her rocking chair in the main room and read her Bible on Sunday afternoons.

In their hot little room, the girls whispered and giggled and drew on their slates. They were supposed to learn their verse for Sunday school, but it was hard to stick to it. Sometimes Grandma would call out from her rocker, "What is going on in there?" and they would stifle their giggles in their pillows. They were glad enough to go to Sunday school at 3:00.

Back to the church they trudged, through the hot streets, where a teacher told them a Bible story and asked them questions to see if they had understood. They went to Sunday school, rain or shine. If it was raining, they would dash from their house to the next one, hide under its porch, and then run to the next shelter. They often arrived bedraggled and muddy, but so did everyone else.

One Sunday soon after Gertel and Marlene had come to live with their grandparents, Grandpa gave them each a shilling and told them they could go to the matinee after Sunday school. The matinee, a moving picture show for children, began at 5:00 on Sunday afternoons.

Right after Sunday school, Lolette said it was time to go to the matinee.

"Shouldn't we go home first and leave our lesson books? We don't want to carry them to the matinee," objected Gertel.

"If we go home first, Grandma will make us stay there," said Lolette with the voice of experience.

They went and watched in fascination as the little Swiss girl, Heidi, slid down the mountain on her toboggan. Although she enjoyed the picture, Gertel felt embarrassed. Not one other little girl wore a hat, and certainly no one else was carrying Sunday school books.

The next time they had money to go to the matinee, Gertel made up her mind to assert herself. "I'm taking my things home first," she said after Sunday school.

"You'll be sorry," warned Lolette.

Gertel marched down the street and, after a moment's hesitation, Marlene followed her.

When they reached home, Grandma looked up from her rocking chair. "Where's Lolette?" she asked.

"She went to the matinee and we are going too, but we decided to bring our books home first," explained Gertel.

"You aren't going all the way back to the matinee. It's too far," said Grandma irritably. "You just change your clothes and stay right here."

"But, Grandma, nobody wears white hats to the matinee," Gertel wailed.

"Carrying Sunday school books to the matinee is nothing to be ashamed of," retorted Grandma. "Now do as I say."

Gertel sighed. Lolette had been right. After this they would go straight to the matinee and not try to come home first.

One Sunday when it was exceptionally hot, Lolette suggested to the girls that they skip Sunday school. They agreed. It was much too warm to go traipsing through the streets in the middle of the afternoon. Uncle Albert, who lived nearby and often ate at Grandma's, had given them money for the matinee, so they thought they would skip Sunday school. Then they wouldn't have to drag their Sunday school things along to the matinee.

At 3:00, the girls were lying quietly in their bed, hoping Grandma had fallen asleep in her chair. All at once Grandma's stern voice came to them from the other side of the door. "What's happening? I don't hear any noise. Are you getting ready for Sunday school?"

"Oh, Grandma, the sun is too hot. It's too hot to walk all the way to Sunday school," Lolette whined.

"I'm so hot, Grandma," Marlene added her endorsement.

"Humph!" came from the other side of the door. But she didn't say anything more. They heard the rocking chair creak as she sat down again.

The girls waited for a long time in their stuffy room. When they figured it must be time for the matinee, they got up and quietly began pulling on their dresses. They hadn't heard the rocking chair creak for a while, so Grandma must have fallen asleep.

"Now what's happening? What are you doing?" called Grandma from her chair.

"We're getting ready to go to the matinee," said Lolette in a small voice.

"It's too hot to go to the matinee," said Grandma decidedly. Her rocking chair thumped as she rocked furiously.

The girls looked at each other. They knew they didn't dare leave the room. That Sunday they did not go to the matinee. After that they always went to Sunday school and carried their books along to the matinee afterward.

One Sunday Grandma sent Lolette to visit her mother and her younger brothers and sister.

"Was it fun?" asked Gertel when she came back.

"No!" said Lolette, looking stormy. "I hate going there."

"Why?"

"Because my mom doesn't love me. She didn't want me. She gave me to Grandma when I was a little girl. I won't call her Mom. She isn't my mom. Grandma is my mom."

Gertel felt sad for Lolette. Sometimes she thought her own mom didn't like her very much, but she had not given her away. She had even acted a little bit sad when Gertel and Marlene left on the riverboat. How would it feel to have your mom give you away? *If I ever have children, I'll never give them away,* she vowed.

.

8

Turtle Soup

The little country girls were used to rainy season, but they were not used to the foul-smelling floods that rainy season brought to the city. When it rained too hard, the canals overflowed, spreading their garbage and filth across the streets and into the yards. Sometimes the girls had to wade through several inches of sludge to reach the outhouse or the wash house. The receding water left all kinds of rubbish behind it. Then the girls had to rake the yard, and Grandpa would dump the stuff right back into the canal.

"It's going to be a high tide tonight," announced Grandpa one night when he returned from the docks, his boots covered with mud. The water that swirled into the yard the next morning was cleaner. Grandpa explained that it was sea water from the high tide.

Most of the houses in the city were built on stilts so the water wouldn't come into the houses. As often as he could, Grandpa would bring home a bucket of sand or gravel that he had gotten from a ship and dump it in the yard. People tried to build up their yards above the constant floods that flowed into them. "Don't know why they built a city on a swamp like this," Grandpa would grumble.

All their drinking and washing water came from a hand pump two blocks away. Usually Grandpa or Uncle Albert carried two big buckets down the street to get the water, but sometimes Grandma sent the girls with empty gallon jugs. The girls loved to jerk the pump handle up and down, but too often other people were lined up to get water. Bigger children would push their way to the front of the line and make the girls wait. Gertel did not like the fights at the water pump. She longed for their wide, clean river with its unlimited water for washing and bathing.

Here she bathed by pouring a calabash of water over herself, and if she used too much water, Grandma would scold.

Naturally there was no swimming. Even though the school was only a few blocks from the Caribbean Sea, she never caught a glimpse of it, let alone swam in it. But she did reap some unfortunate consequences from its polluted floodwaters.

Gertel had seldom been sick, but she hadn't been in Belize City long before she came down with a severe sore throat. Grandma made her swallow herb tea and wrapped a rag smeared with Vicks medicated ointment around her throat. It made her eyes burn. For a few days she lay in bed with a fever and did not want to eat anything because it hurt too much to swallow.

Several times during that first year, her tonsils became inflamed. Parasites had entered her body through her bare feet, and these parasites caused tonsillitis.

"Don't go barefoot," Grandma ordered. "Make sure you have your shoes on. And stay out of the water when the yard floods."

To Gertel, who was used to going barefoot, wearing shoes all the time was a trial. It was hot enough without having to wear shoes.

. . . .

Gertel and Marlene regularly fed some of their food to the dog. Split peas and certain vegetables such as broccoli or beets went over the railing into the yard whenever Grandma wasn't looking. They never went hungry since there was usually plenty of rice or bread to fill the gap.

"Why do you make so much food?" Gertel asked Grandma once.

"Always cook for the stranger," she answered. "The good Lord has blessed us with plenty to eat, and He has told us we should entertain strangers. I make extra so I have some to share with those in need."

Someone always ate up the extra food. Grandma often carried food to shut-ins or poor, elderly people. Uncles and cousins often stopped in, and no one went away hungry. She fed peddlers and dock workers and sailors that Grandpa brought home from the docks, and she handed out buns to the many skinny children who ran about the streets as though they had no one to care for them. Gertel figured Grandma wouldn't begrudge the dog the extra food the girls didn't like.

Grandma washed clothes under the house in large tubs set on a wooden stand. She rubbed soap into them and scrubbed them on a corrugated scrub board. "You girls are big enough to wash some of your own things," she announced one Saturday. "Get your hair ribbons and underclothes."

Gertel carried her armload of clothes to the wash stand and filled a small basin with water. Busily she began soaping and scrubbing and wringing out her clothes.

Lolette came down the stairs, her load of laundry dangling from her arms.

"I want to use the basin," she announced, elbowing Gertel aside and dropping her clothes on the stand. She grabbed at the basin. "Give it to me."

"Wait till I'm finished," said Gertel, clutching at the basin. "I'm nearly done."

"If you don't give it to me right now," hissed Lolette, "I'll tell Grandma that you feed the dog the food you don't like."

Gertel glared at Lolette, but she closed her mouth, angrily fished the rest of her clothes out of the basin, and stepped back. Then she saw Grandma standing right behind Lolette. How long had she been there? Grandma's dark eyes flashed fire. "You throw away my good food?" she exclaimed. "I could have given that to someone who wanted it!" In her indignation over the wasting of food, the wash basin squabble seemed to vanish from Grandma's mind. She grabbed Gertel's arm and yanked her across the lawn to a bush. Breaking off a branch, she bent Gertel over her knee and lashed her.

"Marlene did it too!" Lolette cried, her eyes big.

Grandma paused, considering, and then shrugged. Marlene was nowhere in sight. *It isn't fair,* thought Gertel. *Just because I'm the oldest,*

I have to take the punishment for both of us.

A few evenings later Grandma served them a soup with some strange-looking lumps of meat floating in it. Gertel peered suspiciously into her bowl. "What is this?" she asked Lolette, holding up a spoonful of the meat.

"It's turtle."

Gertel studied the lumps of meat floating in the broth and wrinkled her nose, but she didn't say another word. Outside the dog whined and thumped his tail. Gertel gulped, but she opened her mouth and swallowed a big spoonful. It wasn't so bad.

That night the dog went hungry.

One night Lolette discovered Gertel's freckles. Gertel had forgotten to take a clean dress to the wash house with her, so she ran up to their bedroom with only a towel wrapped around her. The girls always dressed and undressed discreetly, but now Lolette stared at Gertel's bare shoulders and exclaimed, "You've got the pox!" She opened the bedroom door and called, "Grandma, come see. Gertel's got the pox."

Grandma came into the room, inspected Gertel's shoulders, and humphed at Lolette. "Pox, nothing. Those are freckles."

Gertel had always had freckles—scattered dark brown spots on her shoulders, back, and thighs. The only other dark-skinned person she knew of who had freckles was her dad. She figured that was one more reason her mother seemed to like Marlene better than herself. Marlene's skin was light brown and clear—no ugly freckles.

"Listen," Grandma said, shaking her finger at Lolette. "It doesn't matter what color your skin is, black or white or brown or yellow or freckled. God made all of us in His own image, and no one is any better than anyone else because of skin color. Don't you forget it!"

9

Home for the Holidays

Gertel's first year of school went by in a blur, and then it was time to make the trip back up the river to their home. Grandma baked a sack full of johnnycakes and fried some fish for the journey. Grandpa built each girl a lovely wooden valise for her clothes. Like their school boxes, it had a little metal clasp and a handle for carrying. Gertel felt rich with her whole valise full of clothes. They boarded the riverboat at the Swing Bridge like seasoned travelers.

Gertel noticed that the motor pulsed louder than it had on the trip downriver, yet the boat moved more slowly, pushing against the current. Although she was too young to realize it, she was learning that her life was like the boat. If she did not resist the difficult circumstances that came her way, but rather simply accepted what she could not change, her life would flow more smoothly and happily.

On the second day, the boat picked up three *chicleros*.[17] They had been in the jungle for weeks, gathering chicle from the sapodilla trees. The boiled-down resin was shipped to the United States, where it was made into chewing gum. The *chicleros* were rough-looking, loud-talking men who looked and smelled as though they hadn't bathed for a month. The girls shrank up against Grandma and tried to stay out of their way.

The next morning the *chicleros* were gone and so were all of Grandma's johnnycakes. Grandma shrugged. "They were hungry," she excused. "Probably hadn't eaten properly for days."

At the next village, somebody gave the cook a bag of black beans, which he cooked and shared with the passengers. That night when they

---

[17] Men who make or harvest chicle, the gumlike substance obtained from the sapodilla tree.

tied up at a cluster of houses, Grandma told one of the ladies who was washing in the river that their johnnycakes had been stolen. She asked the lady if she would make them some more. "Sure," the lady replied cheerfully. "I just got a bag of flour off the barge, so I will bring you some tomorrow morning."

True to her word, she came down early in the morning and handed Grandma a large bag full of fresh buns. The girls eagerly bit into them. But, ugh! They tasted nasty. "Kerosene," said Grandma, sniffing at her bun. "That bag of flour was riding beside a can of kerosene and absorbed the fumes."

The girls were so hungry and the buns were so soft that they ate them anyway. About an hour later their stomachs started to hurt. "O-o-h," they moaned, holding their arms across their middles and leaning over.

"It's that kerosene," muttered Grandma. She dug in her handbag and brought out a bottle of coconut oil. She spooned out the semisolid oil and sprinkled it with salt from a small jar. "Here," she ordered. "Open your mouth." She administered a dose to each little girl. In a few minutes both of them were leaning over the side of the boat, retching as the buns came back up. Then they felt better, but they fed the rest of the buns to the fish.

"Cast your bread upon the waters," Grandma had often quoted when feeding her extra food to strangers. *I'm casting my bread upon the waters now,* thought Gertel. She hoped it wouldn't make the fish sick.

On the third day they neared a long series of rapids. The boat could never climb the rocks against the tumbling water. The crew members waded to shore and hacked their way through the bush with machetes until they found a sturdy tree on which to fasten their cable. Then they winched the boat until it was alongside the tree. They tied the boat there while they carried the winch hook to another tree farther upstream.

All this work took several hours, and the girls were free to wade along the shore. What a treat to play in the clear, sparkling water! Through the water they could see many beautiful rocks. Some were red, some were marbled, and some had glittery flecks of gold in them. They gathered them up in their skirts and carried their treasures back to the boat, where they lined them up on the narrow platform on which the winch was mounted.

When the man came to turn the winch, he shouted at the girls. "Hey, you, get rid of these rocks. They are weighing down the boat." They had to throw their treasures away, but that didn't stop them from looking for more.

The girls were delighted at the sight of the howler monkeys again, as well as the flocks of bright green parrots that screeched among the treetops. At one place a large turtle lay, tied up on the rocks. Gertel figured she knew where that turtle was headed: into the soup pot. She would have to tell Señora Ramona about all the strange things she had eaten in the past year.

At last they reached their landing. There was the beach, the tree where they hung little Charles' hammock, the path leading up to their house . . . and there was Mom, hurrying down the path with a much bigger Charles in her arms and Myrtle trotting along behind.

"Hello, Mom!" called Gertel.

Mom laughed. "I see you have learned to speak English." Gertel was surprised. She didn't know when it had happened. Living with Grandma and hearing it spoken every day at school had filled her head with proper English. She stumbled at first when she tried to speak Spanish, but after listening to Señora Ramona talk to her mother for a few minutes, it began to come back to her.

Little had changed in Santa Rosa. Gertel washed clothes in the river and swam and bathed to her heart's content. She carried Charles on her hip down to the river and let him splash in the shallow water. She visited Señora Ramona and ate tortillas and cassava and gibnut[18] meat. No split peas or turtle soup here!

Her mother's new friend, Lucinda, often spent time at their house. She and Mom would talk and laugh together as they shelled corn or

---

[18] The gibnut, or paca, is a large tropical rodent widely hunted for its meat.

cleaned beans. They were such good friends that they sometimes ate out of the same dish, dipping their tortillas into a common bowl of chicken soup. Lucinda didn't have a husband. She was a petite Hispanic woman with gold earrings dangling from her ears and bangles that clattered around her wrists. Grandma would not have approved of her. She took care of a couple of children, but Gertel didn't know if they were her own or someone else's.

Marlene and Myrtle returned to their love-hate relationship, playing and fighting together as though Marlene had never been absent.

Their father came home and quizzed them on what they had learned at school. "You make sure you behave good and don't make no trouble for Grandma," he admonished. He didn't talk to them very much, and they were glad when he left again.

Although she knew she would miss the river, Gertel eagerly looked forward to her return to the city for another year of school.

10

City Life

Back in Belize City, Grandpa had acquired a small boat. He kept it tied up along the edge of the canal a block or two from their house. The first time Gertel saw the craft, she read with delight *"Gertel M."* spelled with white-painted letters along its side.

"You named the boat for me?" she asked Grandpa in surprise.

"Yes," he replied, squeezing her shoulder. "I named it for you." Gertel felt warm circles around her heart. She knew Grandpa loved her.

"You know where we found your name?" he asked her.

She shook her head. She knew no one else who had the name Gertel and had often wondered where they had found it.

"I was a stevedore on an English ship just before you were born," Grandpa explained. "A man I worked with heard that my daughter— your mom—was expecting a baby. He said if it was a girl, they should call her Gertel. I told your dad, and he liked the name, so that is how you got your name. Maybe that man knew someone in his own country with that name."

Gertel didn't really like her second name, Gwendolyn, so she often just wrote Gwen if she had to write her whole name.

"Do you catch fish in this boat?" she asked him.

"Not fish," he said, shaking his head. "I catch wood."

"Wood?"

"I go back in behind the city to the swamps and cut down wood and bring it here to sell to people for their cooking fires."

Whenever Grandpa wasn't cooking for the dock hands, he was out in his boat gathering and selling firewood. He never took the girls with him. He said the boat wasn't big enough for both wood and girls. Gertel didn't want to go in a boat on that dirty canal anyhow.

It was bad enough that sometimes Grandma sent Lolette or Gertel to empty the outhouse bucket into the canal. Gertel would hurry along the street in the semi-darkness of early dawn, duck behind a fence or outbuilding if she saw anyone coming, and try not to spill the bucket's noxious contents. When she reached the canal, she would lift the lid, hold the bucket out as far as she could, turn her nose away, and dump it in. Then she ran from the scene as though guilty of a criminal act. The buckets and the dirty canals were what she hated about Belize City.

The girls helped Grandma wash clothes and hang them on lines strung across the yard or, if it was raining, under the house. They swept the floor and raked the yard daily. They washed the dishes, and they stood in line for water at the hydrant down the street. Sometimes that job took a long time.

"Why are you girls so late tonight?" demanded Grandma one evening.

Lolette explained, "We were in line and then the Perkins family came along. They had four or five uncles and aunts and about a dozen children all with buckets to fill, and they all cut into line ahead of us."

"Not a dozen children," Gertel corrected.

"Well, lots then," amended Lolette. "They just shoved and shouted and took hours to get their water."

Grandma said nothing. Even though Lolette was given to exaggeration, Grandma knew that there were a lot of squabbles at the water pump.

School was a joy to Gertel. She learned quickly. Grandma drilled them at night on their times tables and insisted that they write neatly. This year they were allowed to have an exercise book and a pencil in addition to their slates. They used the slates to do arithmetic and practice spelling, but they printed their reading answers and history lessons carefully into their notebooks. Grandpa sharpened their pencils with his knife, shaving off tiny bits of lead and wood so that one pencil lasted for months.

The girls were taught to use every bit of space in their notebooks. One morning Gertel noticed that she had only two lines left on her notebook page from the day before. If she wrote the date on one line, there would be only one line left. She decided to turn the page and start on the next page. Two nights later, as Grandma paged through Gertel's book, she stopped and frowned. "Why did you leave a space here at the bottom of this page?" She didn't wait for an answer but went on scolding, "Paper is too precious to waste. Don't let me see you wasting paper again. You fill up every line in your book, you hear?"

One day after school had been in session for several weeks, the teacher announced that the next day would be Memory Day. "You will not use your pencils or slate pencils. You will do all your work from memory."

The pupils groaned aloud and grimaced apprehensively at each other. Some of the boys pretended to gag. Everything from memory! How could they do it?

Gertel found that she liked Memory Day. The teacher would read off numbers, and they had to add them in their heads and say the sum aloud. They had a spelling bee and had to spell the words orally without writing them down first. She read them a story and then asked them questions to see if they remembered it. From then on, Gertel looked forward to Memory Days.

Lolette, on the contrary, did not enjoy school. She liked skipping and playing marbles or hide-and-seek at recess, but she did not like to study. She soon failed and ended up in the same class as Gertel. The teacher placed the better students at the front of the room, so Lolette always sat in the back where Gertel couldn't see her and tattle on her when she whispered or fooled around.

When they needed new dresses, Grandma would take them to Miss Inez, who sewed their clothes. Miss Inez measured them up and down and around, and then she would sew dresses that fit them nicely. "Make sure it is long enough and has sleeves," Grandma would remind her. "I will not have you dressed immodestly." Lolette and Marlene grumbled because they didn't get to choose their own fabric, but Gertel felt happy to have so many dresses. At home she had had only two or three.

11

Hurricane

*H*urricane. The word struck fear into every Belizean heart. These swirling masses of air moved erratically westward toward land from their origin in the Caribbean Sea. Anytime from June to November the fierce winds and torrential rains could strike, leaving destruction in their wake. During the 1930s when Gertel was attending school in Belize City, weather stations used the radio to warn about approaching hurricanes.

People would fasten down their roofs, board up their windows, stow away any loose boards, and sometimes seek shelter in designated public concrete structures.

The little girls from the country had never experienced a hurricane because their village was far enough inland that hurricanes seldom reached them. But here in Belize City, where the sea lapped at the foundations of buildings and even invaded the streets during heavy rains, hurricanes brought the threat of serious danger. Several times during hurricane season, the radio would broadcast warnings of approaching hurricanes. No one knew when or where the capricious whirlwinds would strike land. They often veered off to the north and followed the coast of Mexico to the United States. Sometimes they fizzled out over the sea and never even touched land.

One day Grandpa came home early from the docks. "A hurricane is coming this way," he said. "It looks like it might hit us this time. It is coming fast."

He directed the girls in carrying all the firewood into the kitchen from under the house. He got a ladder and nailed the shutters on the house shut. Grandma hurried to the market and bought more rice and cooked up a huge pot of it. Uncle Albert made several trips to the pump to get water, and he brought it to them. "I had to push my way into line," he grinned. "Everyone else was trying to save water too." Gertel wasn't sure why.

When they went to bed that night, the wind was howling around the house. The little house shuddered and groaned. Sheets of rain pounded against the house, sending trickles of water through the cracks and under the eaves. Occasionally something hard would bang against the wall, making them jump. The wind whistled through the cracks in the walls so forcefully that the lantern extinguished, leaving them in darkness. Grandma encouraged the girls to go to sleep, but they were too scared. At last the wind seemed to die down, and the girls fell asleep.

Early the next morning Grandma shook them awake. "Hurry, get up!" she said urgently. "We need to go to the neighbor's toolshed."

Confused and bleary-eyed, the three girls got up and followed Grandma down the steps. They stepped from the bottom step into a foot of cold, swirling water. Rain still poured down. The frightened girls hung onto Grandma's dress as they struggled through the churning flood that clutched at their skirts and threatened to carry them away.

At last they reached the stairs leading to Mr. Carlos's toolshed. The shed, a cement building, stood on higher ground than their house.

The girls huddled inside the door, watching the flood waters rise. In a short time they saw the water reach the top of the stairs to their own house. Soon it would be inside. In the yard, only the roof of the wash house remained visible.

With fearful fascination they watched the waters swirl ever higher, toward the door where they stood. "I wish it would go away," whimpered Marlene.

"Here, let's get up on this," suggested Lolette, pointing to the big iron anvil that stood beneath a window. "Then we can watch the water from the window."

She clambered onto the anvil and stood on tiptoe to peer out the window.

"Hey, get off my anvil!" shouted Mr. Carlos. Lolette scrambled down again. Idly they waited out the storm, hungry and scared and bored.

"There's nothing to do," whined Lolette.

"You be glad you are safe and the hurricane is leaving," Grandma admonished. "When I was just married, one of the worst hurricanes in history hit us on September 10."

"What happened?" asked Lolette.

"Everyone was out celebrating St. George's Caye Day, and we didn't have radios then, so no one knew it was coming. The storm hit suddenly, with furious winds and rain. The people rushed into buildings, wherever they could find shelter. Your grandpa was a policeman at that time, so he had to patrol during the storm to assist those who needed help getting to safety. A piece of zinc flew off the roof of a house and caught him in the back of the head. It almost knocked him senseless, but—thank God—he survived.

"Then the storm stopped as suddenly as it had begun and everyone thought it was over. They all came out of the houses to see the damages, and then many of them went back to celebrating the holiday. But the storm turned back. You never know what a hurricane will do. It was worse than before. At the same time, the tide came in, and with all the extra water, it just washed into the city in a big wave and caught many people before they could reach shelter. Some people were carried out to sea, and others were trapped in their houses and drowned."

The girls shuddered. "Look!" said Gertel in a trembling voice, pointing at the open doorway. "The water is coming into the shop."

The water had reached the level of the concrete floor of the shop where they were standing. It crept across the floor toward them.

"Here," said Mr. Carlos. He picked up Marlene and lifted her to the top of a cupboard along the wall. He helped the other girls and Grandma up, and then he perched there as well. By now two inches of water covered the floor.

Marlene started to cry. "Will it come up and drown us?"

"I don't think so," said Mr. Carlos. "It's about time for the tide to turn. That wave your Grandma was talking about came all at once. This is just rising slowly. It will soon start to go down."

"Were you all right?" Lolette asked Grandma, wanting to hear more about the hurricane story.

"I was all right. Between the storms, I had gone to my auntie's, who lived farther from the shore. The water didn't come into our house.

"The next day," she went on, "a friend and I decided to go to the hospital to see if we could find anyone we knew who needed help. As we were crossing the Swing Bridge, we saw these trucks coming, loaded high with something.

"I said, 'They must be bringing back things from the parade—benches and stuff.'

"My friend said, 'Benches, nothing. Those are dead bodies.' "

"Were they?" asked Marlene, her eyes big.

Grandma nodded. "As they passed us, I could see that she was right. I fainted right there on the spot."

The gruesome story sobered the girls, and they stopped fidgeting for a while. They clung close to each other and to Grandma as the water rose higher.

After an hour or two the water started going down. Soon it was running back out the door and they could get down off the cupboard.

Grandpa came in the *Gertel M.* and rowed them back to their house, where Grandma had left her pot of rice in the kitchen. How glad they felt to eat the rice, even without chicken. They were also thankful for the water Uncle Albert had saved. All the dirty floodwater was seeping down into the well under the pump, and the water would not be fit to drink for some time.

The yard was still a pond of brown water the next day, and Grandpa let them paddle around in the boat.

"Let's go out in the street," suggested Lolette. "Can we, Grandma?"

Grandma shook her head firmly. "You don't know what is out there," she said with a grim look on her face.

The girls remembered her story of the dead people on the truck, and they didn't ask again.

Paddling around the small yard got boring after a few days, and they were tired of eating rice. They were glad enough to slosh their way to school through the mud when the water finally drained back into the canals.

Hurricanes were no fun.

12

School Days

School days, school days,
Good old Golden Rule days;
Reading and writing and 'rithmetic,
Taught to the tune of a hickory stick . . .

This was one of the many songs and jingles Gertel learned in those years of school days. They were "good old Golden Rule days." Grandma taught them to do to others as they would be done by, and the stick, although it wasn't hickory, was applied liberally when necessary.

As they progressed through school, they learned to do some of their work in graceful cursive writing with pen and ink. Grandpa added little sections to their wooden boxes for their quill pens and pen nibs. A glass ink bottle rested in a little round hole in the top right corner of each desk. Blotters became a most necessary part of their gear.

Hunching over her desk, Gertel dipped her nib into the inkwell and then touched it to the piece of blotting paper so that all the excess ink could soak into the paper. Then she carefully wrote one or two words. Dip the pen again, blot it, write, dip, blot, write. It took a long time. Whenever too much ink ended up on a letter, she had to carefully press the blotting paper to her writing and blot it up. The teacher was very hard on people who had big blobs of ink in their work or too much ink on their fingers; she made them do it over. It was exacting work.

Gertel, along with the others of her generation, was relieved when someone invented the fountain pen. She used a little lever on the side of the pen to suck ink up into the rubber balloon inside, and then she could write a whole page while the ink flowed smoothly from the nib.

She didn't need to use nearly as much blotting paper anymore.

By this time the girls wore uniforms to school. They looked smart in their white pleated skirts and white blouses with yellow and purple epaulettes on the shoulders. Keeping those uniforms clean took a lot of work. Since the girls had to do their own washing, they learned to be careful.

Each May Day the community held a maypole dance. Young girls, each holding the end of a colored ribbon, would dance around the high flagpole, weaving in and out so the ribbons created a pattern. Gertel reveled in this game and several years in a row was one of those chosen to participate in the maypole dance.

The school always presented a Christmas pageant but, although she would have liked to be an angel, Gertel never did more than sing in the choir. Grandma said she didn't have money for costumes.

One time she did get to dress up. The Ladies' Guild of St. Mary's Church gave yearly benefit programs to raise money for the charitable works they did, and one year Grandma informed Gertel that she was to be a Japanese girl in a play. Grandma pulled her hair straight up into a fluffy ball on top of her head and stuck two big knitting needles into the ball. She placed her own long, dark blue kimono onto Gertel and tied a red sash around her waist. Gertel carried a dainty bouquet of flowers and stood on the stage smiling sweetly while a choir sang a song about a little Japanese girl. She almost had to giggle, thinking that a stocky black girl like herself made a strange Asian.

Miss Hazel was sometimes too busy to plait Gertel's hair when it needed combing. At those times Grandma would do it. She would gather the hair on one side of Gertel's head and braid it into a four-inch braid that hung down right beside her face. Another braid on the other side and then three or four in the back completed the job. Gertel did not like those little braids that dangled against the side of her head all day. She preferred having her hair all caught up tight into cornrows, out of her way.

Grandma took her responsibility as their guardian very seriously. Too seriously, the girls sometimes thought. She rarely let them out of the yard. In all her years in Belize City, Gertel never went out to one of the many *cayes* along the barrier reef, never went swimming in the sea, never went to the market by herself, and never went to a classmate's home after school.

"Your mother trusted me to take care of you. How can I do that if I'm not watching you? If you get into trouble, she will blame me. No. You can just stay right here." This was always Grandma's dictum.

Consequently, the girls' world consisted of the route to school, church, and the matinee, as well as daily treks to the canal and pump. At times Grandma took one of them along to market to help her carry the vegetables and fruit she bought. She took them shopping when they needed new shoes and hats and dresses. They did not have spending money for candy or ice cream unless one of their uncles or Grandpa gave them a few pennies.

Every year the church families went on an excursion to the Northern Lagoon.

"Can't we go, Grandma?" the girls would beg. "Everybody else is going."

"I don't have money for that," was the answer. "It costs too much to send you girls to school and buy your clothes and keep you fed."

Twice during the seven years Gertel lived with her, Grandma did take them on the church excursion. They rode in boats up the canal, into the clean waters of a river, and then into the Northern Lagoon. Swimming in the clear, still water of the lagoon was almost as much fun as swimming in the river at home, but Gertel did not like the sticky feeling the salt water left on her skin.

The outing included a picnic lunch and races for the children. What a day to cherish and remember! Gertel wished they could go every year, but she was grateful that Grandma had taken them at all.

When they were older, they attended Girl Guides, where they learned to say the Girl Guide pledge and were taught to be loyal, dependable citizens. They learned to crochet, embroider, and hem pillowcases. They had lots of fun times at Guides. One day when they were sitting in a circle singing "There's a Hole in My Bucket," one of the girls pointed to the leader's leg. There was a hole in her stocking. Some of the girls started to sing, "There's a hole in my stocking . . ." The leader, thoroughly embarrassed, later told the instigator's mother about it—and that girl got a lashing.

13

Religion

Gertel had always enjoyed attending church services. She listened avidly to the sermons and gave the right answers to Grandma's quizzes afterward. She dutifully memorized her Sunday school verses and tried to be good.

The year Gertel and Lolette were twelve years old, they joined the confirmation class at St. Mary's. Every Saturday afternoon for several months, they met with the Anglican priest at the rectory and studied their catechisms. They learned the Apostle's Creed and the Ten Commandments. They learned that God sent His only Son, Jesus, to earth to die for their sins, and that, if they believed in Him, they would have everlasting life.

Gertel thrived on memory work and eagerly anticipated being confirmed. She had been baptized as a baby at the Anglican church in San Ignacio, and now at her confirmation she would publicly confess that she wanted to be a member of Christ's church. She enjoyed the important feeling the ritual gave her; however, she had not been taught that she needed to make a personal decision to follow Jesus Christ and become His lifelong disciple.

Grandma had Miss Inez make new white dresses for them. The dresses had full skirts that came well below their knees, puffed sleeves that reached their elbows, and dainty collars trimmed with white lace. Before the service, the priest's wife took them into the rectory and fitted each of them with a white veil. *Just like a bride,* thought Gertel, tingling with excitement.

She answered all the questions perfectly and took her first communion. How close she felt to heaven as she received the emblems! From then on she took communion along with the rest of the congregation every Sunday. She and Lolette also began to attend matins, the morning prayer service.

On Ash Wednesday, forty days before Easter, the Lenten season began. During Lent, people put on their best behavior. Uncle Albert stopped drinking after work, and Grandma gave up reading anything but the Bible. The girls were not supposed to play rowdy games. To Gertel it seemed like forty days of tedious Sundays.

"Lent is a time to afflict your souls," Grandma explained. "It is to remember the sufferings of Christ. We need to make some sacrifices so we can understand how He suffered. Now that you have been confirmed, you should practice denying yourself something you enjoy. Gertel, I know you like to buy chocolate bars with the money that Uncle Albert gives you. During Lent you should deny yourself chocolate and put that money in the church offering instead."

Gertel did put her money in the church offering, but she certainly missed her chocolate bars!

After the service on Palm Sunday, the members of the Ladies' Guild handed out little crosses twisted together from palm fronds to remind them of how people had waved palm branches when Jesus rode into Jerusalem a week before His death. The girls took their palm crosses home and hung them on the wall to keep them until the next year. By that time they were dried and shriveled, but then they would get new ones.

Many strange superstitions were connected with the Lenten season. One girl told them that if you break an egg in a glass of water on Good Friday, you could see your future. If you looked into the glass and saw a ship, that meant you would travel; if you saw a bride, you would get married soon; if you saw a coffin, you would die. Gertel thought it sounded silly. She knew Grandma would never spare them an egg to try it out.

"My uncle says that there is a flower—I forget the name—that blooms only on Good Friday, and if you find one and put it under your pillow, it will turn into money," reported a boy in her class.

Gertel figured she never would see such a flower, so she couldn't try out that one either. Another boy said there was a tree back in the bush that, if chopped on Good Friday, would bleed blood like Jesus' blood.

Regardless of the superstitions, Good Friday was a sober day. On that day they fasted; that is, they did not eat meat. Grandma cooked only rice and beans. They went to church and had to be quiet all day.

But on Easter Sunday it was all over. The somber atmosphere transformed itself into rejoicing, merriment, and singing, accompanied by lots of good food, new dresses and sometimes hats, and chocolate. Uncle Albert went out and got drunk, much to Grandma's disgust. "What good does it do to fast and deny yourself for forty days and then go out and indulge?" she complained.

14

Life Lessons

One day after school, Gertel had greeted Grandma and changed out of her uniform into a dress, when Grandma looked at the dress and asked sharply, "How did you tear your skirt?"

Gertel looked down. A small, three-cornered tear hung open in the middle of the skirt. Where had that come from? "I don't know," she said, shrugging her shoulders.

"You go fix it right now," said Grandma, turning back to the kitchen.

Gertel crossed to the main house and found Grandma's mending basket. She picked out a needle and threaded it. Just then the laughter of the other girls drifted up from the yard below. She stepped over to the window and saw that they were playing marbles. She could fix the tear later. She dropped her needle and ran outside to join them.

When Grandma came down into the yard later, she looked hard at Gertel. "Did you fix that tear?" she asked. She stalked over to Gertel, reached out, hooked her finger into the small hole, and ripped it down to the hem. "A stitch in time saves nine," she quoted. "Now go fix that tear."

After that, whenever Gertel tore her dress or found a hole in her sock, she mended it right away.

Now that the girls were older, Grandma decided to teach them to cook. In addition to her gas stove in the kitchen upstairs, she had a fire pit under the house where she cooked beans and corn. She bought several small kettles and showed the girls how to start the fire using dry corn husks for kindling. "After washing the rice until the water is clear, you add water until it comes up to the first joint of your middle finger, like so," she showed them. "Then you add salt and a little coconut oil and put the lid on. When the water starts to bubble out, it is boiling, and then you remove some of the sticks from the fire so that it cooks slowly. Don't lift the lid for twenty minutes."

She taught them to regulate the heat by adding and removing sticks of wood, to cut up chicken and wash it with lime juice or vinegar, to bake tortillas, and to fry plantain.

Often when the girls had cooked a pot of chicken or a beef stew, Grandma would take them with her to deliver it to an elderly lady or a sick person. "My, my," the elderly lady would cluck. "And you girls made this for me. Thank you, dearies. God bless you!" The girls felt a warm glow of satisfaction.

Grandma made regular trips to school to consult with the teachers and make sure the girls were progressing as they should. If their marks had slipped, she would make them spend more time doing homework; if they had misbehaved, she punished them at home.

One afternoon Gertel saw Grandma coming across the schoolyard. *She must be making one of her visits to the teacher,* Gertel thought. Gertel had never outgrown her propensity for eavesdropping, so, without a qualm, she slipped around to the back of the school and stood under one of the windows of her classroom.

"How is Gertel doing in school?" Grandma asked the teacher after a few minutes of small talk.

"Gertel is an excellent student," replied the teacher. "She is careful with her work and gets good marks. She is exceptionally proficient on Memory Day. She is no trouble at all. That girl will go far. I hope she can go to high school in a few years."

Gertel, standing outside the window, felt relief and pleasure at her teacher's praise. She, too, hoped she could graduate and go to high school someday. Then she caught her breath as the teacher went on. "It is Lolette who is the problem."

"What is her problem?" Grandma asked quickly, her voice sharp.

"She and two of the other girls go out into the streets at noon hour, and they are late getting back into class. I have reprimanded them and given them detentions, but they are still doing it." The students were permitted to leave the school grounds to go home for lunch or to buy food at nearby shops, but they were expected to return when the bell rang after lunch.

"I'll take care of it," promised Grandma. Hearing the chair scrape, Gertel ran from her hiding place, scooted around behind the school, and raced to get home before Grandma.

When Grandma reached the yard, she called Gertel into the kitchen. "Does Lolette come in late after lunch?"

Gertel stood with her hands behind her back and looked at her toes. She was tempted to lie, but Grandma had told them that the devil was the father of lies, and they should always be truthful. "Yes," she mumbled miserably.

"That ungrateful girl," stormed Grandma, banging her fist on the tabletop. "Her mother gave her to me, and I've raised her and given her everything and taught her right—and now she acts like this!"

Grandma called Lolette into the kitchen next. Gertel could hear the exchange from outside.

"Lolette, do you come in when the bell rings at noon?"

"Yes, Grandma. I always come in on time."

O-o-o-h, how can Lolette lie so easily? thought Gertel.

Grandma said nothing more, but the next day after noon hour, when Gertel took her seat in the third row from the door, she froze inside. Behind the open classroom door stood Grandma, straight and determined. What was she going to do? The class was unusually silent, all of them noticing Grandma but trying to pretend she wasn't there.

The teacher picked up her history book and started to read about the British in India. After ten minutes, footsteps sounded in the hall. Dorothy walked into the room, followed by Mavis. As Lolette passed through the open doorway, a hand shot out and grabbed her by the hair. She let out a screech. While the horrified children watched, Grandma slapped Lolette and began pounding her shoulders with her fist, keeping a viselike grip on her hair. Lolette dodged this way and that but couldn't escape the blows.

The teacher hurried over to Grandma. "Miss Liza," she urged. "You can't do this in school. Please stop."

Grandma paused long enough to glare at her. "If I take care of her now, maybe the police won't have to take care of her a few years from now." Then she gave Lolette a few more slaps and pushed her away. Without a backward glance, Grandma strode out of the room.

Lolette stumbled to her seat, crumpled into it, and hid her head in her trembling arms. Gertel was shaking too.

Lolette did not come in late for school again, nor did the police ever have to deal with her in later years. Grandma's methods may have been harsh, but they yielded results.

When Gertel had completed Standard Five, her seventh year of school, the teacher announced the results from their final tests. "I was pleased with your test scores," she said with an encouraging smile. "I would especially like to recognize two people. Rose was first in the class."

The children turned to look at the blushing Rose and began clapping to congratulate her.

"And Gertel was second. These two have done very well. If you all work hard, maybe you can do as well next year."

As the children clapped, Gertel felt a surge of triumph. *Next year,* she promised herself, *I'll work really hard, and I'll be first in the class.* She knew that part of her success was due to Grandma's high expectations. Grandma's methods of upbringing, though strict, had helped her to excel.

When she reached home, she tore up the steps and pushed her test results between Grandma's face and the paper she was reading. "Good afternoon, Grandma," she said breathlessly. "I came in second!"

Grandma lowered the sheet of paper and glanced briefly at Gertel's report card. "Good," she said, but she didn't sound very enthusiastic. She looked at Gertel, an expression akin to pity in her eyes. "This is a letter from your father," she said, lifting the paper from her lap.

From my father? Cold apprehension seized Gertel.

"He says he wants you to come home to stay with your mother. Next year both Myrtle and Charles will be in school, and he doesn't want to leave her all alone."

Gertel felt the tears pushing against her eyelids. "But why can't he take Mom along to the bush with him?" she quavered.

"I don't know." Grandma shook her head. "But he is your father, and you have to do as he says."

Gertel turned and ran to her bedroom. She slammed the door, threw herself on the bed, and let the tears come. Her sobs came in huge gulps. *Why? Why?* She pounded the bed. It wasn't fair! She was second in her class. She could be first next year. Now there would be no more school. No high school. No job in the city. Her life was over! She did not want to go home, but there was nothing she could do about it. Her dad had said she must go, so she had to go. She felt the current sweeping her onward, like a riverboat hurtling over rapids. At that moment she hated her dad.

15

Home to Stay

Two months later, after her siblings had sailed away to school on the riverboat, Gertel sat on the top step of their little house on the slope above the river, her elbows on her knees and her chin in her hands. Trees, river, pasture, more trees, one or two houses. What was she going to do in this boring place? She was only fourteen, but now there was no more school for her. No Girl Guides, no matinees, no more giggling under the sheets at night, no more cooking lessons with Grandma, and no more going to Miss Hazel to get her hair combed. She brushed disconsolately at her frizzy hair. She couldn't even comb her own hair. She'd never had to. All she could do was brush it straight back and pin it there with a big clip. She sighed and rose slowly to her feet.

Her days became a round of making tortillas, sweeping the house and yard, feeding the chickens, chopping the weeds around the corn, pounding rice, digging cassava, and washing in the river. The river provided her only recreation; she spent hours swimming, fishing, and sitting on the shore watching the water drift by. She felt that she had been carried out to sea and set adrift with no place to go and nothing to do but float around.

As the weeks rolled by, her natural resilience asserted itself. She adapted to her new role. If her mom needed her at home, she would at least try to make their life comfortable. Gone were her dreams of being a school-teacher or a secretary or a nurse, but she refused to mope. She would try to do her best wherever she was.

"Why don't we go to church?" she asked her mom one Sunday morning.

"I stopped going to the Catholic church. Your father doesn't even go anymore," she answered. "I had enough of it. The priest used to come up here and discuss religion with me when he'd come to Santa Rosa. One time he was after me about attending Mass, and I said, 'Listen. Remember those two men near here who got into a drunken brawl and ended up in the hospital in San Ignacio? I heard that you went to visit them and hear their confessions. You heard one man's confession and gave him absolution, but you didn't make it to the other man before he died. Then you refused to bury the man who wasn't shriven.[19] Both of those men were sinners. They both died and went to the same place. Nowhere in my Bible does it say that a man can forgive sins. Only God can do that. There is only one God and one mediator, and that is Jesus Christ.'

"Another time when he came, I talked about the woman taken in adultery. I told him that all those religious men brought this woman in and Jesus forgave her sins, but what happened to the men? They all went away unforgiven. I told the priest the only way to be saved in the Day of Judgment is to believe that Jesus died for our sins and ask Him to forgive us. I told him, 'Your parishioners don't even read the Bible, so how can they know what to believe?' "

"What did he say to that?" asked Gertel.

Mom smiled with satisfaction. "He said, 'Mrs. Morris, you are a very sensible woman. Can I borrow your Bible?'

"I said, 'No way! If you borrow it, you will tear out the pages you don't teach, and I won't have much of a Bible left.' He stopped coming after that, and I haven't gone to church there since. Maybe when they get the new road built, we can go to San Ignacio to St. Andrew's Anglican Church more often. It won't seem very far then."

"They are building a road?"

"Yes, just up there." Mom waved her hand to the south. "They've been hacking away at the jungle along the walking trail for a few months already. Soon they will bring in tractors and Caterpillars to take out the

---

[19] When someone is shriven, his confession has been heard and absolution, or forgiveness, has been granted.

stumps and make a road big enough for trucks."

Sometimes her mom's good friend, Lucinda, plaited Gertel's hair for her. Lucinda often came to cook and talk with her mom. At such times, Gertel would wander over to Señora Ramona's house and speak Spanish with her. Ramona always cheered her up.

At times she wondered about Marlene and Lolette, dressed in their clean, white uniforms, walking to school, doing their homework, and going to Guides—but that world seemed far away. In an attempt to keep her brain from shriveling up, she read every scrap of printed material she could get her hands on, which wasn't much—a few magazines and newspapers her dad had brought home, her old school books, and the Bible.

Before another year had gone by, the new road became passable, at least in the dry season. For much of the year it remained a muddy track, but slowly it was built up with rocks and gravel.

Gertel's father came home and spent several weeks building a new house for them beside the new road. Gertel did not say much to him. She felt that the more she ignored him, the less chance he had of hurting her feelings.

Gertel did ask her dad, however, why they had to leave the river. He explained that riverboat travel was coming to an end. Goods and people would now be moved by truck along the new road, which ran straight for just over a hundred miles from Belize City to the western border. Most of the people in the village moved their homes close to the new road too. This new village near Red Creek was called Esperanza.

As soon as they had settled into their new home, along with their cow and chickens and all their earthly belongings, Gertel's father prepared to leave for another six months in the bush.

"Here's money," he said, tossing some tattered bills onto the table. Then he was gone.

Mom picked up the money and counted it. Her lips stretched into a rigid, thin line; then she dropped the cash contemptuously onto the table. "There is exactly one dollar and fifty cents a month here. One dollar and fifty cents! How can we live on that? And, he took Lucinda along. I know he gives some of his money to her. Now he took her with him." Her face crumpled as she collapsed into a chair, dropped her head on her arms, and cried.

Gertel let out her breath in a huff. "Lucinda?" she asked. "Why take Lucinda? Why doesn't he take you along to cook?"

"He says you and I have to stay here and take care of the corn and other crops. And I thought she was my friend," she sobbed.

Gertel slipped out the door. How could her father be so mean, leaving them hardly any money? How would they live? They would have to work very hard to raise enough food to stay alive. And to take Lucinda with him! How could he betray Mom that way? Gertel wanted to scream.

In the following months, Gertel and her mom became full-time farmers. Alejandro, an older neighbor, offered that if Gertel would help him plant his corn, he would help them with theirs. Accordingly, Gertel walked two miles through the jungle to the plantation day after day. There she helped to plant corn, jabbing a planting stick into the ground and dropping four kernels into each hole. Then they planted beans and rice. When the weeds started to grow, she swung a machete to chop them away from the young corn. They planted cassava, sweet potatoes, malanga coco,[20] peppers, and okra. The planting, tending, and harvesting of food kept her hands and mind occupied.

· ·

One day as she followed Alejandro down the jungle trail, he suddenly stopped and flung out his arm to stop her. "Look," he hissed, pointing.

Gertel peered around him to see a tiny jaguar kitten pouncing on a twig on the trail. The tawny, spotted kitten stared at them with bright eyes. Then a second one sprang out of the bush and jumped on its brother. They tumbled over and over, snarling and batting at each other.

---

[20] A root vegetable similar to potatoes.

"O-o-o, they're so cute. I wonder if I could touch them." She started to step around Alejandro, but he grabbed her arm.

"Don't move," he warned in a whisper. "The mother is probably right there watching."

Gertel froze. She knew better than to tangle with a jaguar. The two kittens gave them one last glance before scampering into the jungle. Alejandro and Gertel edged cautiously past the place where they had been. Gertel couldn't help wishing she could have taken one of them home for a pet.

All their hard work yielded them enough food to keep going. The work consumed all Gertel's energy, leaving no time for wistful long-ings of city life and more education. When the corn was dry, they went through the field, breaking the tall stalks so they could pick a single cob from each stalk. Then they picked up the cobs and put them in sacks and loaded them, two at a time, on the back of Alejandro's bony horse.

They cut the rice with machetes and gathered the stalks by armfuls and laid them on a canvas tarp. Then they took sticks and beat the dried stalks until all the rice had sifted down onto the tarp. Removing the trash and winnowing the rice was backbreaking, dusty work. Beans were pulled up by the roots and harvested the same way. The corn had to be shelled and ground in a little hand grinder; the beans had to be sorted and all the dirt picked out; the rice had to be pounded in a large mortar to separate the grain from the hulls. Gertel would lift a heavy pestle in both hands above her head and then bring it down hard over and over again on the whole rice in the hollowed-out log that served as a mortar, until only the shiny grains were left.

Her body grew hard and strong. Every night she fell into bed, exhausted. She could almost hear Grandma saying, "The sleep of a laboring man is sweet."

Their new location brought them into contact with more people. Instead of the riverboats, trucks chugged by, sometimes several in one day. More people built houses along the new road, and they made con-versation with neighbors who passed by on their way to their plantations.

Most girls her age were either in school, working, or maybe even married, so Gertel didn't have a social life. Occasionally she and her mom walked the three miles into town to go to church, and she was able to take communion again.

In her second year at home, a Church of the Nazarene minister came into their area hoping to establish a church there, but the Catholic village people would not sell him land on which to build a church. To Gertel's amazement, her dad offered that he could hold services under their house. She couldn't figure her dad out. He could be so generous sometimes, but he still left them only a tiny amount of money to live on. Whatever the reason for his current generosity, she was glad, because now they could go to church regularly.

The Nazarene services were conducted differently from the liturgical Catholic or Anglican services Gertel had attended. Instead of the formal chanting and reading from the prayer book, the minister would preach sermons, explaining passages in the Bible. Gertel liked that. It made the Bible seem more real to her. She also liked the singing. It was livelier and the songs were new, mostly choruses she could learn easily. Few people came to the services, but at least the times of worship gave Gertel a break from the grinding labor of the rest of her days.

16

Locusts

The corn had almost begun to tassel. Relaxing in the house, Gertel sipped a cup of lime juice. Suddenly it seemed as though the lights went out. Although the sky had been cloudless, all at once it was dark.

"What happened?" asked Mom, coming to join Gertel at the open window. "Is a storm coming?" A low, shimmering cloud had blotted out the sun and seemed to be moving rapidly toward them. A buzzing sound filled the air. Then something hit the side of the house, then another and another, as though an invisible hand were pelting the walls with small stones. A greenish brown insect about four inches long landed on the windowsill and stared at them with bulbous eyes.

"What is it?" asked Gertel apprehensively.

"Locusts!" croaked Mom. "Shut the windows!" They hurried to close all the shutters and secure them. Now the locusts were tapping against the walls like raindrops, and above the little pings, Mom and Gertel could hear the sound of chewing. "They'll eat everything in sight," groaned Mom.

"What will happen to our plantation?" asked Gertel.

The locust cloud landed and moved across the land like an army, mowing down everything green and edible. The village men dug ditches and lit fires in them. Some of the locusts, stunned by the smoke, fell in and burned, but far too many of them stayed on the ground, eating, eating, eating.

Then suddenly, after three days, the plague vanished. Gertel and Alejandro walked back to see what remained of their crops. The corn stood stark and naked; only stalks and leaf veins had escaped the insects' merciless mouths. The rice had been wiped out. The beans were stripped of leaves, but the dried beans were still salvageable. Those had been too hard for the locusts to chew. The young malanga coco and cassava plants were gone. What were they going to do?

"It will be a famine," predicted old Alejandro, surveying the devastation.

"What will we eat?" Gertel worried.

"We can eat our seed corn," said Mom, "and Dad will just have to give us more money for seed when he comes. We will have to kill some of the chickens because there is nothing for them to eat. We'll tether the cow out in the bush where there are still some tough green leaves, until the grass grows again."

Together with Alejandro they quickly planted more corn, but they kept most of their seed corn for food. They dug up the small yams, malanga coco, and cassava and replanted some of them.

They ate corn tortillas and beans, then beans and corn tortillas. When Gertel went to the shop to buy flour for some variety, there was none to be had.

"There is a shortage of food everywhere," the proprietor told her.

"We'll eat corn grits," said Mom. She ground the parched corn coarsely and cooked it like porridge. They ate it with the little milk the cow gave. The milk tasted strong from the jungle plants the animal was eating, but they added some cinnamon to disguise the taste. They walked back to the river and caught fish to eat with their grits.

They had no oil or shortening, but Mom taught her how to extract oil from cohune nuts. They picked up the hard, egg-sized nuts from under the palm trees, took them home, and smashed them open in the mortar. Then Mom boiled the meat and let it sit until the oil rose to the top.

"How do you know all this?" asked Gertel.

"I've done it before," was the answer.

Gertel tried to think of some way she could earn a little extra money. At Guides she had learned to crochet. One day she walked to San Ignacio and bought some yarn. She worked every spare minute until she had made a little sweater, cap, and booties out of the yarn. Then she took to the road.

She made her first sale to a young woman with a new baby. The woman admired the little outfit and said, "I don't have money, but would you take a chicken for it?"

"Sure." A chicken they could eat.

They survived the locust famine by hard work and careful planning. What a relief, though, when the new crops were ready!

As she grew older, Gertel became aware that her father bore the blame for the life of deprivation they lived. He earned enough money for them to live comfortably, but most of it was spent on women and drinking. Her father continued to be unfaithful to her mother, and her parents fought constantly whenever her father came home. The tension in her home felt raw, like an open sore that wouldn't heal.

One evening a neighbor stopped by and invited them over to his place for a birthday party. "My daughter is turning fifteen. Come over and have some cake."

Her dad, home at the time, did not want to go, but Gertel and her mom walked up the road to attend the event. When they returned after dark, they found the house locked. Mom was furious. "Why did he go off and lock us out? He has the only key." She clenched her fists. "I know where he is. He is with Lucinda! I'm going over there to get that key."

"Oh, don't go over there," pleaded Gertel. "It will just make trouble. We can sleep back in the kitchen."

Her mom refused to hear reasoning. She stalked off down the road while Gertel sat on the front steps, her arms wrapped tightly around her, waiting for the inevitable fight.

Shortly she heard them returning. They entered the yard, shouting insults and aiming blows at each other. Angrily, her dad stabbed the key into the lock and opened the door. He stomped through the house, out the back door, and into the kitchen, followed by his wife. As Gertel entered the house, she could hear the quarrel mounting in intensity.

Through the open kitchen doorway she saw her mother gripping the collar of her dad's shirt and twisting it with all her might. Her father, not a big man, was attempting to push her arms away, but he was fighting for his breath as his wife wrenched the shirt tighter against his neck.

Gertel had had enough. She charged into the kitchen and forced herself between the two of them. With a hand on each chest, she pushed hard, much as she had always imagined Samson might have pushed the pillars of the heathen temple to bring it down. "Stop fighting!" she yelled. Her youthful strength and the adrenaline that surged through her veins came to her aid, and the two staggered apart, a ragged chunk of shirt coming away in her mom's fist.

That was the last time she saw her parents fight. Although plenty of strong feelings still roiled under the surface, they never attacked each other physically again.

She determined that she would never marry a man who would treat her like that.

17

Year of Reprieve

After three years of agricultural life, Gertel watched Grandma arrive again with her siblings, this time on the back of a truck. "Well," Grandma exclaimed, brushing the dust off her skirt. "I think I prefer boat travel even if it does take longer. This trip took only two days, but such shaking around and choking on dust. I feel black and blue all over." She rubbed her back and winced.

"Where did you sleep?" asked Gertel.

"On the truck. It goes day and night." She shook her head in tired disapproval.

For several days Grandma observed Gertel leaving for the plantation and coming home again, dirty and exhausted. Finally she could stand it no longer.

"I am ashamed of you," she told Gertel's mother. "I sent this girl home with a whole valise full of clothes, and now she is wearing rags. She doesn't even have shoes." True, Gertel had not had a new dress since she left Belize City. Her old ones were much too tight and short. Her dad had brought her a pair of moccasins made out of cowhide to wear for work. Otherwise she went barefoot. "She is working like a slave and not like a young lady," was Grandma's indignant assessment.

"What can I do?" Mom threw up her hands. "Charles gives me hardly any money, and we have to grow our own food or starve."

"I have decided," said Grandma in her no-nonsense voice, "that I am taking Gertel back to the city with me. Marlene can stay home for a year. A young girl needs some social life."

Gertel's eyes filled with grateful tears. *Bless Grandma. Back to the city for a year!* She walked on air for the next few days until the time came to leave.

Marlene wailed and fumed about having to stay home. She had never liked hard work. "There is no way I am going out to grub in the dirt and chop weeds," she stormed.

Gertel knew Marlene would not help her mom like she had, but she decided it would be good for her sister to get more experience with being the primary helper at home.

The little school in their village had closed, but the village children now walked into town to attend the Anglican school there. Myrtle and Charles did not need to go back to Belize City for schooling, so Gertel and Grandma traveled back to the city by themselves.

Back in her old place in Grandma's house, Gertel found that everything had changed. No longer was she a schoolgirl with a rigid schedule to follow. Even Grandma's strict rules seemed to relax somewhat now that she was a young lady going on eighteen.

Grandma lost no time in sending her to Miss Inez for some new clothes. She still insisted on long, full skirts, full sleeves, and high necklines, but Gertel was allowed to choose her own fabric.

"We need to find you some work," said Grandma. "I know a lady from the church guild who needs a girl to clean her house. I'm sure you could do that."

Cleaning houses and washing dishes for other people felt like a welcome reprieve after chopping bush and beating out beans. Gertel picked up several domestic jobs, some of them involving cooking. She also babysat occasionally, earning enough money to give some to Grandma for her room and board and still have some left for herself. She treated herself to an occasional chocolate bar and even bought herself a hat for church. Lolette still lived at Grandma's and went to school, but Gertel didn't envy her. She reveled in her independence.

She made friends with several girls from church, and they would go shopping together or plait each other's hair or just walk down the street together, enjoying each other's company. She had outgrown Girl Guides, but now there were youth programs at church and even parties.

One day a letter addressed to her was delivered to the house. The envelope contained an invitation to a party at her friend Sonja's house. "May I go?" she asked Grandma anxiously.

"Of course. This is a very respectable affair. You must carry the invitation with you and present it at the door; otherwise they won't let you in. Her parents will be present, so there will be no drinking or nonsense."

Gertel attended many parties that year. Most of them included square dancing, which Gertel thoroughly enjoyed. She caught on quickly to the steps and joined in heartily. The only thing she found unpleasant about dancing was when she got partnered with a boy she disliked.

One time Lolette's younger brother escorted her to a party, and that night she didn't have to worry about disagreeable partners. She enjoyed having a set partner.

There were no special boys for her at this stage of her life, but she and her friends had endless discussions about which ones were handsome, which ones were lazy, and which ones were too smart-alecky.

The glorious year of freedom, fun, and fellowship came to an end when, some months after Marlene returned to the city to continue her education, Gertel's father again summoned her home. Her mother wasn't well, he said, and it was her responsibility as the oldest daughter to come home and take care of her.

As she bumped along, seated on a hard bench at the front of the box of a big truck, she agreed with Grandma that although faster, truck travel was not nearly as pleasant as the riverboat had been. This truck carried big bags of flour, rice, and beans as well as several dozen wooden crates at the back of the box. The mud track which they called a road had such deep mire in one place that the truck got stuck in the ruts. Another truck at the top of the incline hooked a rope to their truck and pulled it up the hill. Because of the heavy load on the back, the truck's front end kept lifting, and Gertel feared they would flip over. The passengers had no way to jump out because of the tarp over the top of the truck. They were trapped. At last, to everyone's relief, the truck got out of the muck without tipping over.

Along the way they could see only the muddy road and the jungle that hemmed it in on both sides, viewed out the small opening in the rear of the truck. Whenever they met a vehicle coming the other way, one or the other of the two would have to pull over into one of the spaces cleared at half-mile intervals to allow the other to pass. Here and there the jungle was punctuated by new villages, like their own, that had sprung up along the new road.

Gertel comforted herself with the memories she had made in that year of reprieve. Life would probably not always be drudgery. Maybe someday she would have her own home, but for now she would go and help her mom as a dutiful daughter. Perhaps she could assuage Mom's loneliness and discouragement, the likely causes of her ailment. In the meantime, there were always people who needed a helping hand along the way. A young woman with four small children traveled with them; she looked as though she didn't have enough hands.

"Let me hold the baby," said Gertel, reaching for him. She took the baby and played finger games with him. The next two children came to watch. She shared some of the powder buns Grandma had sent along. She smiled as she recalled how they used to throw their crumbs to the fish on the river journey. Now she was sharing her bread again. All the weary day, she helped the grateful lady keep the children happy.

18

New Hope

Mom smiled as Gertel recounted her experiences in the city. The stories reminded her of her own teenage years. "I wish you could get a job here," she said with a tired sigh. "With the new road, maybe you could get a job in town. You could earn enough money that we could buy our rice and corn. And you wouldn't need to work so hard."

How nice it would be to have a job, Gertel thought. She wouldn't mind the walk to town, and she could see different people every day. A neighbor suggested that she apply for a job at the new hospital. "You could work as a cook or cleaning lady," she encouraged.

The next time Dad came home, Mom asked him if Gertel could try to get a job at the hospital.

"Absolutely not!" he replied.

"But why not?" asked her mother boldly.

"I don't want her gallivanting around town. Who knows what might happen to a girl on the loose in town? No!"

Gertel walked outside to hide her disappointment so her mother wouldn't feel so badly.

For lack of other activity, Gertel began to sew her own clothes. Mom couldn't help her because she had never done it, so Gertel figured it out for herself. She picked an old dress apart and used the pieces for a pattern. At first she sewed by hand, but then her mom resurrected an old treadle sewing machine and helped her oil it and get it running.

A lady from the Nazarene church stopped by their house one day. "We're starting a Bible school for young people down close to Benque," the lady explained to her mother. "We wondered if Gertel would want to go."

Gertel's heart skipped a beat and then began to race. She would love to go to Bible school! Her mother looked excited as well. "I'll have to talk to her father," she said slowly. Gertel tried not to get her hopes up.

"No!" said her father the next time he was home. Slightly drunk, he slapped a few bills down on the table and then collapsed onto the bed. The next morning before he left, he growled again, "Don't let that girl go off and leave you."

But he couldn't stop her from attending the Nazarene services that were held under their house.

That fall a visiting speaker came for a week of revival meetings. Revival meetings had not been a part of the Anglican Church, so they aroused Gertel's curiosity. She attended every night. The evangelist shared God's plan of salvation from the Fall of Adam and Eve to the death of Christ on the cross.

"Ye must be born again!" was his theme on the fourth night. Gertel sat riveted in her seat. She had heard the same phrase in her Anglican confirmation classes, but the priest had not explained what it meant. "We are all born in sin. The Bible says that there is none righteous. We all need to be born again, and God calls every one of us. You will know God is calling you when you feel that you are guilty before Him. When you know that if you died tonight, you would go to hell, that is the Spirit of God convicting you. Then you must respond to the call. Come to Jesus and accept His free gift of salvation. Ask Him to forgive your sins. Invite Him to come into your heart and make you a new creature. That's what it means to be born again. Jesus comes to live in our hearts, and we are changed. All things become new. We have a new perspective on life. Jesus will be there to help us in the trials and tribulations we face. He says, 'Come unto me, all ye that labour and are heavy laden, and I will give you rest. Take my yoke upon you, and learn of me; for I am meek and lowly in heart' " (Matthew 11:28–29).

The preacher wiped the sweat from his face as he pleaded with the audience. "Do you want to be born again? Do you want Jesus to live in your heart? Come to Him now. Come forward and we will pray with you."

Gertel's heart was hungry. She longed for the peace that God could give. She wanted God to guide her life. She stepped into the aisle and went forward as the congregation sang, "Just as I am, without one plea . . ."

"Praise God!" shouted the preacher.

After the service, the pastor and his wife met with Gertel. "How can we help you?" they asked.

"I want to accept Jesus as my Savior," she said.

When they rose from their knees, Gertel felt light and free. She had been born again! She knew Jesus was living in her heart, and God would help her to live for Him.

One thing bothered her. She had heard the evangelist say that a believer should be baptized. "Should I be baptized now?" she asked.

The pastor looked thoughtful. "You are Anglican, aren't you?"

"Yes. I was baptized as a baby at St. Andrew's in San Ignacio and confirmed at St. Mary's in Belize City."

"Then you have been baptized. But now you have confessed your sins, and you have faith that God has forgiven your sins, so I think it is all right not to be baptized again. Just keep on trusting in the Lord and reading the Bible and obeying His commandments. God bless you, sister."

Gertel went home, satisfied and at peace.

Not long after that a neighbor stopped by to chat. "Did you hear that the Ramie Company across the river is looking for a girl to cook and wash for the workers and tend the store?"

"No," said Mom.

The Ramie Company, a new enterprise that had been established across the river in the area known as Spanish Lookout, cultivated an Asian plant called ramie, or China grass, from which silky fibers were extracted and used to make cloth. Gertel's father had recently started working there and usually came home on the weekends, so they knew about the company. But he had not told them about the job opening.

"I think it would be a good job for your daughter," the neighbor went on, nodding her head. "She is strong. She could do it."

Gertel felt a flutter of excitement. Her mom had been feeling better.

How she would love to have a job!

After the neighbor left, her mom surprised her by saying, "If we ask your dad, he will say no. I am just going to go over there tomorrow and volunteer you for that job without telling him. You are almost twenty years old. You can take care of yourself, and you are a hard worker. Besides, your father is right there and can keep an eye on you if he thinks he has to."

Gertel could hardly wait until her mom came home the next day.

"What did they say?" she asked eagerly.

"You can have the job," said Mom with satisfaction.

"When do I start?"

"As soon as you move in."

"Where will I stay?"

"They have cabins for the workers, and your father lives in one of them. Maybe you can stay with him."

Gertel shuddered. What would her dad say when he found out?

He heard the news the next Friday night when he came home, his breath laced with alcohol.

"You did what?" he shouted, slamming his fist on the table. "I wanted that job for Lucinda, and now you got it for Gertel!"

Gertel huddled in the kitchen, ready to bolt if he came after her.

"Why didn't you ask me first?" Dad stormed at his wife. "What is your problem?"

Mom said nothing.

Dad heaved himself into a chair, muttering curses about the crazy women in his house. "Where's my food?" he demanded.

Gertel quickly filled a bowl with rice and stewed beans and brought it to him. If they could get him to bed before he did anything rash, she might still have a job in the morning.

He shoveled in his food and then staggered to the bed, collapsing into a deep sleep. Gertel slipped into her own bedroom and barred the door. "Please, God, let me have this job," she prayed fervently.

19

Ramie

On Sunday afternoon Gertel accompanied her father back to the Ramie site. They rode a truck for a few miles down the road and then walked two miles to the river, where they crossed on a ferry that was little more than a large raft pulled across the river by a cable.

The Ramie Company comprised a small village. The workers lived in a row of tiny wooden houses that looked as though they had been slapped together in a hurry. The owner of the company, an Englishman by the name of Payne, had a larger house where he stayed while on the site. Mr. Longford, the secretary, along with his wife Alice and their family, lived in three rooms in the back of the office building, and beside it stood the company store where Gertel would work in the afternoons. Closer to the ramie fields stood the sheds that held the machinery used to extract and bale the fibers, which were then shipped to the United States to be made into fabric.

Some of the workers had brought their wives and families along, but Gertel had been hired to cook and wash for the bachelors and the men who came to stay for the week and left their families at home.

She shared a cabin with her father and, although he never talked much to her, he treated her civilly, and they got along all right. As a foreman, his responsibility was to plan the work and assign tasks.

Gertel's days began before dawn when she lit the fires in the kitchen beside their house. She made tortillas, refried beans, and eggs for the five or six men who ate around the little table in the kitchen. After breakfast had been cleared away, she tackled the laundry, scrubbing the shirts and pants on a scrub board in a large wash tub. The labor was backbreaking, but she was strong. She thrived on the companionship of other women who stopped by to pass the time of day.

She also prepared and served the noon meal, and at four in the afternoon Gertel took her place behind the counter in the small store to wait on customers. That was fun: weighing out flour and sugar and lard, sorting out nuts and bolts and nails, treating the little children to a gumball, listening to banter and gossip, and adding up the account book at the end of the day.

She became good friends with Bridgett Payne, the daughter of the owner who sometimes came to stay with her parents. The girls would visit, comb each other's hair, and cook treats for the men.

Another friend, Alice Longford, hired Gertel to come and help her clean and iron whenever she had extra time. Alice's husband had his own car, and occasionally Alice would invite Gertel to ride along to town with them. Mr. Longford drove like a maniac, Gertel thought. The car hurtled along, swerving from side to side as he jerked the steering wheel to avoid the worst potholes.

"He was an ambulance driver in England," Alice explained to Gertel, "and he still drives like that. I tell him he will be the death of me yet." She laughed nervously. It was scary but thrilling to go for a drive with Mr. Longford.

"Do you want to go along to Belize City with us?" asked Alice one day.

Gertel considered. Who would cook and wash if she went away for a whole day? Besides, she was trying to save her money to give to her mom. If she went shopping, she might spend it, and she really didn't need anything. In any event, she didn't quite like the idea of riding all the way to Belize City with Mr. Longford at the wheel. She decided to stay home.

That night as she prepared for bed, she looked out her window toward the Longford house. It was dark. She had not heard the car returning, so they must not be home yet. *I'm glad I didn't go along,* she thought. *Imagine driving in the dark with that ambulance driver!* She went to bed.

"Gertel!"

She sat up with a jerk. She thought someone had called her name.

It was the middle of the night. The voice sounded like Alice's. She ran to the front door and peered into the darkness at the Longford house. All was dark, and she couldn't see a car parked in front of it. She must have been dreaming.

The next day they got the news that the Longfords had been in an accident. Driving too fast around a curve, they had crashed head-on into a truck. Alice had flown through the windshield and broken her neck. Her jesting prediction had come true; her husband's driving was the death of her. Their two young daughters riding in the back were injured and taken to the hospital, but they recovered. The accident crippled Mr. Longford, who never came back to work at Ramie.

Gertel believed the accident had happened at the moment she heard Alice call her name. *What if I had gone with them to Belize City?* she wondered. *Why was Alice killed and I was spared? It makes me feel as though God has a special plan for my life,* she concluded.

In February of 1952, Mr. Payne informed his workers that King George VI had died. His daughter, Princess Elizabeth, had been crowned queen. Queen Elizabeth II looked beautiful, Gertel thought when a friend showed her pictures of the coronation. Now the national anthem had to be changed to "God Save the Queen," although the change made little difference to the people living along the banks of the Belize River.

One day when Gertel was bending over the wash tub, her friend Suzanne came and perched on a nearby stool. "The carpenter crew is going to build some new houses," she said.

"I know, my dad told me."

"I wish I could get a new house. My windows won't shut. I have to tie them shut every night."

Gertel laughed. "My shutter opens inside, and if I don't watch it, I crack my head on it when I sit up in bed."

"You should tell your dad to get the carpenter crew to fix your house. Yours is one of the oldest ones. They were slapped together in a hurry."

"I think he's going to do that. He said something about getting them to put a porch on the house too."

"There is a new man on the carpenter crew. I saw him yesterday. Nice, big, handsome fellow," Suzanne remarked.

"I saw him. My dad says he is from Belize City, so he thinks he is not much good. He says Belize City people have no ambition." The girls laughed together.

20
Ernest

A few days later, the carpenters arrived to fix up their house. Gertel watched them as she ironed shirts. The new man appeared to be working hard, even if he did come from Belize City. As she ladled out bowls of food for the men at lunchtime, she sensed his gaze on her. When she turned, she was startled by the intense look in his eyes. Blushing, she turned away, but she couldn't help wondering about those eyes. What was it about them? The next time she caught him looking at her, she noticed that his eyes had a bluish hue. Blue eyes in a black person?

That night after supper, one of Gertel's usual diners approached her. "Ernest, the new man—he needs someone to wash his clothes. You could take one more person, no?"

Gertel looked up from her dishpan and thought for a moment before answering. "Yes," she agreed. "One more won't make much of a difference. I can wash his clothes."

"I'll tell him."

Gertel watched as he relayed her answer to Ernest. She saw Ernest nod and glance toward her. *What kind of man is he?* she wondered.

Over the next few months she began to find out. Ernest Wagner, sometimes called Nesto, stayed longer and longer after supper. He didn't talk much, but he watched her as she cleared the table and washed the dishes. Sometimes he asked Gertel about her work and her family or shared some piece of news with her. Finally one night as she washed dishes, he asked her, "Would you like to go to a dance?"

She turned, startled. "My father wouldn't let us stay long," she said. "He's very strict."

"I noticed," he said. "But George's daughter is turning fifteen. He's holding a pig's head dance in town tomorrow for her birthday party. I'll talk to your dad. We won't stay late." George was one of the Ramie Company employees.

Gertel smiled. "I'd love to go."

The next night Gertel stood in front of her dresses. "Blue, blue, blue," she muttered. "I don't have any other color." She shrugged and chose the newest one. "This will have to do."

As she and Ernest approached the building where the party was going on, music filtered out into the street. *A marimba!* she thought, recognizing the hollow tones of the large wooden-tubed percussion instrument. The marimba, resembling a large xylophone, was played by two players and often used for dances.

They stopped to watch a group of men lower a pig's head wrapped in plantain leaves into a large hole in the ground. Steam rose when the bundle touched the hot rocks at the bottom of the hole. The men threw more hot rocks on top and then shoveled dirt over it.

"Go dance!" said one of the men, waving to them. "We'll pull it out in two hours."

Inside the building the music jauntily accompanied those in the middle of a dance. Ernest and Gertel sat on the sidelines and watched. "Have you danced much before?" Ernest asked her.

Gertel nodded. "When I lived with my grandma in the city, I was often invited to dances."

Ernest smiled and asked if she would like lemonade and cake. She nodded. While he was gone, she thought about the dances she had attended in the city. At least this time she didn't need to worry about who she would dance with. She had an escort.

They joined three other couples for a square dance. As they stepped and turned to the beat, Gertel felt fortunate that she had learned to dance in the city. And this was much more fun than any dance she'd attended before. She wished the night would never end.

After the party, Gertel and Ernest continued to spend time together. He often stayed after supper, and the two would converse around the table by the light of a kerosene lamp. Sometimes other young people joined them. Gertel would have liked to attend more dances, but her father liked to have her under his eye, and he seldom let her go. When they did go, they had to be home at an early hour.

Gertel liked what she saw in Ernest. He was a dependable worker, and she knew he didn't drink—at least not much. She enjoyed his quiet strength, although she knew his sturdy personality sometimes translated into formidable stubbornness. And Ernest had told her that he attended church. Gertel expected that they would do that together after they left Ramie. The company settlement had no church on the premises.

One evening as they sat talking after supper, Ernest turned and looked at her for a long time. His dark gray eyes with the blue halo around the iris held hers intently. After several moments of intense silence, he spoke softly. "Gertel . . . will you marry me?"

Gertel's breath came fast. She swallowed hard, then nodded and whispered, "Yes!"

Ernest's face brightened and his lips spread in a big smile. "I'll write your father a letter, asking for your hand," he said.

Gertel nodded. She supposed they ought to follow the custom, but she wished it weren't necessary. She could just imagine her father saying no, as he so often had whenever she wanted anything badly.

Two nights later she and Ernest sat in the house as her father read the letter. He looked up, cleared his throat, and began. "Well, marriage is a big responsibility," he said in the pompous tone of a preacher.

Gertel stopped listening. *Huh! Marriage is a big responsibility,* she thought cynically. *How did Dad fulfill his responsibility? He didn't take care of my mother because he had another woman. He made me do all the work at home, and now he thinks he can lecture Ernest?* She felt her pulse beat in her neck. She swallowed and clenched her fists under the table. She glanced at Ernest. He sat quietly, his face stolid, impossible to read. She forced her mind to concentrate.

"If you can't treat her the way I treated her mother, then you can't marry her," her father was saying.

Gertel felt something snap inside her. "No!" she interrupted. Ernest and her father stared at her in surprise. Jutting her chin in the air, she gave Ernest a determined look. "If you're going to treat me like he treated my mother," she said evenly, "then I won't marry you. I'm staying home."

Her father frowned. Then he shook his head. "You see what she's like," he said, splaying his hands helplessly.

Ernest looked at her with understanding but said nothing. She had told him a little of her father's abuse, and he had said, "No man should treat a woman like that." She knew she could trust him. He would not be like her father.

When they went for a walk outside later, Ernest told Gertel what his mother had said when he told her that he wanted to get married. " 'She's a simple country girl,' she said. 'Are you sure, Nesto? You'd better be good to her.' "

"What did you say?" Gertel asked.

"I said, 'Yes, I love her and I will take care of her.' " Ernest paused and smiled warmly at Gertel. Then he said, "I would just like to go to the church and get married quietly, but my mother says we have to have a wedding, at least for the family."

Like all girls, Gertel had dreamed of her wedding day. How glad she felt that they would have a real wedding, though she would have married Ernest without a celebration.

"I bought material for your dress while I was in Belize City," Ernest went on. "My cousin Miss Lucille will sew it."

"Good!" said Gertel. Then she added with a chuckle, "She had better make it modest. Even though my grandma is old, she still always checks to make sure we girls are properly covered."

Since the wedding would be catered by the Star Club, of which her father was a member, there was little food preparation to do. She and Ernest went to the city to pick up her dress. His mother received her graciously. Like her son, she spoke little, but Gertel knew they would be friends.

While they were there, they went to visit Ernest's Aunt Elva. When they arrived at the house, Gertel said, "I've been here before."

"You sure?" Ernest looked at her, puzzled.

"One time when Grandma had me make a stew, we brought it here to this house."

When she told Aunt Elva about it, the elderly lady smiled widely. "So you were the little girl who brought me some stew when I was sick. Well, well! And now Ernest is going to marry you. Well, Ernest, one thing I can tell you. That girl can cook."

"I know that already. She feeds me now," said Ernest.

The time passed quickly, and soon she would be Mrs. Ernest Wagner. She smiled to herself. Wagner? It was a German name. Ernest's grandfather had been German; from him Ernest had inherited his blue eyes. Gertel Wagner. She liked how the name tasted as it rolled off her tongue.

21

The Wedding

Gertel smoothed her skirt and turned slowly in front of the mirror on her wedding day. Her dress, made of a lovely embossed white taffeta, had long, full sleeves and a tiered skirt. A short veil hung around her face, making her feel like an angel. She knew she was no angel, but she wanted to be the best wife she could be for Ernest.

"Are you nervous?" asked Bridgette Payne, one of her bridesmaids, as she tied the sash on her own dress. Marie, the other bridesmaid, picked up a bouquet of orange blossoms and handed it to Gertel.

"My heart is beating fast," Gertel admitted, "but I'm not afraid. Ernest is a good man, even if he is stubborn sometimes."

"He is stubborn all right," said Bridgette, tucking her blonde curls under her hair band. "He wouldn't even have a best man."

Gertel smiled and shrugged. "My dad insisted we have a church wedding, and he wanted to invite a lot of guests, but Ernest told him he isn't marrying for show. He didn't want to have a big wedding at all. He told me it isn't going to be any bigger than it has to be, so he isn't having any attendants."

Later, from the back of the church, she glanced over the audience, picking out her family, along with Grandma and Grandpa. Only a few of Ernest's relatives attended. Most of them lived too far away, but his parents and a few cousins had come. Friends from the Ramie Company and San Ignacio filled the remaining benches.

On her father's arm, she walked slowly up the aisle toward her groom who stood all alone, big and handsome in his black suit and white shirt and tie, waiting for her at the other end. Ernest's piercing gray-blue eyes held hers all the way, and at last she let go of her father's arm and took her place beside the man she loved.

With great sincerity they said their vows, and at last the priest intoned, "I now pronounce you man and wife." Hand in hand, their hearts fairly bursting with happiness, they walked down the aisle.

After the congratulations outside the church, Ernest's aunt came and told them it was time to form the procession to the Star Club, where the reception would be held. "You lead out and we will all follow you," she directed.

Ernest stalled. "How far is it?" he wondered.

"Three or four blocks," answered Gertel. "It's not far."

"No," said Ernest. "I'm not walking that far. There's a car here. We'll ride." A friend from the Ramie community had driven them to the wedding and stood waiting by his car.

"But people expect us to walk," countered Gertel. "They'll be disappointed." According to local custom, the bridal party would walk slowly from the church to the reception while people threw confetti. That way the town folks could enjoy the show.

"I don't care. I don't like making a show. If you want to walk, walk—but you can walk alone. I'm riding."

That was her man. Stubborn as a mule. She climbed into the car after him.

In typical Belizean style, the wedding reception was replete with lots of music and lots of food: rice and beans and chicken, followed by cake and lemonade.

After the meal, the dance began. Gertel had been dreading it because she knew she would be expected to dance with her father.

When the music started, her dad stood up. "Come on, Gertel," he called out. Her father had never touched her kindly. She felt sickened by the charade. What a relief when the duty was over and she could stay by Ernest's side. Here she would stay, and her father would never touch her again.

They rode home to the little company house that had been allotted to them. Ernest and his crew had built it recently.

"I don't want my wife to have to earn money," said Ernest. "I will provide for you. You do the cooking and take care of the family."

"Family?" she giggled. "What family?"

"I'd like lots of children, wouldn't you?" he teased.

"Sure. I like children. We'll have lots. But you want me to stop working in the store right now? Whatever will I do all day?" she looked around the one main room that opened into the single bedroom.

"Well, maybe you could work in the store for a while until they find someone else for the job, but no more cooking for men and washing. That work is too hard."

The next morning Gertel unpacked her wedding gifts and spread them on the small table Ernest had built. What would she do with all these glasses and pretty serving bowls? She had only two shelves for storing dishes and food. She picked out one set of bowls and a couple of larger ones and packed the rest away. She put a pretty new set of sheets on the bed, also built by Ernest, and packed the remaining linens in boxes. Maybe someday she would need them. Then she swept her little palace and scrubbed the plain board floor. She liked cooking for only two people, but she often made far too much and had to carry food to her parents. Mom had come to stay with Dad at Ramie by this time.

Before long Gertel was wishing she didn't have to do any cooking. She didn't feel well.

"You'll have to be careful now. If somebody is sick, you stay away. You don't want your baby to be harmed by the sickness," warned Maria, a Hispanic neighbor who had stopped in to visit with her. "And you have to be careful what you eat. Don't eat the rice bun . . ."

Gertel wrinkled her nose. She liked the rice bun, the crust of browned rice at the bottom of the pot.

"And don't sit in the doorway or on the steps . . ." Maria ticked off the restrictions on her fingers.

Gertel thought carrying a baby sounded rather complicated.

Just then they heard a "halloo" from outside. "Hey, Gertel! Come see what I brought you." It was her father. Gertel went to the door. On the grass lay a small brown animal about the size of a dog.

"A fawn!" she cried. "Where did you find it?"

"In the bush. He looks like he needs some mothering. I thought you might like him for a pet."

Gertel knelt, gathering the trembling, spindly-legged creature into her arms. "He's so tiny and so pretty," she crooned, stroking his soft neck. The fawn looked warily at her with his large, brown eyes.

Maria stood in the doorway, watching. "You'd better put a ribbon around his neck so nobody shoots him," she cautioned.

"Good idea," agreed Gertel.

She found a pink ribbon for her little Bambi, as she named him, and put him on a diet of bread and milk. He grew sleek and handsome, running around the camp. At first he never strayed far from the house, but as he grew older, he would venture into the jungle for hours at a time. However, he always knew when to come home for the corn Gertel saved for him. Everyone in camp knew Bambi and tolerated his mischief.

One evening some of Ernest's friends came to hunt in the jungle nearby.

"Don't shoot my deer!" Gertel called after them as they entered the bush. "He has a pink ribbon around his neck, so you'll know he's a tame deer."

"No, Mrs. Wagner, we won't shoot your deer," they called back, adjusting their lights.

Gertel went back to patting corn tortillas. A few minutes later she heard the crack of a gun. "I hope they didn't shoot my deer," she muttered to herself.

But when the men returned, they were shamefaced. "Well, Mrs. Wagner," they stammered, "See, the deer was in the bushes . . . it was dark . . . we saw only the back side of it . . . well . . . we broke your deer's leg, Mrs. Wagner. We're very sorry." There lay Bambi, in the front yard. When he saw her, he struggled to stand up, but he couldn't get onto his three legs.

Maria came running. She had heard the shot.

"We'll have to put him down," said Ernest, looking down at the stricken animal.

Gertel covered her face with her hands to hide her tears and ran into the house. Maria followed her.

"At least you can eat the meat," Maria tried to console her. "Deer meat is very good."

Gertel was horrified. "I won't eat any of that meat. He was my pet."

"You have to eat it," Maria said adamantly. "If you don't eat some of it, your baby might die, or at least he will be marked."

Gertel knew this was likely just another one of Maria's irrational superstitions. Yet the woman was so solicitous for her welfare that, in order to not offend her, Gertel forced herself to eat a bite or two of the stewed meat that Maria brought her the next day.

22

William Alexander III

In time the building contract at Ramie ended. Ernest decided to go back to Belize City and look for work. "Carpenters can always find jobs," he told Gertel. "I know several men who would hire me."

The doctor had told Gertel she had a hernia. "What did you do to get something like this?" he asked. "Were you doing heavy lifting or something?"

Gertel didn't answer, but she remembered how she would push and lift the heavy boxes and bags of supplies at the Ramie store.

"I am afraid it might complicate the birth," he warned. "You should be in the city, close to a hospital where they can take care of you. In the meantime I will give you medication to try to shrink it."

Ernest settled Gertel into her grandma's home in the city. He knew she would be cared for there. Grandma made sure she didn't tire herself or lift anything heavy. Gertel enjoyed visiting some of her old friends and attending church at St. Mary's again.

When she went for her next checkup, the doctor frowned and shook his head. "Your baby is too big. You are gaining weight too fast." He scribbled on a notepad and handed her a paper. "Follow this diet, and remember: no salt, no fat, and eat only bread you can see the light through. It would be good if you could lose a few pounds."

No fat? No salt? What could she eat?

Grandma studied the doctor's instructions. "That man is crazy," she sputtered. "How does he expect you to have enough strength to deliver this child?"

Nevertheless, Gertel attempted to follow the doctor's instructions.

She tried eating a spoonful of unsalted rice. "I can't eat this," she complained. "And this boiled fish has no taste. I can't eat it," she repeated, pushing her plate aside.

"This is what you get to eat," Grandma said unsympathetically. "Might as well get used to it."

Gertel pushed herself away from the table. "I need something with some taste. I'm going to go buy some shaved ice and syrup from the vendor." She got a thermos and put some milk in it. Then she went out and found a man selling iced drinks from a push cart. "Here, fill it with ice and strawberry syrup," she said.

For the next month she practically lived on milk with ice and syrup. She could vary the flavors, and it sure beat tasteless food. Sipping the cool, sweet concoction helped her cope with the increasing heat of dry season.

At her next doctor visit, she stepped on the scale.

"You haven't lost an ounce," he scolded impatiently. "Are you keeping the diet I gave you?"

"Keeping it?" she snorted. "I can't even eat it."

"If you don't stop gaining weight, I'll have to put you in the hospital," he threatened.

Grandma worried about the hernia. At the first twinge of labor pain, she sent Gertel to the hospital. All day long the pain came and went, and all night too. Gertel became frightened when the ordeal went on into the next day. She prayed fervently for the safe arrival of her baby. She wished Ernest were with her, but he was far away. Grandma had sent for him, but he hadn't come yet. As she tossed and turned through the night, she prayed over and over that the baby would be born soon and that everything would be all right. The nurses kept encouraging her to not give up, and the doctor checked on her every few hours. The baby just did not want to be born.

On the third day, she opened her eyes to see Marlene and Adele, Ernest's sister, standing by her bedside. "I didn't know you could pray in Spanish," said Marlene worriedly.

"Was I? I'm praying in any language I know," replied the weary patient.

Seeing how haggard Gertel looked, Marlene began to cry. "What if she dies?" she asked Adele. "Can she go on much longer like this?"

Adele had had a few babies of her own. "She won't die," she assured Marlene, "but I don't think that baby will come until Nesto gets here."

"What if he doesn't come until tomorrow?" sobbed Gertel.

That night, Gertel felt so exhausted she thought she wouldn't make it. "Don't go to sleep now," urged the nurse. "It won't be too long. Don't give up."

Several times through the night, Gertel opened her eyes to see an unfamiliar nurse with long black braids standing at the foot of her bed, regarding her with compassion. The woman's presence gave her the courage to fight on.

The next morning, just as Ernest turned in at the hospital gate, his son was born.

"How was the journey?" he asked when he was allowed to see Gertel.

"Terrible!" she answered. "I don't want another one!"

They admired the baby together. His ebony skin glistened, and his cheeks were full and round. *He's beautiful,* Gertel thought. *All nine pounds of him.* His eyes, when he did peep them open, were a deep blue. "Maybe his eyes will be blue like yours," she said. "I don't know how to take care of a tiny baby, though," she confessed, tucking his blankets around him.

"You'll figure it out," he assured her.

She told him about the strange nurse who had cheered her on that last night. "I never saw her before or since," she said, puzzled.

"Maybe it was an angel," he suggested. "No matter who it was, I am glad you and the baby are alive and well. Thank God for that."

Gertel spent ten days in the hospital recovering from the birth. The nurses were concerned that she would have help for a while. "Do you have someone to help you when you go home?" the doctor asked. "You had a long, hard labor, and you are too weak to do the work yourself."

"I'll be all right," Gertel assured him. She just wanted to get out of that hospital. She didn't really have anyone to help her, and she didn't even know where she would go. Ernest worked away from home, and her mother lived far away in the Cayo District.

Ernest's parents came to visit her and their new grandson. His father cradled the tiny bundle in his arms and smiled down at him. "Does this little fellow have a name yet?" he asked.

"No," said Gertel. She and Ernest had talked about it but had been unable to decide on a suitable name. Ernest figured they would find one that fit sometime.

Ernest's father smiled broadly. "I'll give him my name then. I am William Alexander II, and he can be William Alexander III."

Oh, yes. It was perfect. Gertel felt certain that Ernest would approve.

"I'll take care of registering him at the registry office," promised William Alexander II. "You don't have to worry about it."

"Are you going home to your mom when you leave the hospital?" asked Miss Rose, Ernest's mother, as she took a turn cuddling the baby.

"No, it's too far away," said Gertel.

"You can come home with us," she offered. "We'd be glad to take care of you and this sweet little fellow."

Gertel sighed in relief. It would be nice to live with her in-laws. "I'll go get my things." She stood up.

"You just sit down. I'll get them." Miss Rose handed the baby to his mother and bustled about packing Gertel's clothes into the valise. "I'll just change this baby and get him ready to go too. You need to rest."

As they exited the hospital, Miss Rose hovered at Gertel's elbow, making sure she didn't fall. *I'm not that much of a cripple,* thought Gertel, but it did feel good to have someone looking out for her.

At home, Miss Rose tucked Gertel into a bed and gave her orders to not walk down the steps for anything. "If you want something, just let us know. We'll get it for you. And don't worry about the baby. When he needs to eat, I'll bring him to you. Otherwise, I'll bathe him and change his nappy. You just relax."

For a whole week Miss Rose pampered her, and Gertel slowly began to feel alive again and ready to be up and around. She stayed with her in-laws for three months more, and then Ernest came back to take her home.

But where was home? They had no house of their own. They finally moved to Gertel's parents' house in Esperanza until they could find other accommodations.

One of the first Sundays after they moved, they had little William baptized at St. Andrew's Anglican Church, just as both she and Ernest had been baptized as babies. Gertel prayed that the Lord would take care of her son.

23

Against the Flow

L iving with Gertel's parents was less than ideal. Her dad had a new job at a beef farm a few miles down the road, so he spent more time at home. He still did not have a good opinion of Ernest. Occasionally he would repeat his old litany about people from Belize City having no ambition. Ernest walled in a corner under the house so they would have a bit of privacy. Gertel and her mom cooked together and used the same laundry tubs. Gertel felt uncomfortable with the arrangement, but at least they had their own sleeping space. She tried to stay out of her dad's way when he was in a bad mood, which happened frequently. She feared there might be trouble ahead with two families living under one roof.

One morning she carried little William up the stairs and sat down to nurse him.

"How is the baby today?" asked Mom. "He sure is getting chubby, and he can almost sit by himself already. Soon he will be running around."

"Here, you can hold him," Gertel said when he had finished eating.

Her mom took the baby and tickled him. She bounced him up and down on her knee until he giggled. She ran her fingers over his kinky curls and was quiet for a while, her lips pursed. She seemed to be thinking serious thoughts. Finally she looked up and fixed her eyes on Gertel. "He is the firstborn, you know."

Gertel's heart skipped a beat. "Yes, he is," she replied calmly, although her mind was in a whirl. She knew what her mother was implying, but she refused to give her the satisfaction of a reply.

"Many people give their firstborn to their parents." Mom's voice sounded ominous. "I expect to raise this boy."

"I'll have to talk to Ernest about that." Gertel made an effort to keep her voice steady. Mom glared at her sternly but said no more.

As soon as possible, Gertel excused herself and retired to her little room. "I'll never give my baby away," she whispered fiercely as she clutched little William to her chest. She thought of her cousin Lolette, who had been given to Grandma when she was a toddler. Lolette had no respect for the mother who gave her away. She would hardly speak to her mother when she came to visit. Gertel didn't want that to happen to her little son.

The next time Ernest came home she told him what her mother wanted. Ernest looked shocked. "No way!" he said. "We are not giving our child away. He is ours."

"So I should tell her the answer is no?" asked Gertel, relieved but still apprehensive.

"You give puppies away, but not children," Ernest snorted in disgust.

"That's what I think," Gertel agreed, "but I hate to think what Mom will say when I tell her. I'm afraid she will be vexed. She is counting on it."

"I don't care what she says. He is ours and no one can take him away from us."

Gertel smiled. Stubborn Ernest. This was one time she was glad for his inflexibility. She thought again of the riverboats chugging down the river, going with the flow of the current. But sometimes the boat got hung up on rocks and the current couldn't move it. She tended to go with the flow and not cause a disturbance, but this was one time she and Ernest would hook their boat to a tree and resist the current. They would not give their baby away.

Trying to steady her trembling knees, Gertel told her mother of their decision. "God gave this child to us, and he is our responsibility. You might spoil him. God will hold us responsible for his training."

Tears rolled down her mother's thin cheeks. "I had only four," she pleaded. "You can have more."

"Why did you have only four?" Gertel had always wondered about that.

Her mother stared out the window and replied in a sad monotone. "I had a tumor, and it gave me trouble for many years. Then I went to a bush doctor up at the Northern Lagoon. He gave me bush medicine, and it took care of the pain. But I never had any more babies. That's why I thought . . ." Her voice trailed off as she looked wistfully at William. "But it's up to you," she said, shrugging pathetically.

Gertel's mother said no more about adopting William, but she resented their decision. From her little room, Gertel heard her mother complaining to a neighbor. "Gertel won't even give us one," she sputtered indignantly. "And she is expecting the next one already. How will she take care of two babies? She has no respect for her parents."

The neighbor clucked sympathetically.

Over the next months Gertel's mother reiterated her tale of woe many times, talking about Gertel's selfishness and stubbornness to all her friends. Gertel found it hard to take the black looks and hurtful remarks her mother sent her way. How she wished they could have their own home.

They almost lost William before his first birthday, and all because of an iguana. Gertel had never eaten iguana because of her mother's repugnance for it, but one time when her in-laws were visiting, Grandpa Wagner found a nest of iguana eggs and had Miss Rose boil them for him. He offered the baby some of the soft egg from his plate. William, who loved to eat anything, opened his little pink mouth eagerly. Gertel objected mildly, "We don't eat iguana."

"Oh, this isn't the meat. This is just an egg. It won't hurt him," said Grandpa as he continued to spoon the egg into the baby's mouth.

That night William cried with a tummy ache. His severe diarrhea lasted for several days, and he refused to eat anything but his mother's milk. Gertel began to worry. She could almost see the fat melting from his bones. He whined constantly and seemed listless.

Suzanna, a neighbor, clucked sympathetically over the suffering baby. "Tsk, tsk. Iguana egg be cold. Not good for baby." She ran her hand gently over the top of William's head. His soft spot had sunken in.

Gertel's mother agreed that babies should not be given meat or eggs from a cold-blooded animal like an iguana. Gertel prayed for her little boy and kept nursing him.

After a week he slowly began to improve.

"It was the breast milk that saved him," said Miss Rose. "Without that, he might not have made it."

All the more reason to not eat iguana meat or eggs, thought Gertel, even though she still liked to stand like a trussed iguana.

Little William provided sunshine for her days as he took his first steps and learned to say "Mama" and "Dada." Every time she watched him discover some new talent, she rejoiced all over again that they had kept him. What would life be like without her little roly-poly boy? Since most of the people around him spoke Creole, that is what he learned, but Gertel determined he should learn to speak proper English too. She knew what Grandma would say if he didn't!

Along with the bright spots in Gertel's life came a few things that chafed like the sand along the river's shore. Besides the friction with her mom, she was disturbed that Ernest drank at times. When the men got their paychecks after a hard week of work, they usually went to a bar and celebrated with a few beers. She supposed all men were the same, so she didn't complain too much when Ernest went with his coworkers. At least he never came home drunk or beat her or cursed at her, and he always left enough money for her to buy groceries. She just prayed that he never would get into the habit of drinking heavily.

The Nazarenes had built a small church across the road. Sometimes Ernest and Gertel walked there on Sunday mornings. "I don't mind attending here," said Ernest. "It's too far to carry the baby all the way into town to go to church—but I was born and baptized an Anglican, and I'll die an Anglican." Gertel said nothing. She wanted to worship God, regardless of the name of the church.

"Your father said he will let us build a house beside his," Ernest told her one weekend. "I have been planning a house in my mind for a while. I'll start collecting materials right away."

How nice it would be to wash and cook in my own house without Mom's critical eyes on me! thought Gertel, elated.

While Ernest planned and gathered materials for their new house, Gertel hemmed more diapers for the new baby.

24

Alvan Codwell Godfrey

On a Sunday morning, Gertel sent for the taxi Ernest had requisitioned to take her to the hospital in Cayo when her time came. The baby was born right at noon when the other patients were enjoying their lunch.

"You rude boy," Gertel scolded him playfully when they brought the baby to her. "You come on a Sunday morning so I can't go to church, and at lunchtime so I can't eat my lunch."

The baby was long, lanky, and several shades lighter than his older brother. He also had the same blue eyes except that, by this time, William's eyes had turned dark brown like her own. Again Ernest missed the birth, but he came to see her before she left the hospital. He was pleased to have another son. "I'll soon have my own carpenter crew," he joked.

"Let them grow up first," she protested with a grin.

Gertel's grandparents came to visit the new baby. Grandma hadn't changed a bit. Her hair was now nearly white, but she still wore it pulled back into a knob. She continued to wear modest dresses and use no makeup or jewelry. Her back was still straight, and she handled herself as elegantly as ever.

Grandma laid the baby on her lap and studied his little face gravely. "Do you have a name for this one?" she asked after a few minutes.

Gertel shook her head. "We haven't found a good one yet."

"Ah," said Grandma, a pleased smile spreading across her face, "then I will give him a name." Her finger gently traced the line of the baby's chin. Then her eyes brightened. "His name will be Alvan Codwell Godfrey." She looked up to see Gertel's reaction.

Gertel nodded her head. "That is a good name. It sounds very distinguished. Three names. It is the name of your oldest son, right?"

"Yes, and my son Alvan is a good man."

"It is good to have a family name just like William. He is named after his Grandpa Wagner, and now this little one will be named after his great-uncle on the Morris side." As soon as she could, Gertel registered the birth of little Alvan Codwell Godfrey Wagner.

Nineteen-month-old William accepted his new brother without protest. An easygoing child, he would bring a diaper for his mother or run and tell his grandma if Gertel needed something. Gertel's days flew by, and she didn't have to wonder what to do with her time. Running after the exploring William and feeding the baby took much of her time. Her mother often didn't feel well, so Gertel washed and cooked for her parents too. Trying to keep the house and yard cleaned up became her responsibility as well. Soon she was expecting another child. How she wished their new house were finished!

Her dad continued to insult Ernest. "That boy has no gumption. Why doesn't he build you a house of your own? I warned you about him. He comes from Belize City."

The pile of lumber grew higher, but Ernest had so little time at home that the construction of the house hadn't even begun. She felt thankful that he had work, but she did wish they had their own house before baby number three arrived. However, she didn't complain but kept patiently taking care of her children and her parents.

"No, William, you stay up here while Mama goes downstairs to chop wood," she told him one day. She did not trust him nearby when she was swinging an axe. William whined but finally settled on the top step of the porch to watch her. When she turned her back, he reversed and quickly crawled down the steps after her. Little Alvan sat in the doorway and gurgled excitedly as he watched his brother descend. He paused to consider. Finally he turned around as William had done and reached a leg down for the next step. His leg slipped off the side of the step, and suddenly he was hurtling through the air, ten feet to the bare ground below.

Gertel, her axe in the air, heard the thump behind her. She turned to see baby Alvan on the ground, lying absolutely still. "My baby!" she screamed and ran for him.

From the other side of the yard, her father heard her scream. "That careless girl," he said to himself. "She's hit the baby with the axe!" He grabbed a stick and ran across the yard, ready to beat her for her carelessness.

Her mother came flying down the steps. Alvan lay in Gertel's arms, blue and not breathing. "Alvan!" Gertel called hysterically. "Alvan!" She shook him to try to get him to respond.

"Get some water from the barrel," ordered her mom.

Her father quickly brought a calabash of water, and Mom threw it into the baby's face. Alvan gasped, jerked, sputtered, and then let out a wail. What a relief to hear him cry!

"Take him to the hospital," said Mom, shoving Gertel toward the road. "Go!"

Gertel stumbled to the edge of the road and frantically waved at the first vehicle that came along. She was too distracted to notice what kind of vehicle it was. "I need to get to the hospital," she gasped, climbing in beside the driver. Alvan was still screaming from his fright. Gertel couldn't forgive herself. How had she let this happen? She kept watching Alvan to make sure he didn't stop breathing again.

The driver shifted into gear and took off. "What happened?" he asked in concern.

"My baby fell from the top step," she answered shortly. Under her breath she whispered, "Hurry, hurry!"

He glanced over at the baby. "How old is he?"

"Seven months." She wished he'd just be quiet and drive. What would Ernest say when he found out? She wasn't fit to be a mom if she couldn't watch her children.

"No! He's too big for that," the driver was saying.

"You're telling me I don't know how old my own baby is!" Gertel exploded.

The driver simply raised his eyebrows and said no more. Moments later she looked up and recognized his cap and uniform. She blushed. She shouldn't have spoken to a law officer that way.

When they arrived at the hospital, she thanked him and apologized in a subdued tone before running with Alvan through the doors. "Please, God, let him be safe," she prayed over and over.

After the doctor had examined him thoroughly, he handed Alvan back to her. "He seems fine," he told her. "If he starts to vomit blood, or if he goes to sleep and you can't wake him up, bring him back in. You know," the doctor went on, "some people believe that each child has a guardian angel, and if something bad happens, you shouldn't make a big commotion or you will scare off the angel."

Gertel nodded. She had heard that superstition before.

"I'm glad you made a commotion, though. It is always better to be safe than sorry. If you have any more emergencies with your children, don't hesitate to bring them to the hospital."

Gertel held Alvan close and nodded. She did believe that children had guardian angels, but she resolved to watch both children more closely so their guardian angels wouldn't have to work so hard.

25

New House

The days and weeks marched on in a routine of washing clothes, making meals, tending her babies, and cleaning the house. The tensions beneath the surface continued to boil. Her mother complained if the boys cried at night, her dad scolded her if she didn't bring his meals on time, and both of them favored William with treats and extra hugs as if they were trying to steal his affection.

Her dad had a yellow mongrel that Gertel couldn't stand. The dog would slink around under the house and grab articles of clothing or the boys' toys and run off with them. She didn't trust him around the little boys either. She often picked up a stick of firewood and threw it at the dog to get rid of him. If her father caught her, he would tell her off. "That's my dog. Don't you go throwing sticks at my dog. If you had your own house, you wouldn't molest my dog."

Her mother left to visit Grandma for a few weeks, and Gertel had to cook and wash for her dad. She would carry his bowl of eggs and beans and fry jacks[21] up into the house and say, "Good morning!" as cheerfully as she could. He would just glare at her and not answer at all.

When her mom came home, she scolded Gertel. "Dad says you wouldn't talk to him. Why were you so rude to your dad?"

Living under this pressure wore Gertel's nerves down to the point where she could hardly eat. More than once, she put the boys down for their naps and slipped away down the hill to the little creek and sat on the bridge, watching the water gurgle over the rocks.

Her mom would coax her to eat, but she felt too stressed to swallow

---

[21] Deep-fried dough pieces. A traditional Belizean food.

anything. She didn't gain much weight with this third pregnancy.

The children squealed with excitement every other weekend when Daddy came home, and when Ernest was around, she felt as though she had a defender against the negative attitudes.

"I think I have enough material here now to start the house," Ernest announced one weekend when he had a few extra days off. He surveyed the pile of lumber and posts with satisfaction. Gertel breathed a sigh of relief. They would have the new house before the next baby arrived.

Ernest marked off the spot for a ten-by-twenty-foot house two hundred feet to the east of her parent's house. In the next two days he set the posts and nailed the long framing pieces between them. Gertel helped him plant a row of young malanga coco plants and another of cassava between the two houses. "These bushes will grow high and give us some privacy," he said. "When I come back in two weeks, we'll plant some corn and beans so we have our garden right here, and you won't have to go far to tend it."

"I still can't believe that Dad is letting us build on his land," said Gertel, leaning on her shovel. "I can hardly wait to move into our own house."

"I'll finish it when I come back in two weeks," he promised. "Until then the malanga and cassava can start to grow."

One day about a week after Ernest had started the house, Gertel felt a strange tension in the air when she went up the stairs to her mom's house. Mom's lips were pressed together in a grim line, and she didn't want to talk. Then a motor started up outside, and all of a sudden her mother started talking animatedly. "Did you hear about Sofia's sister? She is in the hospital. They think she might have appendicitis. She has been sick for three days and . . ."

Gertel looked out the window to see what engine was running so close to the house. "What is he doing?" she gasped. Her father was running a bulldozer right through their newly planted rows of cassava and malanga.

"I—I think he plans to make his garden bigger," stammered her mother.

"But we just planted that!" She wanted to run down and stop her father, but she knew it would do no good. Her dad obviously did not want them to use the land for a garden. She might as well not say anything. She would wait until Ernest came home and let him decide what to do. She hoped there wouldn't be a fight.

When she showed Ernest their ruined garden, a shadow crossed his face. He turned and walked toward the new house he had started. He stood there for a while, his arms crossed, his jaw clenched, while Gertel watched him anxiously. Then he turned to her, a resolute look on his face. "Come," he said. "We need to talk to someone else."

"Who?" she asked, nearly trotting to keep up with him.

"Mr. Benjamin Peters, the pastor from the Nazarene Church."

She nodded. That would be a good idea. He lived on the other side of the creek and across the road.

Together they walked down the road, each carrying a little boy. The pastor would be able to give them some advice.

Mr. Peters listened to their story, including Gertel's struggle to live harmoniously with her parents. He shook his head slowly. "It sounds as though you live too close to Gertel's parents." He thought for a moment. Then he offered, "Why don't you build your house here on my land?" He waved his arm toward the creek.

They stared at him in amazement. "Are you serious?" asked Ernest.

"Yes. There is plenty of land here. I will never use it all. I can lease part of it to you. Take your house down and bring the materials over and build here. There is even room to plant a garden."

Ernest looked at Gertel and she looked back at him, her eyes shining with hope. She nodded. He looked away for a moment, considering. Then turning back to Mr. Peters, he said, "We'd really like that. I'll dig up the posts and start planting them tomorrow, if it's all right with you. I'd like to get at least one room closed in and get Gertel settled before I leave again. We do need to get away from her parents."

The pastor nodded wisely. "Farther distance, better acquaintance," he said.

Gertel happily swung a machete to clear the tall grass from their new

house site while Ernest transported all the materials from her parents'
place. They left some of the pine and cohune trees standing for shade.
As she worked, Gertel planned how she would plant flowers in front of
the house, and the cassava could go beside it. The land sloped down to
the creek, where she could wash if she wanted to cool off.

Before Ernest left for another two weeks of work, he had framed the
house, thatched the roof, and closed in one room. "I paid José to come
and finish putting the boards up," he told Gertel. "He should be along
in a day or two, and then you can have the rest of your house."

Gertel nodded. "I hope he comes soon. It will be hard to be squished
into one room."

Three days later, José had yet to make his appearance. Gertel stood
outside her unfinished house and studied the stacks of lumber and
rolls of wire.

"What you do?" asked William, tugging at her skirt.

"Mama's gonna make our house," she told him.

"I help," he offered brightly.

"No, dearie. You watch Alvan." She pointed under the roof where
Alvan was crawling in the dirt. "You might get hurt out here, and then
what would your pa say?"

William reluctantly sat himself down near Alvan to watch the
operations.

Gertel lifted the first board. She stood it on end and wired it to the
horizontal supports at the top and bottom. The next board went beside
it. Interruptions kept her from working quickly; she had to stop to feed
the boys and take care of her chickens. In a little over a week, she had
put all the boards in place, and she had even sawed holes for the windows. Holding Alvan, she stood and surveyed her work with satisfaction. "What do you think, William? Is it a good house?"

William ran in and out of the door opening. "Mama make a house,"
he sang. "Mama make a good house."

"Now we need to fix the floor," she told the boys. While Alvan napped,
she and William walked down the slope to the creek, where she dug red

clay out of the bank and carried it home in buckets. The next day she poured water over the clay and mixed and pounded it with a wooden stick. Then she got down on her hands and knees and smoothed it over the floor with the palms of her hands. She gave up trying to keep the boys out of the clay, and they delighted in helping her. They were soon covered in red clay from head to foot. When the floor was smooth and shiny, she told the boys to stay off it for the rest of the day so it could dry. Then they all went down to the creek to bathe. It took a lot of scrubbing to get all that clay out of their clothes, but it was worth the work to have a house with a nice floor. Only doors and windows were still needed.

When Ernest came home, he walked slowly around the house, inspecting it and checking the wire ties. Gertel watched in silence.

"When did José come?" he asked.

"He never did come," she said.

He looked at her, startled. "Then who built this house?"

"I did," she said.

He looked again at the walls, the window holes, and the floor, which by now had hardened until it was nearly like cement. "That's amazing. Good job," he finally said with a grin. "I'll make the doors and shutters and put up some inside walls."

Gertel hummed happily as she stirred the pot of beans over the fire pit. Tomorrow she would build a real fire hearth with a stone base covered with hardened clay and finished off with mortar made from ashes. Then she would feel like a queen in her little kingdom.

26

Robert Linsford

On one of the weekends when Ernest was at home, the family was sitting around their fire on low stools, eating their rice and beans, when they heard a *"Buenos"* from the road. Ernest went out and returned shortly, followed by a dust-covered, unshaven man with a bundle over his shoulder.

"This man has walked from Guatemala," Ernest explained to Gertel. "He's hungry. Do you have some food for him?"

Gertel wanted to be generous, but she was a bit doubtful. While she dished out a bowl of rice and stew beans, she grumbled to herself, "Ha! You don't know anything about this man—where he comes from, where he's going, and what he's going to do."

"I hear there are jobs to be had in Belize City," said the traveler in Spanish. "I'm looking for work."

Before the man left, Ernest pressed a bill into his hand. "Here, friend. Catch a ride on a truck; you will get there quicker."

"How do you know he won't spend that money on alcohol?" she asked him after the man had gone.

"Cast your bread upon the waters: for thou shalt find it after many days," Ernest quoted. "I believe in helping people out. If we have it to give, we will give. I want you to cook plenty of food so you always have some to share if someone needs it."

"That's what Grandma always used to say," Gertel said.

"It's the Christian way," Ernest replied. Although he did not talk about God in a personal way, he was familiar with how a Christian should act.

Gertel remembered how she used to scatter bread crumbs on the water when she traveled by riverboat. She thought of the many people along the river who had freely shared food with the travelers on the boat, and of how Grandma always "cooked for the stranger." Now it was her turn. They had their own home and Ernest wanted her to share their bounty with the "fish" that came by.

. . . .

Alvan had just learned to walk and William had not quite turned three when she brought home her third baby boy. Grandma Liza came to see the new baby. "I'll name this one too, if you want," she offered.

Gertel nodded. They didn't have a name yet.

"Such big eyes," commented Grandma, studying the baby. "But he is tiny. He's the smallest baby you've had yet. I think Robert Linsford is a nice name. I saw an actor by that name once, and I liked the name. Do you like it?"

Gertel thought a minute. "Yes, I like Robert. We'll call him Robert."

Ernest took pride in his three little boys. A content baby, Robert didn't demand much attention.

Their relationship with Gertel's parents had drastically improved. Several times a week Gertel would walk the short distance down and across the road to her mom's house, Robert in one arm and Alvan holding onto her free hand while William trotted along behind. Her mother was always glad to see the little boys, and her father let William follow him around the yard and garden. Little by little, Gertel was learning to forgive her father for his unkindness. Forgiveness was not instantaneous or complete, but Gertel knew God was sanctifying her, helping her heart to change.

Sometimes one of her sisters would be there. Marlene had graduated from business college and was working in an office in the city. She always dressed in stylish clothes and didn't like to get dirty. Myrtle would soon graduate from Saint Hilda's College and had applied for a job at the new telephone company in Belize City. The telephone lines hadn't reached their district yet.

The aunties fussed over the children and brought them treats and gifts. When she cuddled her babies, Gertel didn't envy her sisters with their careers and modern lives. She had never finished her education, but she had a good husband, and God would give her wisdom to raise these precious children. She often told herself she would raise them with the same firmness and love her grandma had shown. That was the way to raise children.

Although little Robert was a complacent baby, the other two kept her on her toes. When Alvan toddled toward the road, William would go after him and drag him back. A responsible three-year-old, he had inherited his father's quiet, gentle disposition. In contrast, Alvan hurtled through life in the same rude way he had entered it. Always on the go, he gabbled constantly. Gertel did not worry much about Robert. He contented himself with lying on the bed and watching the lights and shadows caused by the waving palm leaves outside the window. He didn't wave his arms or kick his legs much. He didn't hold his head up for several months. He seemed slow. He would learn to roll over and sit up in time, she reassured herself.

But he didn't. When Robert was nearly a year old, Grandma Liza came to visit again. Gertel caught her studying Robert as he lay flaccidly on a blanket on the floor. Robert's dark eyes focused on a toy his mother had hung from the rafters.

"I think something is wrong with this baby," Grandma said at last. "He should be sitting up and crawling by now. I think you should take him to a specialist and get him checked out."

Gertel nodded slowly. "Yes, I've been wondering if something is wrong. The other boys were saying 'Mama' and 'Dada' and 'bye-bye' at this age. I keep hoping he will learn after a while. Maybe he is just slow." Her eyes filled with tears as she watched her baby.

"Take him to the doctor," urged Grandma.

"Do you think it's necessary? It's so hard for me to go anywhere with the children, and the next one is due in another month. But then if there is something we could do to help him, we should try. I would love to see him learn to walk and talk."

Acting on Grandma's advice, Gertel took Robert to the doctor. He took some X-rays and then examined the child carefully, shining lights into his eyes and gently manipulating his limbs.

When he had finished, he handed the baby to Gertel and sat back in his chair, his fingers smoothing his mustache thoughtfully.

"What is wrong, Doctor? Is there anything you can do for my baby?"

The doctor sighed and leaned forward. He shook his head. "I don't know how to say this, Mrs. Wagner, but I'm afraid that nobody can do much for Robert."

Gertel felt her heart drop into her stomach. "Isn't he just slow?" she pleaded. What did the doctor mean?

"Robert will never walk or talk. Although this is not the medical term for it, maybe you can understand better if I tell you that he has only half a brain. The only thing you can do is to teach him right from wrong. Teach him to obey you. He can learn that, just like a puppy can learn it. He will always be a child, but if he learns to mind your rules, he will be much less of a burden."

Tears pushed against Gertel's eyelids. Only half a brain! Robert would never walk. Never talk. How would she ever take care of him? She bowed her head over Robert's little one in despair. But then she straightened her shoulders. The doctor had been kind. "Thank you, Doctor. Don't worry. I'll try to teach him right from wrong."

She stood up and carried the limp Robert from the room. She would do all in her power to love this little one and teach him to obey. She didn't know where she would find the energy, with another baby coming in a few weeks, but she would call on God for help and take one day at a time.

"It's because you hated my dog," said her dad when he found out what the doctor had said about Robert.

Gertel doubted that, but she did wonder if her poor diet while pregnant with Robert had caused his deformity. At any rate, she couldn't change the past. She determined not to have any favorites among her children. She remembered the feelings of inferiority she had suffered because her parents seemed to favor her siblings over her. Each of her little boys was different, and she would love each one in his own special way.

27

Two Louises

Gertel left her boys in the capable hands of Frieda, a kind neighbor lady, when she went to the hospital to have baby number four. To Gertel's delight, Louise, an old school friend of hers who had become a nurse, cared for her during the birth.

While she scurried around arranging pillows and trying to make Gertel comfortable before the delivery, Louise said, "Maybe you will have a little girl this time. You know, I always said that if I ever had a baby girl, I would name her Sandra Louise. I like that name."

"That is a pretty name," Gertel agreed. "We never manage to choose names ahead of time. Maybe it will be a girl. My husband has three men for his carpenter crew now, and I think I need some help in the domestic department." The two laughed together.

As usual, Ernest was not at home. He was working in the Pine Ridge with his carpenter gang. She knew he would be of no use in the delivery room anyway; he couldn't stand to see anyone in pain. The sight of blood and the smell of medicine made him sick. A few months ago Alvan had cut his hand on a machete, and Ernest had taken him to the doctor to get it stitched. He had nearly passed out, and the doctor had needed to send him out of the room and call on another patient to hold Alvan's arm steady. So Gertel gave birth to her babies alone; she had grown used to it by now.

Several hours later Nurse Louise wrapped the tiny bundle in a pink blanket and handed the girl to Gertel. "Are you going to name her Sandra Louise?" she teased.

Gertel studied the little round face. "I think I *will* name her Sandra Louise. I like that name." Light-skinned like her brother Alvan, little

Sandra had fine hair unlike the woolly crops sported by William and Robert.

"She hardly looks like your baby," observed Nurse Louise. "She looks European."

"Well, she has an English and a German ancestor, so I guess those genes have come through." Regardless of the baby's features, Gertel delighted in her first little daughter.

A year later Gertel prepared for another of what she had begun to call her "annual vacations." Only when she gave birth did she have a chance to get off her feet and be waited on hand and foot. The doctor had told her the baby was in a breech position, but one morning she felt a violent churning inside and didn't know what was happening. Ernest had not yet left for work, and he wondered if he should stay home. Certain nothing would happen that day, she assured him that she would be all right.

Later that morning she still felt a strange apprehension, yet she had no pain. She consulted an older neighbor lady, who advised her to go to the hospital. Gertel sent William to call her mother, who was washing down at the river. When Mom came panting up from the river, she insisted that Gertel get to the hospital right away.

"But I don't have any pain," she protested.

"Go anyway. With a breech baby, you might have trouble. They will know what to do with you."

Urged both by her mother and the neighbor lady, Gertel picked up the bag she had previously packed, hailed the taxi Ernest had arranged for, and rode to the hospital. When she walked in, the nurse at the desk asked her what she wanted. "I'm not sure. A bed, maybe," came her ambiguous reply.

The doctor ordered a dose of castor oil. Nothing happened. A few hours later the nurses had her take a warm bath. Nothing happened. She thought about returning home.

Suddenly Gertel felt something release in her abdomen, and only a few minutes later she delivered a baby girl who had indeed turned herself the right way.

"Well, I wonder if you will continue as you began," she whispered to the baby. "You were sure in a hurry."

This second little girl, a miniature copy of herself, had dusky skin, a broad nose, full lips, and tight black curls. Two little girls. How nice! They could grow up together.

Ernest called on the telephone to the hospital to see if Gertel had had the baby yet. "How was the journey this time?" he asked as he always did.

"If they were all like this, it would be easy," she said. "We have another little girl."

"I want to name this one," he said decisively. "I never had the chance to name any of the others."

"Okay. You got a girl name?" she asked.

"Yes, I do. Name her Glenda Louise."

"Oh my," Gertel gasped. "We already have a Louise. Sandra's middle name is Louise. Did you forget?"

She could hear the stubborn tone in Ernest's voice. "Well, I guess you could make it Glenda Marie, but I really wanted Glenda Louise."

She chuckled. She knew he would be offended if she didn't use the name he had chosen. "All right. I will register it as Glenda Louise, and we will have two Louises."

. . . .

Gertel's heart swelled as she watched William walk down the road with the other children from Esperanza for his first day of school. This milestone began a new stage in her life. No longer would all her children be under her wings all day, every day. They were starting to venture out into the big world. She prayed that the world would be good to them.

William liked school and learned quickly. She had taught him to be respectful and to not pick fights with the other children. Alvan eagerly awaited his brother's return every day, and then the two boys would run off and play with their toy cars.

Robert sat, his spindly legs curled under him, and watched them. He was always left on the sidelines when they played, although both of his brothers took care of him, carrying him in to their mother if he cried and defending him if anyone else made fun of him.

Feeding the stranger became a fairly frequent chore. Many foot travelers passed their house, and if Ernest was in the yard, he would often invite them in. When he walked through the door, looked hard at his wife with his piercing gaze, swiveled his eyes to the cooking area and around to the strangers behind him, she knew it meant, "Feed these men." She called it his "look." She cooked up a mess of food every morning, and they ate from the pots for lunch and supper. Anything left over at the end of the day went to the pigs. Sometimes she resented the intrusion into her busy schedule, but she knew Ernest wanted her to do it, so she did. She didn't know how the bread that she cast would return to her, but that was God's end of the bargain.

Sometimes she wished Ernest would give less freely. One time he was asked to build a coffin for a child who had died. He wouldn't take anything for it. "Those people have enough trouble," he excused himself. More than once she saw him slip some money into the hands of the vagrants who stopped by for a bowl of food. *So far we have never gone hungry, but you never know when you might need something set aside for a rainy day,* she thought. *If Ernest gives everything away, we might get in trouble sometime.* She brushed her worry aside, thankful that they had food to eat and a roof over their heads.

Ernest also loved giving to his own children. Buying them toys for Christmas was one of his delights. He had bought little trucks for the boys and even a doll for Sandra, who was barely old enough to play with it. He had bought Gertel a gas stove too, because he often didn't have time to chop firewood, and he didn't want her to have to do it. She no longer had to get up early in the morning to get the fire going before she made breakfast, although she still kept a fire in the hearth for simmering beans and stewing meat.

28

The River Flows On

Anna Marie joined their family in June of 1959, just fifteen months after Glenda. The Mexican wife of a brother-in-law had just died, and her name had been Anna Maria. Remembering Ernest's second choice for a middle name for Glenda, Gertel changed it to Anna Marie. Now their family numbered six, three boys and three girls. William was learning to read; Alvan was four and a half; Robert, who still didn't walk or talk, was three; Sandra, two; and Glenda was just taking her first steps.

Gertel's life had become a dizzying round of feeding the children, keeping them in clean clothes, settling their little quarrels, and taking care of her chickens and the pig. When Ernest came home Friday nights, the little ones swarmed all over him, riding on his back while he played horse and trotting after him as he split firewood or patched up the house. He would bring the groceries home and always leave enough money to pay for the water that was delivered and emptied into fifty-gallon drums.

Sometimes a neighbor would stop by to visit, but Gertel seldom left the yard. With all the little ones, going out to visit seemed much too complicated. However, they usually attended the nearby Nazarene church on Sundays.

The road had slowly been improved by widening it and adding more gravel. Now there were fewer delays over mud and ruts. More vehicles frequented the road, and a big chunk of her child training involved teaching the children to stay away from it. William and Alvan helped her mind the two little girls. She had so many children that she didn't have to spend much time entertaining them; they entertained each other.

She tried to follow the doctor's instructions about teaching Robert to obey. Since he couldn't move about, he didn't get into too much trouble, but he did have a temper. If he was trying to do some simple task like putting a block into a tin can, and he couldn't manage it, he would get frustrated and fling the block as hard as he could. She feared he would hurt one of the little girls sometime. If he wanted something or felt threatened by one of the others, he would scream and thrash his legs and arms about. She would pick him up, hold him tightly, talk sternly to him, and spank him, letting him know that temper tantrums were not permitted.

Her parents disapproved of her methods. "Don't lash him," her mother would scold. "He's innocent. He doesn't know what he's doing, poor boy." But Gertel determined to teach him what was acceptable behavior and what was not.

When Anna was still very small, Ernest decided to move the whole family to Augustine, the lumber camp where he was working, far out in the Pine Ridge south of San Ignacio. The crew Ernest worked with built houses for the camp, as well as fire towers on the hills. Following the long, dusty drive to their new home, they settled into a nice cabin with a large stone fireplace at one end. The fireplace fascinated the children. They wanted to stand in it and look up through the chimney. "You'll be glad for that fireplace in December," Ernest told Gertel. "It gets pretty cold up here in the mountains."

How pleasant to have Ernest home every night! Sometimes Gertel felt as though she spanked little bottoms all day long. Ernest, on the other hand, rarely lashed a child. If they misbehaved, he would look at them with his signature look, hard and steady, and they just shriveled up. They didn't mess with Dad.

They had been in Augustine only a short time when she received a letter from her father. "We need you to come and take care of your mother. She is sick," read the letter.

Gertel's shoulders slumped. How could she? She had six little children, one of them just a few months old. William went to the little company school every day, but the other five stayed at home. How could she leave them and go to take care of her mom?

She used the community phone to call her dad. "Can't Marlene come and take care of Mom?" she pleaded.

"Marlene is busy with her children and her chickens," he answered. "Mom wants you."

Children! thought Gertel resentfully. *I have children too—six of them.* To her dad she said, "I'll talk to Ernest about it."

When she told Ernest, he didn't answer for a long time, considering. Finally he said, "The Bible teaches that we should honor our parents. I really think you should go. I can stay here and take care of the other children if you take the baby with you."

Gertel pursed her lips and eyed him doubtfully. "I know you can cook, but what about the washing and dressing the children and all?"

"I can do it." He set his stubborn jaw.

"I can ask Miss Rosa to come and help sometimes," she suggested. Miss Rosa lived two houses down and her children were older. Ernest nodded soberly. It would not be the most enjoyable job he ever did, but his philosophy was to do what he had to.

As she hugged her children and rode off on the truck with only little Anna in her arms, she felt as if she were leaving part of herself behind. Once again circumstances defied her attempts at control; she bowed her heart and yielded to the current.

She found her mom in the grip of severe depression. She sat and cried most of the time and couldn't seem to get her wits together enough to cook a meal or even comb her hair. Gertel felt compassion for her. She knew her mother had had a hard life. She wasn't sure if her dad was still philandering, but he often acted cantankerous when he was at home. She did her best to be kind and get the house cleaned up so it would look more cheerful. With her mother improving on medication, Gertel felt free to return to her family after several weeks.

The children greeted her with squeals of joy. The little girls both wanted to sit on her lap, and the two older boys had so many things to tell her. She smiled, happy to be back in the midst of the noise and turmoil of her own brood.

Miss Rosa came over for tea. "You should have seen Ernest," she said enthusiastically. "He cooked and washed dishes and even combed the girls' hair. He washed their clothes as well as I could. But then," she added with a chuckle, "he'd ask me if he was doing everything all right. He said he could wash his own clothes, but the children's clothes were harder. I helped him out sometimes. I'd guess he's happy you're back!"

Gertel nodded. "I'm glad to be back too. I know Ernest did fine, but I kept worrying about the children back here. Robert can't walk yet, and Glenda is only one and a half. I just hoped they weren't burning the house down or falling into the creek or something.

"We decided that when Ernest goes to Punta Gorda for the next job, I will go back to Esperanza to be closer to my folks. Then, if they need me, I am there and my children are right there too."

Before he went off to work in Punta Gorda, far in the southern end of Belize,[22] Ernest built a new house next to their previous one in Esperanza, with a thatched roof and a real cement floor. His work took him away from home for several months at a time now.

Not a very social person himself, he didn't want Gertel to spend a lot of time visiting. "I don't like the idea of ladies going about the neighborhood, gossiping and stirring up trouble," he said. To compensate, he supplied books and magazines for Gertel to read in the evenings after the children had gone to bed. Gertel loved to read and devoured anything he brought, but she particularly enjoyed lawyer stories. She thought she might have liked to be a lawyer herself. She almost felt like one at times when she had to settle the children's spats.

"Mom, he took my red crayon! I was using it and he just grabbed it." That was Alvan.

"This is *my* crayon," retorted William, holding it above his head as Alvan tried to snatch it back.

" 'Tis not."

" 'Tis too." William kicked at Alvan, who started to pound his brother.

---

[22] Though British Honduras was not renamed Belize until 1973, the new name is used from this point forward.

"Here, you two." Gertel took each little boy by a shirt collar and dragged them apart. She thought about Solomon and the babies. "I'll just break this crayon in two," she said, prying it out of William's hand. "Then you can each have a piece."

"Don't break it," yelled William, dancing up and down. "None of my crayons are broken yet."

Alvan scowled but said nothing.

"I think it *is* William's," she said. "Now, Alvan, go get your own crayons."

Ernest brought her a battery-operated radio. Listening to the news every day made her feel connected to the rest of the world. She used it sparingly in order to save the batteries.

Night always fell early in the tropics, so the family rose early and retired early. Gertel felt safe in the village; she had never heard of thieves or child snatchers in the area. One evening when baby Anna had a bad cough, Gertel remembered the medicine her mother had for coughs. She asked William if he was afraid to stay with the little ones while she ran to Granny Morris's to get medicine. Always responsible, William, not quite seven years old, said he could watch them. The youngest three were asleep and Robert didn't move much, so she felt safe leaving them in their brother's care while she went to get the medicine.

In May of 1961 Gertel had another baby girl. She named this one herself. She knew that everyone called Ernest's mother Miss Rose, but she wasn't sure of her full name. She thought it might have been Rosemarie, so that is the name she registered—Rosemarie Yvonne. When she called Ernest, he said his mother's name was really Rosamund.

"Oh, dear. Do you think we should change it?"

"Up to you," he said.

She decided not to change it. "Rosamund is such an old-fashioned name. This little Rose might not like to be saddled with a name like that," she reasoned.

So far every other baby had been lighter-skinned. True to the pattern, baby Rosie, as she came to be called, was dark-skinned like Glenda.

All the children had blue eyes at birth, but none of them stayed blue.

Both Alvan and William attended school now, but that still left five at home every day. Robert, at five years old, still did not walk, although he could sit and move about on the floor. He could get his own tortillas into his mouth, but did not handle a spoon well yet, so she usually fed him.

29

Hurricane Hattie

The batteries in Gertel's radio had died long ago, and she had never replaced them, so she completely missed the warnings of a severe hurricane threatening Belize in the fall of 1961.

Sweat rolled down the preacher's face as he exhorted the little Nazarene congregation that Sunday morning. Everyone felt the mugginess in the air. Some little girls were playing right outside the church. When their laughter became too riotous, Mr. Peters stepped to the window and rebuked them. They quieted down for a few minutes, but soon their noise again competed with the preacher's voice.

Mr. Peters stepped outside and spoke seriously to the girls. "You girls should come inside and listen. It is very calm now, but God could send a big storm, and then you would wish you had listened to God's Word."

The girls just laughed and said, "Sho'. That no happen."

The people inside nodded in agreement with the girls. Some of them had heard the warnings of a hurricane, but hurricanes never reached them here in the Cayo district, so they didn't worry. Gertel thought back to the hurricane she had weathered in Belize City. She remembered the fear, the floods, and canoeing in the yard. But this was Cayo. Surely they wouldn't have a bad storm here.

The sermon ended and the preacher announced, "We will have our harvest service here tonight. The Lord has been good to us and has given us a bountiful harvest. Bring something of your bounty to sell and be prepared to buy. The money will be distributed to the widows and needy around us. God bless you as you share."

That night as Gertel walked home from the harvest service, carrying the eggs and tomatoes she had bought for their breakfast, she noticed a deep, black cloud with a strange red center hanging in the east.

"That looks like a terrible storm," she commented to Miss Anna, her neighbor walking beside her. Not a leaf moved in the oppressive stillness, and the humidity wrapped itself around her like a blanket.

She set the eggs and tomatoes on the table near the stove and got the children ready for bed. With baby Rose asleep on the big bed and Robert and Anna on her lap, the other children clustered in a circle at her feet as they did every night. She prayed with them, asking God to protect the people who would have to endure the storm. Then they sang "Jesus Loves Me" and a few other favorite choruses.

When Gertel awoke in the night, a stiff breeze was rustling the thatch on the roof, and raindrops whispered across the dry leaves. She drifted back to sleep. The next morning when she tried to open a shutter, the wind wrenched it out of her hand and slammed it back against the frame. When she finally wrestled it open to look across the road, she saw trees swaying violently through a veil of driving rain. What a storm! *And I'm alone with the children,* she thought. *Oh, how I wish Ernest were here.*

Then she noticed the traffic. Trucks moved up and down the road, loaded with people clutching bundles and buckets. *They must be carrying people to hurricane shelters,* she surmised. *Well, I can't go anywhere with all these children. I will just have to stay right here and trust God to take care of us.* Resolutely she turned from the window. She had to keep busy and stop worrying.

She woke the children, got them dressed, and fried the eggs and tomatoes she had bought the night before. She prayed under her breath as she went about her duties, sensing the danger of the storm raging outside.

The children were just finishing the last of their breakfast when a strong blast of wind ripped the center row of thatch from the ridge of the roof.

The children looked up with round eyes as the rain poured in, creating a long puddle down the center of the floor.

"Get into the bed," she ordered the children. She grabbed a tarp and covered her own bed and then threw some plastic sheets over the children in the other bed. "Now stay there," she commanded. They whimpered and complained, but they obeyed.

The door blew open with a crash, and her dad stepped into the room. "Are you all right?" he asked.

"Yes," she assured him, although she was quaking inside. "What is happening?"

"It's a hurricane," he said, his voice laced with worry. "We are going to the shelter. You should come too."

Gertel hesitated, frowning. She hated to leave.

"Your neighbor over there," he said, gesturing to the far side of the road, "the one with the little baby, she went already. You should go."

Gertel shook her head. Surely it wouldn't get much worse. She just couldn't imagine herself packed into the concrete hurricane shelter with fifty or a hundred other people, trying to keep all her babies quiet. It would be bedlam.

Anxious to get to safety himself, her dad soon left.

When he had gone and the rain continued to pour through the hole in the roof, she almost panicked. *What if the rest of the thatch tears off? I'm here all alone with the children. What would I do if the roof goes, and sticks and branches start coming in? I can't even light the oil stove or a lantern because of the wind.* Suddenly paralyzed with fear, she didn't know what to do.

In her fright she started to quote the twenty-third Psalm. " 'Yea, though I walk through the valley of the shadow of death, I will fear no evil: for thou art with me . . .' " The words forced her to slow down and think rationally. She knew what she had to do now.

Quickly she packed two sets of dry clothes in plastic bags for each child. She gathered up all the groceries and put them into a cupboard to keep them dry. Now they would at least have dry clothes and dry food if the roof blew off. She watched anxiously as the thatch heaved and strained at the thongs that bound it.

A "halloo" came from outside, and the next minute a dripping Mr. Peters stood in the doorway. "Are you all right here?" he asked.

She nodded. "Only the ridge blew off." She pointed to the roof.

"Best you come over to my house. It's cement block with a tin roof, and I have lots of room. My wife is gone, so you and the children could have our bed."

With relief, Gertel picked up the baby and instructed the two boys to carry the bags of dry clothes. Mr. Peters carried Robert and took Anna by the hand. With the other two girls clinging to her skirts, they fought their way against the wind and rain across the yard to the Peters' house.

They were just getting settled when they heard a knock on the door. A family with three children stood shivering in the rain.

"Come in, come in," invited Mr. Peters heartily, pulling the children into the dry house. They were not the last. More and more stragglers arrived, and soon the house overflowed with people.

Outside, the storm increased in fury. The wind blew so hard that the men who went out to bring in firewood could hardly stand against it. When Gertel looked toward her own house through the curtains of slashing rain, she could see that the custard apple tree had been stripped of leaves, and its branches hung at crazy angles, broken and twisted.

About mid-afternoon, the wind died down and the rain settled down to a drizzle. Some of the children clamored to go outside.

"Why do you want to go out?" she asked her children.

"Look!" William pointed. "The tangerines all fell off the tree." Orange spheres carpeted the yard.

"No," said Mr. Peters. "Sometimes a storm like this comes back. You just stay right inside."

The children were getting hungry. "I don't know what we will feed them," Mr. Peters confided to Gertel. "My wife went to Belize City last night, and there is hardly any food in the house."

"I have food," she said, "and it is dry. I put it in the cupboard. I'll go get it."

Fearful of what state she would find her house in, she felt relieved to see that it remained as she had left it—a wet strip down the middle. She emptied her flour sack into a basin and added shortening. She took the rest of the eggs she had bought the night before and some okra she had picked earlier. *What a pitiful amount to feed all the people crowded into Mr. Peters' house!* she sighed. *It will be like feeding the five thousand. God will have to make it stretch.*

When she had made a stack of tortillas and fried the eggs and okra, Mr. Peters told her to take out for herself and the children, and they would divide the rest among the other people.

"Oh, my children don't eat much," she said. She took a bowl of fried eggs and a few tortillas for them and didn't eat any herself.

She noticed one mother with a small baby in soggy clothes. "I don't have no dry clothes for him," explained the mother hopelessly.

"He will get sick if you don't get him into dry clothes. Here," and Gertel fished out a shirt, a diaper, and a blanket from the bag of clothes she had brought.

A volunteer from the hospital auxiliary arrived with a kettle of rice. The other people crowded around and dug into the kettle with their hands. Soon they had polished it off, and Gertel had not been offered any of it.

"You see how it is," said Mr. Peters, shaking his head sadly.

"It's all right. Don't worry about me. I don't need it," she assured him.

When night fell, Mr. Peters told her, "You and your children take our bed. You deserve it. The rest of them will just have to bunk down on the floor."

Worn out with fatigue, Gertel didn't protest. She lay down beside her children, grateful for the hospitality extended to them.

The next day her father came to tell her to come and stay with them. Their roof had not been damaged. She stayed there for three days before gathering enough courage to return to see what needed to be done to move back into her own house.

· ·

Gertel was walking around the yard picking up sticks and wondering how she would get the roof fixed when she spied a man striding down the road at a fast pace. It looked like—could it be? Yes, it was . . . Nesto!

He engulfed her in a relieved bear hug. "You're all right," he whispered gruffly.

"Oh, Ernest, I'm so glad you came," she sobbed into his shoulder.

"We heard down in Punta Gorda that the hurricane had wiped out Cayo, that nobody had a house anymore. I just had to get home and see if you were all right."

"We are all right. The children are all right. Only the roof," she said, pointing to it.

"That we can fix," he assured her. "They say that Belize City was nearly wiped off the map."

Her hands flew to her face. "Oh, no!" She wondered about Grandma Liza and Mr. Peters' wife.

Ernest had scrambled onto the roof to assess the damage. He soon slid down. "I'll get some of my friends and we'll fix it right away." In a few hours he had replaced the missing leaves, and their house stood ready to shed rain again. He helped Gertel move the children and their belongings home again. After they had eaten, they had time to talk.

"We heard warnings of the hurricane on the radio," he related. "When it had passed, we heard that Belize City and the Cayo district had been hit, many people were dead, and most of the houses were flattened. Quite a few of us come from this area, and we were worried about our families. We couldn't get through on the telephone; I guess all the lines are down. So we decided to come home as fast as we could. We went out and bought food because we didn't know how long it would take, or if there would be any food left here.

"But when we got out onto the road, we were able to hitchhike only as far as Deep River. There was a lake across the road, and we had to wait for a dory to take us across. Nearly all the rivers were flooded, and after we got past Stann Creek, the road was blocked with fallen trees. We had to chop our way through the tangle. We were glad for the food we had brought because a lot of the shops were out of supplies, and no trucks are getting through to bring more. It was a hard journey, and I'm tired." He yawned, stretched, and went straight to bed.

Gertel surveyed the broken trees and scattered limbs in her yard, the smashed corn in the garden, and the mud tracked throughout the house. Then she swept her eyes over the seven children safe in their beds and her dear husband, sprawled in exhaustion on their bed. She thanked God for keeping them all safe. She never wanted to see another hurricane.

Due to the devastation and disruption of communications systems, it was several weeks before they heard that Gertel's grandparents had managed to travel inland before the hurricane struck and Mr. Peter's wife was also safe with friends.

That hurricane of 1961 was the worst one ever to hit Belize. It wreaked such devastation in Belize City that it was decided to build government facilities farther inland. Belmopan, halfway between Belize City and San Ignacio, became the new capital city. It was a planned city, with a ring road surrounding a central area that housed the government buildings, and many parks and walkways giving access to residential areas on the periphery.

The many homeless refugees from Belize City were housed in an instant barracks town located approximately seventeen miles west of Belize City along the Western Highway. It grew into what is now known as Hattieville. The AMA (Amish Mennonite Aid) organization from the United States was one of the charitable groups that came to the rescue of Hurricane Hattie victims. Gertel Wagner, living west of Hattieville in the Cayo district, knew nothing of the Mennonites who came to minister there at that time.

30

Robert Walks

Ernest had had enough of working so far away from his family. He contracted to work at Augustine again, fourteen miles south of Esperanza, and moved the family there so they could be together. Once again they settled into one of the quaint cabins with a fireplace. More cabins like theirs lined the dirt street, and the children enjoyed playing with their little friends in the spaces between the houses.

It was a time of contentment and satisfaction for Gertel. William and Alvan attended the small school, learning to read and think for themselves. The three little girls played with their dollies and "cooked" many muddy messes in the old chipped dishes Gertel had given them. She had two babies: one-year-old Rosie and six-year-old Robert. He was a handsome little boy with intense dark eyes and curly hair, but he still had to be fed and diapered and carried everywhere. She had been strict with him and he obeyed her. When she told him not to touch something, or to come to her, he did as she said. He seemed to understand instructions but could not talk. Gertel felt sad to think that he would always be a baby.

One evening Ernest brought a coworker home for supper. John watched as Gertel fed Robert and set him back down on the floor. "How old is that boy?" he asked, curious.

"He's six," replied Gertel.

"What's wrong with him?"

Gertel explained that the doctor had told them Robert would never walk or talk. "I teach him to obey, though," she asserted. "The doctor told me to teach him right from wrong, and I'm trying to do that. He listens to me."

John leaned forward in his chair and studied Robert. The little boy had his hands curled around the rungs of his mother's chair and, with guttural noises, seemed to be trying to pull himself up beside it. "I wonder . . ." John mused. "I wonder if that boy could walk." He sat up straight with a determined air. "I think we could teach him to walk." He turned to Ernest. "What do you think, Wagner? Don't you think we could teach him to walk?"

Ernest pushed his chair back and fixed his eyes on his son. He didn't speak for a long time. Gertel could almost see the gears turning in his brain. Then he nodded and sat up straight. "Maybe," he said. "Maybe we could teach him. Let's try."

The men went outside, and Gertel watched them conferring. Then Ernest went for a shovel. John started to dig a hole in the sandy red soil. The children stood in a circle and watched him.

"What are you doing?" asked Alvan.

"Teaching Robert to walk," replied John with a grunt as he flung a shovelful of dirt to the side.

"But why are you digging a hole?"

"You watch," said John.

When the hole was a little over a foot deep, Ernest carried Robert to it and set him in it. The men pushed sand around his legs to support them. He stood there grinning, pleased to be the center of attention.

"Now we'll just leave him there for a while so he can soak up the strengthening rays of the sun," said John.

The children went back to their play, and the men sat around on stumps, visiting, while Robert stood in his hole in the ground.

After half an hour they lifted him out and, holding him between them, they began to walk him across the yard like a baby learning to walk. His feeble legs buckled and swayed, but they kept him going.

Gertel watched from the doorway, a tiny spark of hope rising in her heart. Could the doctor be wrong? Would Robert actually learn to walk? She knew how determined Ernest could be. Once he started a project, he wouldn't give up. "Please, God, let Robert learn to walk," she prayed.

Every evening, John would come over, and he and Ernest would plant Robert in his hole for a while and then walk him around the yard.

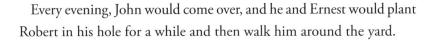

One day a neighbor lady came running. "Miss Gertie," she panted, her eyes big with fear. "There's a snake in my house."

Like most women, Gertel hated snakes. She noticed that the lady's arms were empty. "Where is your baby?" she demanded.

"In the house." She wrung her hands and looked about wildly.

"What!" exclaimed Gertel. "Are you crazy? You left your baby in the house with a snake?" She grabbed up a stout stick of firewood and ran after the lady. She peered nervously inside and saw the snake, coiled up on a bed in one corner. Now where was the baby? She spied him on a bed across the room. She darted in, snatched up the baby, and carried him safely to his mother. Then she tiptoed into the room and nervously approached the snake. With a quick movement she slipped the stick under it and flung the creature onto the floor. As it writhed and twisted, she flailed at it, hitting it over and over again, aiming for its head, until it lay still. She picked it up with the stick and carried it outside.

"Oh, thank you, thank you!" repeated the lady tearfully.

Gertel scolded her. "If this ever happens again, you get your baby out of the house first. Children don't know the danger, and they might take hold of the snake, thinking it is a plaything."

"I was so scared, I just ran," whimpered the lady.

Gertel nodded. She hated snakes too, and many of the snakes in that region were poisonous. But she had learned long ago to kill them rather than run from them.

That Christmas season they lit the fireplace in the evenings and mornings. It was cozy to gather the family around the fire and sing and read to the children from the Bible; they worshiped at home since the only church in town was Catholic.

A lot of the neighbor ladies were making *bollos*[23] for Christmas.

"We want *bollos,*" Alvan told his mom a day or so before the holiday. "Make us *bollos* for Christmas!"

"But I don't know how," she protested.

"Pablo's mom could teach you," he suggested helpfully.

Pablo's mom gladly taught Gertel how to make *bollos.* They spent a day together, butchering and boiling chicken, making the spicy recado paste that surrounds the meat, and then forming the masa[24] around the meat and wrapping it in a plantain leaf. She carried the potful of *bollos* home that evening.

The next day, Christmas Day, Ernest gave the boys a new soccer ball, and the two older girls each a doll with hair. Sandra's doll had blonde hair and Glenda's had brown hair. Anna and Rosie got teddy bears. The boys ran out to kick their ball around the yard, and the girls immediately got busy combing their dolls' hair. Robert contentedly pushed his new truck back and forth in the sand in front of him.

At noon Gertel warmed up the *bollos* and passed them around. They each devoured one or two and then went back to their play. Gertel settled down with a good book, ready to enjoy the holiday.

About 3:00 the two boys came in. "We're hungry."

This brought the girls, carrying their dolls wrapped in blankets. "We're hungry too," they complained.

"What?" Gertel threw up her hands and looked at Ernest. "They wanted *bollos* for Christmas, so I made them *bollos.* Now what do you want?" she asked the little beggars.

"Rice and beans and chicken," said the boys together.

She shook her head. "Rice and beans. Next time I will make rice and beans and chicken for lunch, and we'll have *bollos* afterward. *Bollos* are not a meal, it seems." And she got up and cooked some rice to fill their tummies.

---

[23] Like tamales. A corn-based dough filled with meat, wrapped in a corn husk or other leaf.
[24] Dough made from ground corn.

． ．

A few weeks later Ernest called her from the yard. "Come and see Robert!"

She hurried out to see Robert, standing between the two men. While she watched, they let go of him and he stood, swaying on his own two legs, a big grin on his face. Then Ernest moved in front of him and held out his hands, coaxing him. Robert took one wobbly step toward him before collapsing onto the ground.

Ernest snatched him up and threw him into the air. "He is learning to walk," he exulted, looking at Gertel. "He will soon walk on his own."

Robert did learn to walk. His gait remained clumsy, as though his joints were not quite connected. But he walked—and it was a relief not having to carry him everywhere.

He also learned to talk, after a fashion. His words came out garbled, as though he were talking around a mouthful of marbles, but the family learned to understand what he meant. The doctor had been wrong. What a blessing from God!

31

Ernest and Andrew

Soon after Robert learned to walk, the Wagner family moved back to their home at Esperanza.

Gertel sadly surveyed the furniture that Ernest had built. They had stored it at her parents' house, and her dad had moved some of it outside, where wind and weather had ruined much of it. Ernest had to build another table and a bedstead.

"One of these days," mused Ernest, tilting his head to survey the thatched roof over their heads, "I'm going to build us a real house."

"That would be nice," agreed Gertel.

"It will be up on stilts, out of the mud. I'll make two bedrooms along one side, and it will have real glass windows that open and shut. It will have a metal roof. I will build it so well it will last a lifetime, and we won't have to build another one."

Tingling with excitement, Gertel nodded eagerly. She doubted it would happen before the next baby arrived, but hopefully soon after that. Ernest started to set aside a part of each weekly paycheck for the new house. As soon as he had enough money, he bought lumber for the posts and floor joists.

She knew he always went to the bar Friday nights with the rest of his crew, having a drink or two before he came home. She wished he would bring home the whole paycheck instead of spending it on liquor. Sometimes he would be sullen and depressed when he got home after one of these occasions. She feared he was drinking more than he used to.

The new baby arrived, a fine-featured, dark-skinned little boy. The nurses said he looked like a coolie.[25] Gertel overheard some of them

---

[25] A person of East Indian descent.

discussing the baby and wondering if Ernest was really the father. It bothered her. What if he wondered the same thing? She felt anxious about showing him the baby.

But her fears proved groundless. When Ernest heard that some people questioned the child's pedigree, he snorted. "Huh! I know you, and I know my family, and I know my own child. We got coolie blood in our family. He comes by it honestly. Don't worry about what people say."

With delight, the children welcomed a new baby brother into the fold. Even Rosie, not quite two, wanted to take a turn holding him. What should they name this one?

"It's not fair," one of Ernest's brothers told him. "You have all these children and not one named after you."

"You're right," agreed Ernest. "Shall we name this one Ernest Henry, Jr.?" He looked at Gertel, a question in his voice.

"Sure," she agreed.

Their faithful neighbor lady, Frieda, came to help with the heavy work, and she stayed for a number of weeks.

In time, Gertel returned to her kitchen again. That seemed to be where she spent most of her time. She took pride in keeping her fire hearth swept clean and the clay sides plastered smoothly with fresh ashes. She let the little girls wash the dishes, but she liked to cook and clean up her own kitchen.

One day she looked up to see three strangers walking into the yard. They came to the door, and one of them addressed her in Spanish. "Please, Miss, we have no food. Do you have anything we could eat?"

"Come in," she invited. She dished up bowls of stew beans and quickly mixed up some flour tortillas for them.

"Where are you from?" she asked as the men ate hungrily.

"We're from Honduras, and we are going to Belize City to look for work."

She nodded sympathetically. The economy in Belize was better than in most of the other Latin American countries, and many immigrants came looking for jobs. The men cleaned up their plates and prepared to leave. They couldn't get done expressing their gratitude for the food.

One of them chuckled and said, "It reminds me of the Bible where it says you might feed angels unawares when you feed the stranger. I didn't believe it when they told us we could get food here. God bless you, sister."

Gertel waved goodbye and went back to her work, wondering if she would ever see them again. She thought it unlikely, but it didn't really matter to her. She remembered that she used to get a little frustrated when Ernest repeatedly asked her to share the food they had. By now she had gotten used to it and even felt a sense of satisfaction in being able to share in this small way.

That Christmas, Ernest had not had work for a month or two. He had bought some pork and some apples for their Christmas, but there had been no money for the toys he loved to give the children. On Christmas morning as they sat down to eat, he looked at all the little faces around the table, and tears started rolling down his face.

The children stopped eating and looked at him fearfully, not understanding. "Why are you crying, Pa?" asked Sandra finally.

"I'm so sorry. I don't have anything to give you this Christmas," he said, hanging his head.

Sandra slipped out of her chair. "Don't worry, Pa," she said sweetly, standing by his chair and flinging her arms around him. "You gave us lots of presents before. See, I still have my dolly from last year." She quickly ran to snatch up her doll from the corner where it lay. She brought it to him and held it up. Everyone burst out laughing. The doll's hair, which had originally been blonde, had turned green from frequent washings. Their laughter dispelled the sadness.

The pile of building supplies grew, but ever so slowly. Andrew joined the family in March of 1964 before they had even begun building the new house. Now they had five children with birthdays in March. "I guess we will just have to have one big birthday party every March," joked Gertel.

William, ever an exceptional scholar, had completed grade school before he turned twelve. He loved to study and wanted to go on to high school. However, the Wagners did not have money for high school, and William was too young to qualify for a scholarship. The Anglican priest suggested they apply to St. Michael's College, the parochial high school in Belize City, for a scholarship. Gertel made the trip to the city, taking William and baby Andrew along.

Although the road had improved somewhat, it was still a grueling, rough trip as they bounced around in the back of a truck and made many detours around half-finished bridges. Gertel noticed that more and more land had been cleared and many small villages lined the roadway. People had moved up from their settlements along the river and were clearing the jungle for farmland.

To apply for the scholarship and register William, she needed his birth papers. She waited in line at the registry office, and when she finally got to see an officer, they couldn't find any record of his birth.

"He was obviously born," she insisted. "He is standing right here."

"Did you register his birth?" they asked.

She thought for a minute. Then she remembered. Ernest's father had assured her he would take care of registering William's birth. Had he never done it?

She went to see Ernest's mother, but she had never seen any evidence of William's birth papers in her deceased husband's records.

When Gertel went back to the office, they were harsh with her. "You could be charged for not registering this boy when he was born. You have to present in writing a good reason why you did not." She figured she could do that. She also needed to bring in her own marriage certificate and William's baptism and confirmation certificates. This required another trip to the city, but finally all was in order for William to go to the city to school. They arranged for him to board with one of Ernest's sisters.

Although he was a rather young boy, William was still older than Gertel had been when she left home to go to school. It tore a hole in her family when her firstborn left to go to school. William missed his family too. When he came home for the summer, he always wanted to know what everyone had been doing. He felt as though he missed out on a lot.

On one of her trips to Belize City, Gertel went to visit her grandma.

"Where did you find this boy's name?" asked Grandma Liza as she held Andrew.

"I hadn't thought of a name before we took him to be baptized," explained Gertel, "so I just decided to name him after the church itself: St. Andrew's. Then I thought Noel sounded good with it, so that is his second name."

Grandma sighed heavily. "Well, the Anglican Church sure isn't what it used to be. Longer ago, they wouldn't even serve communion to anyone with lipstick on. Last Sunday a girl with a skirt that didn't even come down to her knees went up and took communion, and I see makeup every Sunday. The morals of the younger generation are going down fast."

"It's not the way you taught us," Gertel agreed.

While Gertel was shopping in the city the next day, a stranger walked up to her. "Do you remember me?" he asked.

She scrutinized his face for a few moments. He didn't look familiar, yet she had a feeling she had seen him somewhere before. "I don't recognize you," she admitted finally.

He smiled, showing a row of fine white teeth. "Remember the day three strangers stopped at your house and you fed them? I am one of those men. I came here to Belize City, and God helped me get a job. I'll never forget the way you gave us food when we were so hungry. It was just like a Bible story. It was like something Jesus would have done. God bless you, ma'am."

When she told Ernest about it later, he gave her an "I told you so" look. "You never know what the rewards will be for reaching out to help people," he said.

32

The Curse of Liquor

Ernest had been working closer to home and coming home every night. The skeleton of the new house rose slowly, stud by stud. Gertel kept tucking the children into their beds in the corners of the one-room house, sweeping around the toys that never seemed to stay in their box, and crowding the bowls of food onto the one small table, all the while dreaming of how she would arrange things in the new house.

One Friday evening he did not come home for supper. Normally he stopped at a bar for a few drinks with his friends after getting his paycheck, but he had always been home by this time. Maybe he had been delayed somehow. At bedtime he still had not returned. *What if he was hit by a car?* she fretted. *He had to walk out from town, and if he was a little drunk . . .* Her imagination ran away with her.

Trying to hide her concern, she coaxed the children to go to sleep. She had to get help—someone to go to the hospital and see if Ernest was there, and maybe to the police. She did not want to call her dad, because she knew how derisive he would be. She went out into the dark night and across the road to a nearby house. Neighbor Lucas said he would go look for Ernest. "I'll take a flashlight and check the ditches," he assured her. His teenage son took another flashlight and headed down the road in the other direction. Gertel stayed on the road, watching the lights bobbing up and down and back and forth across the road.

When her dad's dog barked, he came out to find out about the commotion. He noticed her standing by the roadside in front of her house. "What's up?" he asked gruffly, coming up to her.

"Ernest isn't home yet," she admitted.

"Humph! Likely lying drunk by the side of the road," he muttered.

Gertel turned away. The thought had occurred to her, but she hoped it was not so.

Just then Lucas gave a shout. Gertel hurried down the road. Through the darkness she could make out four men coming toward her. They were stumbling, bumping up against each other and weaving back and forth across the road. One of them was Ernest. Her heart dropped and she felt sick. He was drunk.

"Humph!" grunted her dad. "There's your good-for-nothing city man."

Lucas helped Ernest into the house, where he dropped onto the floor. Gertel left him there and went to bed, heartsick.

The next morning he sat up to the table, nursing a cup of strong coffee while Gertel stirred the oatmeal on the stove.

"How did I get home?" he asked contritely.

She told him briefly. He expected her to scold, but she didn't say any more—just stood by the stove, stirring and stirring. He could sense her vexation.

"I wasn't at the bar very long," he defended himself. "I didn't really drink that much. If you don't believe me, go ask Ronaldo." He knew she would not walk into town to question his friends.

"Just don't let it happen again," she said severely.

Impatient, Gertel wondered when the new house would be completed. It stood like a skeleton, framed and roofed, needing only the siding to close it in. It was taking a long time to save enough money to buy the siding.

"One more paycheck should do it," said Ernest.

But that Friday night when he came home, once again he was noticeably drunk. He stumbled into the house and dropped into a chair. Sensing something amiss, the children stayed out of his reach. He didn't even ask where they were. He shoveled in his food as Gertel watched him in silence. When he finished, he stood up and moved toward the door.

"Where are you going?" she asked.

"Back to the bar," he muttered shortly.

"You drank already," she said, moving in front of him.

He glared at her with fierce eyes. "Get out of my way." He swore at her.

She stood her ground. She knew that if she could just get him to go to sleep, he'd forget all about this in the morning. He tried to dodge past her, but she blocked his way.

He shouted at her, but did not hit her. Finally she steered him to the bed, where he collapsed and fell asleep almost instantly.

Gertel shook as the heaviness of the situation pressed upon her mind. How she wished Ernest wouldn't drink! He had not been an alcoholic when she married him. He had always been a good husband. He worked hard and provided for them. He loved the children, and he had never raised a hand against her. This was the first time he had cursed at her. Tears pushed at her eyelids at the memory.

Ernest had always gone to church with her, but she doubted that he really had a personal relationship with Christ. Once, after sitting through an invitation to come to Christ at the Nazarene church, she had asked him if he had ever been born again. He had gotten a bit huffy as he replied, "I am a good Christian; I am a member of the Anglican Church."

"But being a Christian is more than just being a member of a church," she had replied. Then his face had taken on that closed look, and he had marched off down the road ahead of her. End of discussion. She feared Ernest's stubbornness kept him from surrendering to God.

The next morning as he sat at the table, bleary-eyed, trying to recover from his hangover by drinking a cup of strong coffee, she asked him, "Do we have enough money for the rest of the siding now?"

"Of course we do," he said peevishly. He fumbled in his shirt pocket. "Where . . . ?" He spread the top of the pocket and tried to peer inside. Then his face took on that closed, blank expression that she knew so well. He pushed back his chair and strode from the room.

Gertel watched him go, and tears ran down her cheeks. She could guess what had happened. He couldn't have spent his whole paycheck on whiskey. More likely someone had stolen the money while he was drunk.

"Oh, God," she pleaded, "please make him stop drinking."

The work on the house continued ever so slowly, it seemed to Gertel.

She watched as Ernest fitted each siding piece precisely onto the one below it. He worked meticulously. She wished it were finished, but at least it was getting done.

Only the interior walls were lacking when Ernest's work took him out to Benque.[26] He would be gone for a week. Gertel sighed. Now it would take even longer to finish!

He did hire some men to put up the ceiling. When he returned, he surveyed their work indignantly. They had not done it correctly, and they had run out of boards. He had to buy more and redo it himself. He decided it didn't pay to hire someone else to do the work. He would finish it himself even if it took longer.

"Can't we just move in without the walls?" she pleaded as she folded his shirts and packed them into his valise.

"You don't want to do that."

"I do," she insisted. "It's so crowded with nine children in this little house. Can't we just move our beds and chairs in there and I can put up blankets . . . ?"

"No," he said with that stubborn set to his jaw. "I'll finish it up on weekends."

Gertel gave up. She knew he wouldn't budge when he was in one of those moods. Again she chose to accept her lot and make the best of it.

---

[26] Benque Viejo del Carmen, a town at the Guatemalan border.

33

Wildfire

April was dry season in Belize. The sun beat down from a cloudless sky, the ground lay smothered in dust, and no rain relieved the oppressive heat. Farmers chopped the jungle growth, salvaged the larger trees for firewood, and left the remaining brush to dry out in the hot sun. Then they burned the debris off their plantations.

One day in late April, Alvan came running into the house. "Come see the big fire!"

All the children crowded with Gertel into the yard to watch the wide column of black smoke billowing into the air, just behind the hill. "That is close," she commented, "but I don't think it will come this far. Keep an eye on the fire," she cautioned Alvan. "Sometimes fires get out of control and go where they aren't supposed to."

Almost every day they saw more clouds of smoke. The air grew hazy and the smell of smoke lingered everywhere. Gertel watched the pillars of smoke nervously. She prayed that none of the fires would get out of control and threaten the village.

A few days later Alvan rushed into the house, panting. "The fire is close," he said, waving his arms. "It is almost at our banana trees."

Gertel hurried outside. *Oh, no!* she thought. The fire had nearly reached the back of their property. She could see the flickering flames crawling along the ground, devouring the dried grass. She looked up at the cohune leaves. The brisk wind fanned the fire their way.

"Go to Grandpa's and phone your pa!" she told Alvan. Oh, how she wished Ernest were home! She sent a hasty glance at the three fifty-gallon drums that held their drinking water. That amount of water would be of no use if the thatched roof of their house caught fire. The bare ground around their house should stop the fire, but it would take only one spark to set the whole roof ablaze. They would lose everything they had.

As if to confirm her fears, a burning leaf landed on the ground in front of her. She beat it out with her broom. More sparks were flying their way.

"Come, children! Let's get everything out of the house. Each of you grab what you can carry and bring it out here onto this bare patch of ground." She ran in and out, carrying chairs, mattresses, dresser drawers. When Alvan came, he helped her with the table while the little girls clutched bundles of clothes and basins of cups and dishes.

They could hear the fire crackling now, and Gertel knew it was just a matter of time until the roof would be ablaze. Pushing a chair close to the eaves, Gertel stood on it, grasped hold of a handful of thatch, and pulled herself up onto the roof. Starting at the peak, she used her butcher knife to slash at the vines that bound the long leaves to the rafters. The leaves slid to the ground as she worked her way across the roof. Slash, slash. She worked feverishly until one side lay on the ground. The children tried to drag the leaves away from the side of the house.

Just as she finished the other side, the wind changed, and the smoke began swirling in the opposite direction. Gertel straightened up and watched, breathing heavily. She peered down between the rafters into the bare house below. She had just destroyed their roof. Where would they live now? She glanced at the new house across the yard and gave a guilty little chuckle. Shakily she climbed down and sat on one of the chairs in the yard. That is where Ernest found her when he arrived.

"Are you all right?" he asked, mentally counting heads. Then he gestured to the pile of thatch on the ground. "Who did that?"

"I cut it down," she said.

He stared at the roofless house and then looked toward the new house.

"Guess we'll have to move in there," he said. He threw her a knowing glance.

She could hardly hide her elation. Her smile broadened.

"That's what you wanted, right?" he asked.

She didn't answer.

They moved their belongings into the new house. Before long Ernest had framed up one long wall through the middle of the twenty-by-twenty-foot house and divided one side into two bedrooms, one for the children and one for themselves. Over the next few months, he hung the doors and built the tall windows. For the construction of the windows, he crafted frames around many small panes of glass—a labor of love. The windows swung out like shutters to let in the breeze.

On the end facing the road, a long set of stairs led up to a square landing outside the front door. There was a back door, but it had no stairs yet.

At one end of the main room, Gertel set up her gas stove and a small table for her cooking supplies. Two shelves on the wall above the table held their dishes and cooking pots. Under the house she could do her laundry and build a cooking fire. The crowning fixture was the addition of light bulbs on the ceilings. Ernest brought home a small generator and a gallon of fuel. For many evenings they had bright light without the burden of keeping kerosene lamps clean. She could read in comfort with the luxury of electricity. When the fuel ran out, they were in the dark again until Ernest bought the next gallon of fuel for the generator.

34

A New Prayer

Gertel enjoyed her new house, but the specter of Ernest's drinking cast shadows over their happiness. He came home drunk nearly every Friday night. As soon as they heard him stumbling up the stairs, the children would dash into their bedroom and lock the door. They would huddle on the bed, the older ones hugging the younger ones tightly to keep them quiet.

Ernest would drop into a chair, look around blearily for the children and ask, "Are they all sleeping already?"

She wouldn't answer. She knew they weren't sleeping, but they didn't like to play with him when he was drunk because he got too rough.

She hated that the children had to hear the repeated drama when he tried to leave again to return to the bar. He would stumble toward the door, and she would stand in front of it, barring his way. "Move!" he would roar, lurching to the right.

Frightened but determined, she would step in front of him and try to reason with him. "Ernest, you are already drunk. If you go out there on the road, you might get hit by a truck. Then what would your family say? They would blame me for not taking care of you."

At this, Ernest would respond with more shouting and swearing, trying to dodge left to get around her.

She would counter the move, praying fervently under her breath that he would soon give up. "I'm not moving," she would say as they danced back and forth while he tried to dodge past her.

"What do you want, then?" he would finally growl, scowling menacingly.

"Go to bed."

Muttering threats, he would collapse onto the bed, and she would pull off his shoes and throw them under the bed, exhausted by the struggle.

He never drank at home, nor would he let his friends bring the stuff onto his place. Although it was inconsistent with his own behavior, he didn't seem to want anyone in his family to begin drinking. She had once heard him threaten to thrash a man who tried to bring some bottles into their yard.

After the effects of alcohol had worn off, Gertel would plead with her husband to stop drinking. She pointed out what it was doing to their children and how they could use the money for other things, but he would get that stubborn, closed look on his face, and she might as well have been talking to a stone. She prayed fervently that he would see the error of his ways and give up the vice.

William still attended high school in Belize City, and every day Gertel sent Alvan and the three little girls to school. The morning routine included combing the girls' hair. She would part their hair from north to south and then from east to west in four sections, make two braids on the two front sides, and tie them together on the tops of their heads. Then if there was time, she would plait corn rows on the two back sections. If not, she would just braid them quickly. For some reason, the girls hated the two braids tied together on top of their heads. Sometimes they would untie them and pin the little tails down to their heads with a barrette.

"Why don't you do corn rows on top?" they complained. "Nobody else has braids tied together on top. They look funny."

"Just be glad your hair gets combed every morning," she scolded. "I don't have time to do fancy plaits."

They all knew the rules about walking by the side of the road to stay away from traffic, and Alvan made sure they followed them. They walked two miles into San Ignacio and across the big bridge. Young Glenda lived life as she had begun it. She never held still, dashing from one activity to the next, more excitable than any of her siblings. That long bridge terrified her. The planks forming the deck of the bridge had an inch or two of space between them. The swirling waters of the river far below could be clearly viewed between the planks. Glenda felt sure she would fall through the cracks into the river someday. She would stand at the end of the bridge and wail. Sandra had to take one hand and Alvan the other, and they would drag her across as she fought and screamed the whole way. She had nightmares about falling between some missing slats on the bridge. She never quite got over her fear of bridges.

Every morning Gertel packed five school lunches. A typical lunch consisted of powder buns and a boiled egg or two. After a time, she noticed that the lunch pails were coming home full, and the children were whining that they were hungry.

"Why don't you eat the buns and eggs I give you?" she demanded.

"I'm tired of powder buns and eggs," Sandra complained.

"What do you want instead?"

"I want rice and beans and pig tail," said Sandra. "Moira has rice and beans and pig tail."

Gertel threw up her hands. "All right! I'll make rice and beans and pig tail."

"Hooray!" the children cheered.

Pig tails were bought at the market in bulk, pickled in brine. For a while the children considered them a treat, lunching happily on rice and beans and pig tail, but soon they began to complain again.

"I give them rice and beans and pig tail," Gertel told Ernest indignantly, "and now they still come home and say, 'I'm hungry.' I ask them how they can still be hungry. Alvan says he is tired of rice and beans, and he just eats the pig tail and gives the rice away. This is nonsense!"

Ernest grinned and shrugged. He knew she would solve the food problem. For a while she made *bollos* for them, but that got old too.

Then a bakery opened up right beside the school. For ten cents they could buy a loaf of bread and for another five cents a pat of butter to go with it. One loaf of bread filled up her gang, and it relieved her of having to make lunches every morning.

Robert wanted to go to school. Every morning when the others started down the road, he would follow them to the edge of the yard. Sometimes he tried to sneak along with them, but Alvan would bring him back, or Gertel would hold his hand until they vanished from sight. She wondered if she should send him to school, but she didn't know how it would work. Although he could walk now, he lost his balance easily. Two miles would be too far for him.

Ernest had inquired about a school for handicapped children in Belize City, but they said that if Robert could walk and talk, he was not sufficiently disadvantaged to qualify for their program. Gertel felt relieved because she did not want to send him far away to Belize City to live with strangers.

Robert helped her in many ways. She could send him over to her mother's to borrow an egg if she wrote her request on a piece of paper. Robert could pull the clothes from the wash line if rain threatened, and he tended the baby lovingly. Although he still got frustrated and angry at times, he always treated small children with gentleness. He would sit and hold baby Andrew patiently for a long time while Gertel cooked.

Other people did not trust him, however. He looked normal, but when they saw his stumbling walk and heard his grunting speech, they pulled back. One day a lady with a nine-month-old baby came to visit Gertel. She set the baby on the floor to crawl around. Robert came in from outside and immediately crouched down beside the cute little girl. The baby reached for him, and Robert put his arm around her, intending to pull her into his lap. The alarmed mother quickly snatched the baby up, out of his reach.

Gertel said, "It's all right. Robert won't hurt the baby. He loves babies."

But the lady did not set the baby down again, and Robert had to be content with watching her from afar. His aunts and acquaintances knew that he would not harm a baby, and they let him play with their little ones.

The other children had a healthy respect for him. One day Gertel went downstairs to do laundry, leaving Sandra to finish giving baby Andrew his bottle. A little later, Robert came along and tried to push the empty bottle into the baby's mouth. Sandra grabbed the bottle and tried to pull it out of Robert's grasp. He pulled back and whacked her on the head with it. They learned to get out of his way when he got angry. Gertel continued to punish him for unacceptable behavior.

. . . .

During one season of the year, Ernest did not drink.

"Hey, Waggie," George, one of his drinking buddies, called from the front porch one Saturday evening. "You coming with us?"

Ernest shook his head.

"Why not? You going on the wagon?"[27] asked Walter, peering over George's shoulder.

"It's Lent," replied Ernest quietly.

"Lent!" scoffed George. "What does the church calendar have to do with Ernest Wagner and his drinking?"

Ernest shrugged his shoulders. "I don't drink during Lent."

The men cajoled and teased, coaxed, and even promised him they'd buy the drinks, but Ernest would not budge.

"Fine. We'll go without you," said George, giving up. "But just wait," he flung over his shoulder as the two descended the stairs. "We'll be back next week, and by then you'll be ready to go along."

Gertel had been listening from the kitchen end of the room, holding her breath and praying that Ernest would not give in. When the men walked off, she prayed again, "Please, God, don't let Ernest listen to them."

The next week when Ernest again refused to accompany them to the bar, the men changed their tactics.

Gertel was washing dishes when she heard George's and Walter's voices under the house. She knew they were here to persuade Ernest to go drinking with them. She couldn't hear what they were saying, but

---

[27] A term that means "to quit drinking."

suddenly she heard Ernest's angry voice, "Don't ever bring that stuff to my place again!"

Just then Alvan slipped in from the porch, a big grin on his face.

"What happened?" she asked him.

"George brought some beer here to the house, and Pa got mad at him. He told him to get out and not bring any of that stuff here again."

Gertel breathed a prayer of thanks. She knew that Ernest did not want the children to see him drinking. He would not let anyone bring liquor onto his property. He never drank at home, only at the bar. He didn't swear at home either, unless he was drunk. She had heard him threaten Alvan with dire punishment if he ever heard him use a curse word again. His values contradicted themselves. He didn't want his children to curse or drink, but he allowed himself the liberty to do it occasionally. Gertel knew the devil had him trapped; only the power of God could release him.

Life had been so good the last few weeks, and she wondered hopefully if Ernest would keep his resolution when Lent was over. As she scrubbed little dresses on the washboard, she prayed again, "God, please make him stop drinking." Then she stopped, her hands idle in the soapy water. She had prayed that so often, and it seemed as though her prayers fell on deaf ears. Ernest hadn't drunk so much when they were first married. He just had the wrong kind of friends now. Maybe she was praying the wrong thing. Maybe she should pray that Ernest would find different friends.

From that time on she prayed the new prayer.

35

Sandra Cooks

William had come home for the summer, and there had been some ripples until he and Alvan got their roles figured out. Alvan, always big and aggressive, had been the man of the house in William's absence, and he was not about to relinquish his position. William, more retiring, felt detached from their lives, so it took a while for him to feel a part of the family. Gertel prided herself in the scholastic achievements of her oldest son, but her heart always ached for him because he had to live away from home so much.

Feeling somewhat overwhelmed with her workload and the fatigue of another pregnancy, Gertel set the boys to scrubbing the never-ending piles of laundry. She had to find ways to keep them busy anyhow. Keeping them all fed was another major job. She decided it was time to teach Sandra to cook.

Ernest didn't like it. "I don't want children messing with my food," he complained.

"She has to learn sometime," Gertel argued. "She might as well start."

"She's too young."

When Ernest was at work, Gertel taught Sandra to cook rice, season beans, and butcher and dress a chicken. Sandra enjoyed cooking, and it relieved Gertel of some of the cooking responsibilities.

Gertel couldn't understand why she was feeling so poorly. She tired quickly and sometimes felt suspicious pains. She had never been like this with her other pregnancies. She pushed away the niggling worry that something might be seriously wrong with her this time. After all, she was getting older, although she was only thirty-six. Ernest thought she should go to the doctor before she normally would have.

The evening after her appointment she told him, "The doctor says I have to rest or I might lose this child." Her tone of voice indicated that she didn't believe it.

He stared at her, shocked. She could see the apprehension in his blue eyes. Finally he found his voice. "Pack your bags," he said tersely. "I'm taking you to the hospital."

"The hospital!" she exclaimed. "I'm not going to the hospital. I'm not sick. I can't leave. Who will take care of everything here?" She looked about her in agitation.

"I'll figure something out," he promised.

"But the children!" She threw out her hands in a helpless gesture.

"William is home. And maybe I can get Frieda to come help out. I can cook too, you know. Work is slow right now. I'll just stay home when I can."

She kept on arguing. "William has to go back to school in a couple of weeks, and Frieda's husband is sick. I don't think she can come right now."

"Don't worry about it. You'll stay right there in the hospital until the baby is born. I know you. If you stay at home, you won't stay in bed. You'll be up working. If you are in the hospital, I know they'll take care of you."

Tears dripped as Gertel packed her bag. How she hated to leave them all! How would they ever manage without her? Who would wash their clothes? Who would comb the girls' hair and mind the baby and see that they were all fed, clean the house and . . . ? She hated being in the hospital. She knew she would just lie there and worry about them. But Ernest had made up his mind and there was nothing she could do about it. She just had to float along with the current and let it take her where it would.

When Ernest came to visit her the first Sunday, she peppered him with questions.

"Everything's all right," he assured her. "Sandra can wash diapers and change the baby and get the little ones dressed. Glenda sweeps the floor."

"Who cooks?" she wondered.

"I do," he said with a decided thrust of his chin. "I cook up a mess of food every night, and they eat it cold the next day. Today I cooked rice and beans and chicken before I came here so they have plenty to eat. I don't let Sandra into the kitchen. I don't like children messing with my food."

She didn't say anything, but she wondered what was happening to the unguarded pots full of food sitting at home. Knowing her children, they might gobble it all up and then be asking for more.

The next time he came she asked him again how everything was going at home.

"Well," he said with a lopsided grin, "you remember I told you last Sunday that I had cooked food and left it at home for them?"

She nodded.

"Some neighbor boys came in, and Robert was the only one in the house. The others were all outside playing. These boys told Robert they were hungry and wondered if there was anything to eat in the house. He showed them the pots of food I had made. They 'paid' him a useless metal ring, and he let them eat up all the food! He thought the ring was a treasure. I had to cook another whole meal when I got home."

"I know those boys," Gertel said with a smile. "They often come over looking for something to eat. I think they like my cooking." They laughed together.

"You have to keep an eye on Robert all the time. He doesn't know any better. Anybody can talk him into anything," Gertel reminded him.

"He sees you doling out food to anyone who stops by, so I guess he figured it was the thing to do," concluded Ernest. Then he added, "Your mother comes over nearly every evening and brings something for the children."

"My mother?" Gertel asked, surprised. Her mother was usually the one needing help.

"Yes, the children like to watch for her. She usually comes after dark, and they stand in the yard and watch for her lantern swinging down the road. One of them will shout, 'Here comes Granny Morris,' and they all run out to meet her and see what she has in her basket."

When Gertel was a child, her mother had seemed to prefer her younger sisters to her, but with the passing years she had come to depend on her oldest daughter. At last their relationship had become comfortable.

Gertel felt blessed to think that her mother was reaching out to her children. "What does she bring?" she asked.

"Oh, sometimes it is cupcakes, or sweet buns, or mangos or papaya, or maybe some fresh eggs."

Gertel sat back with a relieved sigh. Maybe her father would also soon be ready to accept Ernest even if he had come from Belize City.

The next week when she asked for a report, he said everything was going well.

"You still cook?" she asked.

"Sandra cooks," he said shortly.

"Sandra is doing the cooking?" she repeated in disbelief. "You let her cook?"

"Uh-huh. And she cooks better than you!" he teased.

Gertel couldn't help saying, "I told you so. And you didn't want me to teach her to cook. It's a good thing I did it anyway." She smiled.

36

Michael Anthony

The weeks dragged by. Gertel became more and more restless. She felt incarcerated in boredom in the hospital, but when she walked too much, she would start to feel pain. When the birth was only a week or two away, Ernest told her that he would be going farther away to work. That decided it.

"I'm coming home. Somebody needs to wash your clothes before you go."

"It doesn't matter," he said tentatively. "I can take what I have."

"No," she said. "The children can't stay alone if you aren't there. I'm coming home. If the baby comes now, it will be all right. I can't stand it here any longer."

Ernest didn't protest much. He actually looked relieved. "If you're sure . . ." his voice trailed away uncertainly.

Gertel had a premonition that the baby might come quite soon if she went home, but she wanted to get out of that hospital. "Let's go," she said, swinging herself out of bed.

After a big, hearty welcome from all the children, she washed up Ernest's clothes. By the time she had finished, she felt the pain again. *Now what am I going to do?* she thought.

When Ernest left at 3:00 the next morning, she didn't tell him that she was in labor. She knew he would not want to go to the hospital with her anyway, and he didn't have his own vehicle to take her. He had told her to go the neighbor's house and have him call a taxi when she needed to go.

As soon as he had gone, she walked across the road and hailed the neighbor. He appeared at his door, bleary-eyed and out of sorts from being awakened so early.

"I'll call the taxi driver," he muttered with a yawn. He left her standing there for fifteen minutes before he came back to report that the taxi was out of gas and couldn't come.

Gertel clenched her teeth. "Can't you call another one?"

"There are only two taxis in Cayo, and I don't know who the other one is."

"Then I'll walk," she said, pressing her lips together and turning away.

The neighbor man watched her walk to the road and disappear into the dark. He shrugged and went back inside.

It was two miles to the hospital. Gertel put one foot in front of the other. At first it wasn't so bad, but soon the pain began coming more often. "I-will-make-it, I-will-make-it," she chanted to herself. She just kept her legs moving, focusing on getting one step nearer each time she set her foot down.

At times she nearly panicked when she thought about what would happen if she had to lie down at the side of the road in the dark and have a baby. "Lord, have mercy," she prayed, reverting to a Catholic phrase she had learned as a child, but praying it fervently. "Just wait," she told the baby. "Just one more mile. Hang in there." On and on she plodded.

Finally she saw the lights of the hospital ahead. Her legs were quivering as she dragged herself through the double doors and leaned up against the counter under the "Admissions" sign.

A white-clad nurse looked up, startled. She threw a glance toward the glass doors. "How did you get here?" she asked in surprise.

"I walked," said Gertel.

"You walked?" The nurse's eyes opened wider. "From where?"

"From Esperanza."

"But it isn't even light yet."

"I know. At 5:00 I was crossing the bridge. Can I have a bed?"

"What for—oh!" she exclaimed as she took a good look at Gertel. "Are you really in labor?"

"Definitely," Gertel said with some exasperation.

"Then follow me," said the nurse, all business now. When she had settled Gertel in the maternity ward and checked her, she said, "It won't be long now. You want me to call your husband?"

Gertel gave them the number that Ernest had left with her, but she could have told them it was a waste of time. He wouldn't want to come now.

Still trembling all over, she promised herself, "Never again will I do that!"

Ernest did come to see the new baby boy, their tenth child, the next day. "I'm renovating a house for Miss Eliza, and she said she wants to give the baby a name. She likes you and all your children."

Gertel nodded. "I remember when she came to visit us, she was so interested in all of them, wanting to know their names and what they liked to play with. So we'll have to wait and see what his name will be."

Nearly a month went by, and Miss Eliza still hadn't announced her choice of name. Gertel didn't like to wait so long to register a birth, so they finally decided on "Michael Anthony" without Miss Eliza's help.

When Ernest went to work the next week, Miss Eliza asked him how the new baby was doing. Ernest told her that they had just given him a name.

"Oh," she replied, a little disappointed. "I was going to name him. What name did you choose?"

"Michael Anthony."

She beamed. "Why, that was the name I was thinking of! Only I would have used the Spanish spelling: Miguel Antonio."

Gertel thought it an amazing coincidence that they had both chosen the same name.

Granny Morris and Frieda had kept the gears turning in her absence, but Gertel soon returned to her daily round of duties.

When Michael was a few months old, a German man named Hugo Griple traveled to Cayo all the way from San Pedro, a town on Ambergris Caye off the coast of Belize City, to look for Ernest. He had been impressed with Ernest's work and offered him the job of designing and building a house on his land on the *caye*. Ernest couldn't pass up such an incredible offer; he asked Gertel if she would mind if he accepted. It would mean he would be working far away, but he could probably come home nearly every weekend.

"I'll see what I can bring you when I come home," he promised the children, bouncing Andrew on his knee.

Gertel shrugged. She had gotten used to managing on her own.

37

Answered Prayer

On Monday morning the children and Gertel waved goodbye to Ernest when he left for his first week of work in San Pedro.

Gertel sometimes felt as though she didn't have enough eyes to keep track of the children all the time. Consequently she made strict rules about where they could play. "You stay right here in the yard," she ordered. "There's enough room right here to play, and there are enough of you that you don't need to go looking for company somewhere else. If you wander off, I can't watch you."

For the most part they did stay in the yard with the exception of walking to and from school and visiting Granny Morris.

She often let them all walk the short distance to Granny Morris's together in the evening, crossing the little bridge over Red Creek. Sometimes Alvan and his friends would hide under the bridge and jump out at the girls. More than once the girls came flying home, shrieking like cicadas. Alvan had told them so many fantastic stories about the ghouls that lived under that bridge that even in daylight the girls would tear across the bridge, Glenda always maneuvering to keep between Sandra and Anna so that nothing could reach out and grab her.

All that week they anticipated their father's return.

"Whatcha think Pa will bring us from San Pedro?" Anna asked Glenda.

"Maybe candy," Glenda blurted, her eyes sparkling.

On Saturday they all wanted to stay in the yard to watch for him.

But he did not come home that weekend. The children stayed up late to wait for him but had to go to bed disappointed. Instead of walking into town to the Anglican church as they usually did when he was home, Gertel and the children worshiped at the nearby Nazarene church.

Ernest called her Monday night on her dad's phone to explain. "We were pouring cement and wanted to finish the job. We worked until late Saturday night."

Gertel bit her lip and only answered, "Oh," trying not to show her disappointment. She knew that George, one of Ernest's drinking friends, was also working on this job. She was afraid the two of them had spent Sunday drinking.

"Lord," she prayed again, "please give Ernest some different friends that will keep him from drinking."

When Ernest didn't come home the next weekend, Gertel prayed even harder. The children wondered when he would ever come.

The third Saturday he hopped off a truck in front of the house and ran into the yard, waving his arms and shouting hellos. The children swarmed around him, and he took turns swinging the little ones up in the air and tweaking the girls' braids. From his backpack he pulled a whole box of chocolate bars and handed them around.

"And this is for you," he said, handing Gertel a rather soggy plastic bag.

"What's this?" she asked, holding the bag cautiously between her finger and thumb and wrinkling her nose. It smelled fishy.

"Shrimp!" he exclaimed. "Rich man's food."

"I don't know how to cook shrimp."

"I do. I'll cook it and teach you how. Next time I'll try to bring some lobster. That is good too."

After they had eaten a meal of stir-fried shrimp over rice, he had an amazing story to tell. "I spent the first weekend drinking with George and some other fellows," he admitted, glancing sheepishly at Gertel. "On Monday morning I didn't show up for work. Hugo asked one of the boys, 'Where's Wagner?'

" 'Oh, he has a hangover. Whenever he's like that, he can't work,' they told him.

"The next weekend we had to stay in San Pedro again, and I went to the bar with George and the boys. When Hugo found out, he and his wife came after me. They found me, bought a flask of whiskey, and said, 'Let's go back to our house.'

"When we got there, Hugo sat me down at the table and set the bottle of whiskey in front of me. He said, 'Mr. Wagner, if you want to drink, here's the stuff. You don't need to go to the bar to drink. Better you drink it right here.'

"The man himself, he doesn't drink. Me, I don't drink alone. So I never touched that bottle.

"Now, Mr. Hugo says that when I have to spend a weekend on the *caye,* he or Lydia will come and pick me up and bring me back to their house, and I can stay with them. It's much easier not to drink if I'm with others who don't drink."

Gertel's heart sang. Was God answering her prayer? He had given Ernest different friends. But what would happen when his old friends came around?

Several weeks later, when Ernest got home on a Friday night, she found out.

George and Walter found him under the house. "Come on, Waggie. We're going in to town. Coming along?"

Ernest shook his head and kept on tinkering with the bicycle he was fixing.

"Wha-sa-matter? Ya got another church holiday?"

Ernest shook his head again. "I quit," he said. "I'm not going to drink anymore."

"What!" they exclaimed together. The men looked at each other and laughed.

"You just quit, cold turkey?" Walter exclaimed in disbelief.

"You'll get sick," George warned.

Ernest remained adamant. "I'm through, boys. No more."

The men finally waved their hands in dismissal and went off, flinging over their shoulders, "You'll be back. It won't last."

Up in the house, Gertel lifted her floured hands in prayers of thanksgiving. God had truly answered her prayer.

In the weeks and months that followed, Ernest kept his resolution. He was through with drinking. *Stubbornness can be a good thing at times,*

Gertel thought. But she knew he was still living on his own strength, not wanting God to be Lord of his life.

38

Those Girls!

For the first time in fourteen years, Gertel had no diapers to hang on the wash line. However, keeping track of those four girls of hers gave her more headaches than tending babies.

"Just look at them!" she appealed to Ernest as they sat at the table enjoying a cup of tea.

"Race you!" shouted Glenda as she darted out the front door. Rosie jumped up, sending her doll and its clothes flying in all directions, and dashed for the back door. Glenda hurtled down the long flight of stairs in two or three gigantic bounds, while Rosie leapt straight out the back door to the ground ten feet below. In a minute both girls were clambering at top speed up the stairs and doing it all over again.

"They'll break their necks one of these times," complained Gertel. "Make them stop it."

Ernest grinned and shrugged. "Let them play," he said mildly. "They haven't broken any bones yet."

"And yesterday," she went on indignantly, "I heard Miss Elsa, the neighbor across the road, hollering, 'Miss Gertie! Miss Gertie!' When I went to the porch, she pointed to the roof and shouted, 'Glenda's on the roof!' "

"How did she get there?" asked Ernest.

"She stood on the windowsill and somehow got up on the roof." Gertel shook her head in exasperation. "Those girls! I never had to haul the boys down off the roof! Girls are more trouble than boys!"

"She didn't fall, did she?"

"Just because she didn't fall this time, doesn't mean she won't the next time. She has no business up on the roof. Miss Elsa said it nearly gave her a heart attack."

"Yeah, you're right. She shouldn't be on the roof. Glenda, come here," he called out the open window.

Glenda ran up the stairs to stand before him.

Ernest fixed her with his stern eye. "You stay off the roof, you hear?"

"Yes, Pa," she answered docilely.

Gertel sighed. She knew she wouldn't have to worry about the roof anymore.

But the next week the girls climbed a tree instead. Miss Elsa yelled for Gertel again, and when Gertel hurried to investigate, she saw Glenda more than halfway up the tall, slender pine tree in front of the house. Seven-year-old Rosie, agile for her age, clambered right behind her. "I'll get you yet!" she yelled, reaching for the next branch and pulling herself up. The top of the tree began to sway with their weight.

Gertel raced down the steps and planted herself at the bottom of the tree. She glared up at the little monkeys and yelled, "You get down this instant!"

The girls paused and considered whether it might not be wiser to stay where they were, but they knew they would have to face her sometime.

Reluctantly they began a careful descent.

"We weren't getting hurt," Glenda insisted.

When they finally had both feet on the ground, Gertel broke a slender twig from the same tree and switched them well to the tune of their loud screeching.

"Don't climb that tree again," she told them sternly.

Ernest rarely punished a child, but he stood behind her when she did.

One hot Saturday in May the girls begged, "Ma, may we go to the river? Alvan said he would come along. It's so hot. We want to go swim."

"No," said Gertel. "I don't trust you at the river by yourselves, and I have too much work today to go with you. You stay right here."

They tried their dad. "Pa, may we go the river? We want to swim. Alvan and Rob too."

Ernest stopped running his planer over a board and looked at them hard. "What did your ma say? Did you ask her?" They wilted under his fierce gaze.

"If your ma said no, then it is no."

They never argued with Pa. One stern look from him sent them cowering into corners.

Alvan's monsters-under-the-bridge stories sparked their imaginations. One evening Gertel heard suspicious giggles coming from the girls' bedroom. After a bit the door burst open and a figure draped in a white sheet glided across the floor to where four-year-old Ernest, Jr., was quietly coloring a picture. When the figure said, "Boo!" he looked up, gasped, and was so petrified he couldn't get his breath again.

Gertel ran to him, picked him up, slapped his back, and shook him while he struggled frantically. At last he went limp, and his eyes started to roll back in his head. Terrified, she dashed toward the door with him—what for she did not know—when he pulled in a raspy breath and revived.

As soon as she felt certain he was safe, she dealt with the girls. Not only Glenda, who was under the sheet, but the others also got punished for planning such a nasty trick.

Gertel tried to enforce the Sunday rules she had grown up with. On a typical Sunday afternoon, she ordered the three older boys to play quietly while she hustled the girls into their bedroom. By this time Ernest had divided the children's bedroom into two, and the girls had their own small corner room.

"Why do we have to rest?" complained Glenda. "We want to play."

"Sunday is supposed to be a day of rest," Gertel decreed, locking the door. "Go to sleep now."

What I really meant, she admitted to herself, *is that it is supposed to be a day of rest for me. The only way I can relax is if those girls are under lock and key.*

She waited until the whispering died down and all was quiet in the little room. Then she stretched out on her own bed and let out several long, slow breaths. Ah! What a luxury. Several hours just to sleep.

In their little room the four girls lay on their bunks, breathing quietly. They waited until their mother's even breathing indicated that she had fallen asleep. Sandra poked Glenda. "Your turn," she hissed.

Glenda rose quietly and tiptoed to the open window. She swung her leg over the sill and then slid down until she was hanging from her fingertips. With a soft plop she dropped onto the grass below. She picked herself up and dusted off her skirt. Then she ran around the house and crept cautiously up the steps and across the main room to the bedroom door with the key still standing in the lock. A quick turn of the key and all four girls were sneaking past their mother's door, stifling giggles as they acted out the scene they repeated every Sunday afternoon.

"Who shall we visit today?" asked Sandra. Although not as much of a tomboy as Glenda or Rosie, Sandra often masterminded their escapades.

"Let's go visit the Olsons," suggested Anna.

They did not walk down the road. They crossed the road, cut through Miss Elsa's yard, and followed a tractor path that ran parallel to the road, a short distance to the back of the Olsons' property.

They picked up green mangos from under the trees, chatted a bit with the old couple, played with their dog, and kicked some coconuts around in lieu of a ball. After an hour, Sandra decided they'd better get home before their mom woke up.

At home, Gertel stirred, woke up enough to assure herself that all was still quiet in the girls' room, then rolled over and drifted back to sleep.

The girls were just ready to cross the road into their own yard when—oh, horrors!—here came old Mr. Reyes with his big, fierce German Shepherd dog at his heels. The girls cringed in the scant protection of the hibiscus hedge as the man and dog drew nearer. Suddenly the dog growled in their direction.

Glenda began to whimper and then wail. Sandra clamped a hand over her sister's mouth. Anna and Rosie clung together. The dog darted at them, barking and growling. All four of them started screaming and crying. The dog barked, Mr. Reyes shouted, and the girls yelled.

Gertel awoke with a jerk. What was all that caterwauling about? She ran out to the porch to see the four girls, who were supposed to be in their bedroom, on the far side of the road, hanging onto each other and screaming in terror. "You get over here!" she bellowed.

The shrieks doubled in volume, but the girls came, dashing past the big dog, who was being restrained by his collar. Gertel met them at the bottom of the steps, switch in hand. She bent them over her knees one after the other and switched them all.

"There are enough of you to play together. You don't need to go all over the neighborhood. If you go into other people's yards, you just get into trouble. You stay right here and play nicely," she scolded.

Later Gertel didn't always insist that they stay in their room, only that they stay in their own yard. But they failed to heed this command as well. They would cross the creek on the slender tree trunk that spanned it and wander about in the pasture for several hours while Gertel rested on Sundays. If they didn't get too dirty, they could keep their shenanigans from their mother.

Little Andrew, who spent his days trailing after their kind neighbor, Mr. Benjamin Peters, had taken to calling himself Benjie after his hero, and the name had stuck. For the rest of his life, he would be known as Benjie.

Benjie followed his sisters across the sagging tree trunk one Sunday afternoon. As the last girl, Anna, trotted across it, the rotting wood cracked and nearly split in two. Trailing behind them, their little brother ventured across, but the bridge collapsed and landed him in the water. Hearing his cries, the girls ran back and fished him out. Sandra escorted him back to the house and, with a shake and an admonition to be quiet, she went inside to get him into dry clothes.

Gertel always told the children they could play whatever they wanted, but they were not to fight and for sure not to draw blood. Alvan kept track of the girls. He took it upon himself to break up their quarrels and distract them by turning cartwheels or standing on his head. A natural clown, he often amused the family with his jokes and riddles. He could impersonate his teacher, the priest, or even his own father so well that sometimes the others thought it was their dad scolding them.

In caring for her children, Gertel found that they were following their own "currents." Although she could not control all their choices, she knew she had to intervene in the natural tendencies of her lively children. They, too, needed to learn to guide the boats of their own lives wisely down their personal rivers.

39

Mr. Peters

To keep her four lively girls out of mischief, Gertel devised a plan to involve them in the housework. She divided them into two teams, partnering the less mischievous Sandra and Anna each with one of the livelier girls, Glenda and Rosie. If paired together, the latter two would find too many ways to get into trouble. One week Sandra and Rosie would work with her in the kitchen, which by this time was a small thatch-roofed room on ground level next to the house. The other two, Glenda and Anna, had to clean up the house and help with the laundry. The next week they would switch around.

Sandra, nearly twelve, enjoyed cooking, but neither she nor Rosie, who was only eight, liked to wash dishes. When it was their turn to clean the house, it took them all day. Sandra would get the broom and scoop out all the junk that had accumulated under the beds. She would pick up the books, toys, shoes, backpacks, clothes, and rumpled papers and toss them all on the bed. About that time, the job would look so overwhelming that she would throw herself down on the pile and fall asleep.

One day her dad found her there, sprawled across the debris. He exclaimed to his wife, "What ails this girl? I think she could sleep on nails!"

Rosie had plenty of energy but would rather race in and out of the house, leaping the stairs or dropping out the back door, than swing a broom. When those two did the laundry, it took them a whole morning of splashing and fooling around.

Glenda always operated in overdrive, and Anna, who loved nothing better than to curl up on the bed with a book, caught her enthusiasm and got the job done so that she could go read her book.

Mr. Peters, the elderly Nazarene minister who lived beside them, aided Gertel tremendously in managing the children. An avid gardener, he grew enormous flat Dutch cabbages, which fascinated the girls.

"How do you make them grow so big?" asked Sandra one day as the four girls helped him pull weeds from around his cabbages.

He stopped working and mopped his forehead. "I just plant the seed-lings and God makes them grow," he said. "You have to take care of them. You have to give them enough water, and then you have to do what we are doing now—pull the weeds so the sunshine can get at the plants. It's just like your parents raising you children. They give you food to help you grow, and they pull the bad weeds by keeping the bad things of the world away from you so you can grow up to be true and honest as God wants you to be."

He contemplated for a minute. Suddenly he said, "Would you girls like to try growing some of these cabbages? I have some small plants ready to put in the ground. You could make a garden and have your own cabbages and maybe some other things."

The girls jumped up and down and clapped their hands. "We'll go ask Ma," Sandra told him as they scampered across the yard.

With Gertel's consent and the labor of Alvan's and Rob's muscles, Mr. Peters helped them dig up a patch of ground in one corner of their yard. Then he helped them plant the young cabbage plants, some string beans, and radishes. Those gardens gave the girls something construc-tive to do and helped put food on the table.

Mr. Peters served as a substitute dad in Ernest's absence. Sometimes when Gertel had reached her wit's end with the children, she would appeal to him, and he would sit them down and admonish them.

One time she had some trouble with one of their pigs. The pigs nor-mally ran loose, finding their food where they could. Although they sometimes ranged far into the bush behind their yard, they always knew where they were fed, so they came home at night. One pig, however, didn't want to roam and forage. He hung around the kitchen house, snorting and rooting. Then he would put his front feet up on the low windowsill when Gertel was cooking, and squeal. If she hit him with the broom, he would come right back, squealing loud enough to make her head ache.

"I don't know what ails that pig," she complained to Mr. Peters. "Why does he act like that?"

Mr. Peters chuckled. "I think I know. Remember when the girls had the measles about a month ago?"

She remembered all too well. They had been very sick, and she had gotten tired of carrying bowls of soup and slices of toast and jam up the stairs to tempt their appetites. As soon as their fevers were down, she had let the girls come down into the kitchen and lie around on blankets and eat whenever they felt like it. She always worried when the children wouldn't eat, and she tried to cook tempting dishes for them. The girls had little appetite then, but Gertel kept urging them to eat. "Eat. You'll never get strong if you don't eat."

Now Mr. Peters told her that he had seen the girls dumping full dishes of food out the window to the pig. They did it so often the pig knew where to come for some easy food.

"Those girls!" she exclaimed, throwing up her hands and shaking her head in exasperation. At the same time, she couldn't help but remember the dog-feeding escapades of her childhood.

Fortunately her brood was seldom sick—except for Anna. Quiet and sweet-tempered, Anna was chubby, almost fat, but she was pale and lethargic, and she complained of stomachaches much of the time. She didn't eat a lot, but she did like to eat meat. She would even eat raw meat. Some years earlier, a doctor had told Gertel that the child had parasites. Since parasites were a common problem in a warm climate like theirs, Gertel regularly dosed her children with worm medicine, but Anna continued to have problems. Gertel hated to see her suffer. Finally she found an elderly Mexican man who gave her a concoction that seemed to cure Anna. She started to eat, and her stomachaches became a bad memory.

When Ernest was home, he and Mr. Peters often worked together on woodworking projects under the house. The two of them built a number of coffins over the years. One day the children came back from playing at the creek and went over to look at a nearly finished coffin resting on two sawhorses.

Glenda and Anna peeked over the edge. The next moment they screamed in unison. "A-a-a-gh!" A man lay inside! They turned and ran.

Then they looked at each other. "Who is it?" asked Sandra.

"It was Mr. Peters, I think," stammered Glenda.

"Is he dead?" asked Rosie.

"I don't know."

"Let's go look again," said Sandra.

The four of them tiptoed nervously up to the coffin and peeked in. It was indeed their Mr. Peters, lying like a dead person with his hands folded together over his stomach.

The girls looked at each other in horror. All of a sudden the corpse gave a loud snore.

The girls shrieked and ran. Mr. Peters chuckled and unfolded himself from the coffin. "I just wanted to see if it was the right size," he told the girls, who were watching from a safe distance.

Keeping her children safe was Gertel's biggest concern in those years. She did not want them playing in the creek when she was not home. Sometimes she walked into town to buy groceries and left Sandra in charge. "Now you stay right here and watch this corn cooking, and nobody is to go to the creek, you hear?"

She would no sooner be over the hill and out of sight than the children would be down at the creek. Even Sandra, who was supposed to watch the corn, would dash out for ten minutes and then run back and give the corn a stir before leaving again. Sandra always made sure to return to her post before her mom came back. In this way she often escaped the punishment the others got for going down to the creek. But sometimes one of the neighbors, Mrs. Peters or Miss Elsa, would report that Sandra had been down at the creek too.

The jumping-out-of-windows stunt came to a stop when Glenda

herself suddenly came to the conclusion that she might break a leg doing that trick. Gertel was relieved when she saw that her children could make wise choices. Training her offspring could be exhausting, but it was rewarding when her efforts paid off.

40

Robert Goes to School

Robert, despite all his limitations, helped Gertel faithfully at home, taking care of the little boys, splitting firewood for her hearth fire, and keeping the yard raked clean. She could even send him to the shop down the road to buy sugar or soap. She would write her list on a piece of paper and give him the money. He always came back with the right change. He never used the change to buy anything for himself, but brought it all back to his mother. Going to the shop made him feel important.

But he longed to go to school like the rest of the gang. He loved to pretend to read, having a special preference for the Bible. He would get a Bible and flip through the pages in rapid succession for half an hour at a time. At times he held the book upside down or backward; it was all the same to him. Back and forth he would page furiously, muttering to himself as he pretended to read it. When he had practically worn out her Bible, Gertel gave him an old one and told him it was his. He ruffled its pages so often that he had soon worn it to tatters. Robert went through more Bibles than all the rest of the family put together.

A neighbor man who drove his pickup into town every day offered to give the neighborhood children a ride to and from school. Now Robert would not have to walk if he went to school, so the Wagners decided to send him. The doctor had said he would never walk or talk, but he could now do both—after a fashion. Maybe he could learn to read and write a little.

How proud and excited Robert felt the day he climbed into the back of the truck in his new school uniform, with his four sisters and his little brother, Ernest, Jr. Gertel watched him go with an aching heart.

A twelve-year-old, he would have to start in the first class with little children half his age. She hoped he wouldn't lose his temper and hurt someone. She'd have to trust the teacher to deal with him. She breathed a prayer for her special boy.

When Gertel sent her children off to school, she let them know that the teacher was always right. If they got into trouble, they were not to expect her to bail them out. "The teacher knows what she is doing. If she punishes you, you likely deserve it. Don't come crying to me," she told them. She never went to school to defend one of her children. Knowing this, they never came home with complaints about the teacher.

One day Mrs. James came to visit. One of her grandchildren was in the same class as Anna.

"I hear the teacher was giving Anna some trouble yesterday," she began, sipping at the cup of iced tea Gertel set before her.

"I don't know," said Gertel. "I never heard anything about it."

"Yes, my granddaughter Flora told me that Anna asked to go to the bathroom, and the teacher hit her with her ruler. Anna cried. The teacher never let her go. Maybe you should go and talk to the teacher. She's a mean one."

Gertel chuckled gently. "No, I won't go and talk to her. She knew the child could wait. I never heard about it because I always tell the children, 'The teacher knows best. You just obey.' Anna knew it wouldn't do any good to tattle to me."

She didn't worry about their interaction with other children, either. She knew her gang hung together. If anyone teased one of his sisters, Alvan found out and put a stop to it. "What's going on here?" he would say, coming up to the scene of the squabble. His large and threatening presence quelled the disturbance.

But now she worried about Robert. He attended the infant class, held in a different building out of view of the rest of the school, so his older siblings could not keep track of him. At first he loved school. He came home singing the little jingles and rhymes he learned in school. "Here we go 'round the mulberry bush," he would growl in his raspy voice.

Every night he practiced writing his name. With his tongue hanging out, a crayon clenched in his fist, he would slowly and laboriously print in large and wobbly letters, "B R T."

"Look," the other children would cry, crowding around him and leaning over his shoulders. "Robert can write his name! Good job, Rob!" They patted him on the back, and Robert beamed in triumph. He wrote "B R T" on everything—his Bible, his shirt, the floor, the walls, the others' exercise books. It took quite a few lashings before he learned to keep his name in the right place.

After he had attended school for several months, Gertel noticed that he came home hungry every night. She packed him a lunch since his school was a few blocks from where the others attended, with its nearby bakery. His lunch bucket came home empty, but he could eat a whole plateful of food and several tortillas after school. She asked him if he didn't eat his lunch, but he didn't seem to know. She worried that the other children were taking advantage of him. Was someone else eating his lunch? She also worried about whether he got teased. None of his siblings were on hand to protect him.

One morning a friend from town climbed the stairs to the house.

"Come in, Mary," invited Gertel cheerily. "How are you?"

"I'm good," replied Mary, taking a chair. "How is your family?"

"Well, most of them are in school right now. I have only Benjie and Michael at home now. Seems quiet around here when they are all gone."

Mary stirred uneasily. "Actually, I came to talk to you about Robert." Immediately Gertel tensed.

"You know I live right beside Robert's school," Mary hurried on. "I am a seamstress, and I have my machine out on the verandah, so I can see what goes on in the schoolyard. I wonder if you should be sending Robert to school."

Wrinkles appeared on Gertel's forehead. She leaned forward. "Why? What is wrong?"

"The other children take advantage of him," Mary told her. "They take his lunch. I see them do it. And when he tries to hold onto it, they hit him."

Gertel felt anger rising in her, but she said quietly, "Maybe you are right. Maybe I should take him out of school."

After Mary left, Gertel sat and mulled it over. At first she wanted to pull him out of school immediately, but she hated to deprive him of the opportunity to learn. True, he didn't seem to be learning much. He knew a few songs and could write a few letters of his name. That wasn't much for half a year of school, but maybe he could learn more. She decided to wait and see if the problem got worse.

That night she asked the children if Robert got teased on the truck that took them to school. They shrugged.

"There's a girl named Dusty who always teases him," Sandra volunteered.

"What does she do?"

"Well, you know Floorf?"

Gertel nodded. Floorf couldn't talk or understand people; he could only make a lot of noise. Robert knew Floorf was different from most people, and he knew Floorf was different from him.

"She teases Rob and calls him Floorf. Well, she does it most. Some other children do too," Sandra said. "He doesn't like it. He gets mad and they think it's funny. We try to make them stop, but it doesn't help much."

Gertel bit her lip. Maybe she should keep Robert home. But no, she wanted him to have a chance.

Only a few days later the children got off the truck boiling mad. Gertel heard them hollering for her and hurried down the steps. Their driver parked the truck so he could talk to Gertel as well.

"It was that Dusty!" proclaimed Anna, breathing hard. "Today she waited till the truck was right at her door, and just before she jumped off, she turned around and hit Robert and called him Floorf."

"She didn't know Robert was so quick," Glenda interrupted, "and he hit her back. She jumped out of the truck and started screeching. Her ma came running and said, 'What happened? What happened, Dusty?'"

Rosie cut in and continued the story. "And she said, 'Robert hit me!' And her ma actually walked over to the truck and slapped Robert!"

The children still on the truck all looked indignant. The driver nodded. "It's true. I saw it all. I couldn't stop her," he said. "Ignorant woman."

Gertel nodded. "I'm glad to know," she said. The driver raised his hand to motion goodbye and started the truck. Gertel hurried the children up the steps to the house. "I'll go talk to that woman!" she promised as she stomped up behind them.

When their dad came home that night, the children poured out the story to him. "Ma says she's going to go talk to that woman," they finished.

Ernest shook his head. "Don't go. Don't say anything to her."

"But she hit Rob!" Gertel protested.

"They're just ignorant people. It won't do any good to talk to them. It will just make more trouble. Leave it alone."

Gertel stuffed her ire down inside. Maybe Ernest had a point. She didn't think Dusty's mom would listen to her anyway.

"All right," she agreed. "I won't go. But I don't think I'll send Rob to school anymore. He shouldn't have to take that kind of thing, and he isn't learning much anyway."

Ernest nodded in agreement.

41

Paul Emmanuel

The fall that Benjie started to attend school and Michael turned four, Ernest escorted Gertel to the hospital for the birth of their eleventh child.

The staff knew what to do with Ernest. "You just go on to work," the nurse told him. "We'll take care of her and call you when the baby has arrived."

A few hours later they called to tell him he had another healthy son.

They could not find a name that everyone liked for this baby. The children had ideas, but somebody always had an objection. They seemed to have run out of relatives after whom to name a baby.

Finally, little Michael had a brilliant idea. He sometimes played with a grandchild of their neighbors whose nickname was Chachi.

One day when Gertel was feeding the baby, Michael came up and leaned on her knee, watching his little brother. "Ma," he said suddenly.

"What?"

"Let's call the baby Chachi. Chachi's a good name."

"Silly boy," she said, giving him a hug. "That's not even a name."

"We do have to give this boy a name," she told Ernest. "Next they'll be calling him Chachi, or something worse."

She determined to find a name. But what name would fit this little boy? The baby, fair-skinned and content, hardly ever cried. When they went to church, one of the girls usually held him. One Sunday when he was six weeks old, an older lady, seeing Gertel nurse the baby, exclaimed, "Well, I didn't even know you had a baby. Where did he come from?" People wondered if he had been adopted when they saw his light skin.

He seems almost saintly, Gertel thought, so she named him Paul Emmanuel.

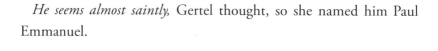

Gertel was unable to attend William's graduation from college. He continued to go to school in Belize City, training to be a mechanic.

Alvan, who always disliked studying, had to try two years before passing the primary school exam. By that time he was done with school forever, so for a year or two he stayed around home, helping her and working for his grandpa.

Sandra had also failed at her first attempt to pass the government exam, so now both she and Glenda were in Standard Six, the eighth year of school.

Gertel's grandmother, now bedridden and nearly blind, had come to live with her daughter. The children called her Grandma, since their grandmother was called Granny Morris. Grandma had a lively temperament and took interest in the children, but she didn't take kindly to nursing care. Sometimes when Gertel's mother tried to get her to use the bedpan, she would get upset. The Wagners could hear her holler all the way from their house on the other side of the creek. "Help! Help! Are you trying to kill me or what?"

"You'd better go, Ma," the girls would say to Gertel.

Gertel would drop whatever she was doing and hurry down the road. When she reached Grandma's bedside, she would talk softly to her and get her calmed down. Then Grandma would cooperate. Grandma always complained that her daughter was too rough. A special bond existed between Gertel and her grandmother, probably because Grandma had been her substitute mom during her school years and had always treated her fairly and kindly.

With the older girls to help with the work, Gertel found herself less busy than when the others were babies, but she had to keep an eye on Robert. He loved nailing scraps of wood together. He imagined himself a carpenter like his dad. He would pound away happily, but when his creation didn't turn out the way he expected it to, he would get frustrated and fling the hammer. Several scars on the wall bore testimony to the extent of his temper. Usually the other children gave him a wide berth when he was hammering.

One Saturday when Gertel came home from a shopping excursion in San Ignacio, she heard the younger children crying before she got into the house. The older ones crowded around her, all trying to talk at once. An unusually subdued Robert skulked in a corner.

"What happened?" she asked anxiously. "Where's Sandra?" Her most dependable babysitter was missing from the group.

"She's at the hospital."

"Rob did it."

"He hit her with a hammer."

"She was bleeding all down her face."

Finally Gertel got the story straight. The baby had started crying, and Rob had wanted to hold him. Sandra had told him he couldn't because she was going to change Paul's diaper. Rob got mad and threw the hammer at her and hit her in the forehead.

"See, he bust the wall too," added little Ernest.

"Who took Sandra to the hospital?"

"We went to Granny's," explained Glenda.

"And when Grandpa saw Sandra, he got mad and whipped Robert hard," supplied Rosie.

"Then Grandpa took Sandra to the hospital. Do you think they will sew her up?"

"I'm guessing they will," Gertel answered slowly, trying not to worry about how Sandra's forehead looked and felt.

"And Grandma Liza, she told Grandpa, 'Don't hit that boy. He doesn't know any better,' " said Anna with a giggle. "She called Robert 'poor boy.' "

"He has to learn," said Gertel. "If we don't teach him, he'll just do it again."

She sighed as she sank into her rocker to feed the baby. Would she ever get these children safely raised?

Robert had another way of dealing with his frustrations. When life got too stressful at home, he would move to Granny Morris's. If he felt slighted by the others, or if they were playing a rough game of soccer that he couldn't keep up with, he would stomp into his room, drag out a little wooden valise that Grandpa had made for him, and stuff some of his clothes into it. Then he would trudge down the road to Granny's house. The others would say, "There goes Rob. He's moving to Granny's again."

Grandpa Morris tried to put him to work. Once, he gave Robert a machete and ordered him to chop the grass in the yard. Robert, not very discerning about what he chopped, whacked off everything in his path, including some young fruit trees.

Angrily, Grandpa took the machete from him. As Robert sat brooding under the house, his grandfather scolded him, telling him he was lazy and saying he wouldn't feed a lazy man.

Later, when Granny Morris set a plate of food in front of him, he wouldn't eat it. She couldn't understand why. She did not realize that his feelings had been hurt. Grandpa had said he wouldn't feed him, so he did not want to eat. After a day or two of not eating, he got hungry and decided to move home again.

This pattern repeated itself often. Back and forth between home and Granny's house, down the road he would trudge, his little valise banging against his legs at every step. The others would see him coming and announce, "Here comes Rob again."

. . . .

One day when Gertel was changing the sheets on her grandma's bed, they heard a voice outside the house. A peddler had come to sell dishes, pots, pans, and accessories. The man called out, "Good mawnin," then went on to enumerate what he had to sell. Grandma sat up in bed. "That man comes from Jamaica," she said eagerly. "That is exactly the way people in Jamaica used to talk when I was a little girl. Tell him to come up here. I want to talk to him."

Gertel leaned out the window to see the peddler from Jamaica. She burst out laughing. It was Alvan, doing one of his imitation acts. Where he had learned to talk with a Jamaican accent, she didn't know, but it was authentic enough that he had fooled Grandma.

Little Paul, a favorite with everyone, learned to sing when he was very young. He would stand by the bedside of his old great-grandmother, stroking her hand gently and singing for her. "When the roll is called up yonder . . ." he would warble in his high, sweet voice. She would say, "Who is singing for me?"

"It's me, little Paul."

"God bless you, child," she would say, patting him on the head. "You are like a little angel."

One night when all the children were in their bedrooms with the doors closed and the lights out, some of them decided they were thirsty. "I want a drink," said Glenda.

"Me too," chorused several other voices.

Then followed a spirited argument about who should venture out into the dark living area to get the drink. Nobody wanted to go. They had heard too many ghost stories.

"You go," Michael urged little Paul finally.

Paul stood up straight. "I will trust and not be afraid," he quoted from a verse he had heard the older ones learning. And out he went to get the cup of water nobody else would.

42

Postmistress

In 1970, the Overholts, a Mennonite family from the United States, had moved into the village. About twenty years before, a colony of Mennonites had settled across the river in Spanish Lookout, but Gertel had had little contact with them. She admired the simple lifestyle of the newcomers. These women covered their long hair with white scarves and wore modest, full-skirted dresses. Grandma would approve of their clothes, she knew. The newcomers had built a house on stilts and started raising chickens and butchering them to sell. They invited the neighbors to attend the Bible studies they held under their house.

In the meantime Gertel's oldest daughter had reached the age to be confirmed in the Anglican Church. The boys had gone through the ceremony at the age of twelve. Now Sandra's turn had come, and she eagerly looked forward to wearing the veil and the white dress her mother was making for her. Gertel made Sandra's dress modest, as her other dresses were, but the day of the confirmation she felt disappointed to see some of the girls in sleeveless and even backless dresses.

"I had to wonder if they were confirming them to God, or to the devil," Gertel confided to Grandma later. The Anglican Church had changed a lot in her lifetime. No longer did it provide the safe sanctuary of faith that it had to her as a girl.

The friendly new Mennonite neighbors came to visit and invite them to attend services. Because they lived so near, Gertel's family often walked over on Sunday evenings.

The children reported that some of the neighbors poked fun at the Wagners because they spent so much time going to church. They usually rose early Sunday mornings to attend the 6:00 service at St. Andrew's in

San Ignacio. After breakfast the children would walk with the Peters to the Nazarene church for their morning service. For a few years, the girls went with Mrs. James to the Seventh Day Adventist Sabbath school on Saturdays, and Sunday evenings they all attended the Mennonite service. To Gertel, the name of the church did not matter as much as the encouragement she got from hearing the Word of God taught and preached.

One day her father stopped by with some surprising news. "Your mother and I are going to the States for a while, and I am going to resign from the post office job," he stated.

"Who will mind Grandma Liza?" she asked.

"Oh, Aunt Em will move in, and you can help her." He dismissed the concern with a wave of his hand.

Yes, she could help. He always did expect her to help. She had been helping them anyway, so this would be no different. But what about the post office?

"You have been with the post office for a long time," she commented, remembering the old canvas mailbag that always hung beside their door in the house down by the river when she was a girl. Although mail was scarce in those days, the village had a post office with a duly authorized postmaster. "So who will take the job now?" she asked.

Her dad eyed her from under his bushy eyebrows. "They asked me to recommend someone I could trust, so I recommended you."

"Me!" Gertel's hands flew up in astonishment. "I can't be postmistress! I have my children to take care of."

"It isn't a lot of work," her dad went on, dismissing her objections. "All you have to do is put the mail that people bring into the mailbag, put it on the mail bus to go to Belize City, and sell stamps. It's not hard. You could do it. Your house is right here by the road and very convenient."

"The worst part of the job would be keeping stamps around," Gertel pondered aloud. "I'd have to go in to town to buy them; but I go in for groceries anyway, and Sandra is here to help." She hooked her hands together behind her back and stared out to the road as she thought about it. It would bring in a little extra money. Then she turned and said, "I think I could do it."

"Good," he said as he smiled and stood up. "I knew you would."

Gertel watched him descend the stairs. *That's my dad,* she reflected. *Always roping me into doing what he wants. Whoever thought I would be postmistress of Esperanza?* She smiled to herself as she turned back to her work.

Ernest approved of her new role. "You won't have to leave the house to work," he said. "I never did want you to go out to work." They re-arranged the front room to accommodate the post office. She had a drawer in a small table where she kept the stamps, the money, and the letters that came in. On the wall hung the old canvas mailbag, which she carried out to the bus three times a week.

Along with the post office came a telephone. It had always been installed at her parents' house, and they'd had to walk over there to use it. Now it hung in her front room, and other people came at all hours to make calls. Sometimes she would get a call and have to send one of the children with a message to someone else in the village. Fortunately her children were usually available, so she didn't have to run every time.

In order to be instated as postmistress, Gertel had to procure a copy of her birth papers. This required a trip to the registry office. To her great astonishment, she discovered that she had been living under an assumed name all her life! She had always thought her name was Gertel Gwendolyn. According to the official birth record, it was spelled Gerthel Gwendoline. That explained why she had never heard of anyone else with the name Gertel. Hers was actually a German name that should have been spelled with an H in the middle.

And she was Gwendoline, rhyming with *fine,* instead of Gwendolyn rhyming with *bin.* "You married the wrong person," she told Ernest. The name on her confirmation certificate and her marriage license was spelled incorrectly. Now, after more than forty years, she finally knew who she was.

. . . .

Over the years, Ernest and Gertel had continued to share freely of their blessings. Sometimes Gertel thought she might as well have put up a sign saying "FOOD HERE" for all the people who stopped by to eat. But they really didn't need a sign. One group of men from Honduras found their way to the Wagner doorstep and were rewarded with cow's foot soup and tortillas. They told Gertel, "Somebody told us back in town that if we stopped at this brown house beside the road just before the bridge, we would get food. It's true. God bless you, ma'am."

Because of civil wars in El Salvador and Guatemala in those years, many refugees, homeless and often penniless, fled across the border to seek asylum in Belize. Not only did Gertel feed them, but she often caught Ernest slipping money into the hand of a despairing man. She knew he'd give away his last dollar if someone needed it.

For her part, every morning she prepared a large amount of food. The family ate out of those pots for the rest of the day, and there was always enough for the stranger, as Grandma used to say.

Gertel found she rather enjoyed the society the post office job brought to her. Neighbors would come to buy stamps, mail letters, and pick up their mail. They would stop to chat while doing their business. Gertel always greeted them with a cheerful face and a listening ear. She often shared a cup of tea or lime juice with her customers. She functioned as the village newspaper, learning about who had a new baby, whose cows had gotten into the neighbor's corn, and who was going on a trip. For once, her father had handed her a burden that she did not resent.

As she smiled and listened, comforted and advised, little did she realize how many hearts she warmed and how many lonely souls she encouraged in her role as postmistress of Esperanza.

43

Churchgoers

Gertel's girls, as she lumped them in a group in her mind, possessed varied temperaments. Sandra, her mother's dependable right arm, had taken over much of the cooking and the care of her little brothers. Gertel knew she had to watch Sandra, because she could be sly—blaming the others for misdeeds she had instigated. Since Glenda often got into trouble, it was easy for Sandra to blame her for any infractions the two of them caused.

But Sandra was growing up and, at fifteen, was an attractive and capable young lady, standing several inches taller than her mother.

Glenda still charged through life in high gear. She worked as hard as she played. She could clean up the house in a hurry. If she wanted a shelf in her bedroom, she would hammer one together. Her laugh was infectious, and she loved to play tricks on the others.

Anna would bring in flowers for her mother and with an impulsive hug would say, "I'm never going to leave you. I'm going to live with you forever." It was rare to see her without a book in her hands.

Rosie, the most precocious of them all and a regular tomboy, earned the nickname "Picky-Picky" at school because of the short, stiff braids that stood out around her head. At one point in her school career, she became such an expert marble shooter that she came home every night with another bag of marbles she had won from the boys, even though playing with marbles was almost exclusively a boys' activity. Gertel began confiscating the marbles because there were so many of them, but Rosie would just come home the next night with another bagful. She acquired so many marbles that Gertel forbade her to play marbles anymore.

Sandra had finally passed her primary school exam and entered high school. Like most girls her age, she longed to fit in with the crowd. When she appeared in her new Easter dress, one of her school friends taunted her, saying she wouldn't be caught wearing something so old-fashioned. Sandra shriveled up inside, wishing she could dress more like the other girls.

One day when her mom was pinning the hem of a new uniform skirt, Sandra rebelled. "Ma, my skirts are way longer than everyone else's. Make it shorter."

Gertel, her mouth full of pins, continued to fold the hem a few inches below Sandra's knees. "The school rules say the skirts should come to the knees," she mumbled around the pins. "Your dad says I should make them a little longer, just to be sure. Those mini-skirts that are becoming all the fashion right now are shameful."

Sandra didn't say anything, but later, in the privacy of their bedroom, she pinned and hemmed the skirt up a couple inches shorter. Gertel noticed but let the matter ride. As she had expected, after a few weeks Sandra's conscience smote her, and she let the hem down again.

Gertel confided to Mr. Peters her concerns about Sandra's attitudes. He had a talk with Sandra, telling her that a girl can have pretty clothes and be rich, but if she has no morals, she is ugly on the inside where it really counts. On the other hand, a girl could be plain and poor, but if she has nice character, having respect for her elders and a modest demeanor, everyone appreciates her, and nobody thinks about how she looks.

After two terms of high school, Sandra tired of studying and of trying to deal with peer pressure. All her life her parents had taught the girls to be obedient, unselfish, courteous, modest, and God-fearing. Sandra quit school and became friends with Estella, a neighbor girl who had joined the Mennonite church.

"Why don't you give your heart to the Lord?" Estella encouraged her friend.

Sandra had responded at a revival meeting at the Nazarene church years before, but it had been a half-hearted, childish commitment. As a teen, she hadn't been living a victorious Christian life. She decided to join the instruction class at the Mennonite church. Her parents approved of her decision. "At least if you are in the Mennonite church, I'll know you are safe. They'll watch out for you," said her dad.

Part of the Wagner family after they began attending the Mennonite church. **Back (L to R):** Hugo, who had helped Ernest stop drinking and became a family friend, Ernest, Glenda, Gertel, Rosie. **Front (L to R):** Mike, Ernie, Benjie (Andrew) with Paul.

The family continued to be avid churchgoers, attending services at several churches. They had their own home worship too. All of the children sang well; Alvan, Anna, and Ernest in particular could harmonize. On evenings when the generator had no fuel, the family would sit around the table and sing. When they ran out of songs, they would take turns reciting Bible verses they had learned.

One evening they had been singing like this for an hour or more. When they stopped, they were startled to hear a round of applause from the yard below. The family crowded onto the front verandah to see the yard filled with clapping neighbors who had come to hear the improvised concert.

"Listenin' to you Waggies is better 'n a radio," called out one old lady.

The other girls in their turn all passed through the confirmation class at the Anglican church, but Rosie dug in her heels.

One day when Gertel was ironing the boys' uniforms, Rosie parked herself in front of the ironing board and declared, "I am not going to confirmation class anymore."

Gertel did not look up but kept on moving the hot iron evenly over the back of a shirt. "Why not?" she asked calmly.

"Father Lee doesn't know anything," Rosie stormed. "I asked him what confirmation means, and he couldn't even tell me. And after class he goes out behind the church and smokes. I don't think a Christian should smoke." She lifted her chin defiantly. "I'm not going to get confirmed. I want to join the Mennonite church."

"All right," said her mother. "Do, if you want." Secretly she wished she could do the same, but she feared Ernest would be displeased.

Two or three weeks later, Father Lee appeared at the post office. After the usual cordial greetings, he proceeded, "I am wondering why your daughter Rosie is no longer attending confirmation class. She needs to attend every class if she hopes to be confirmed."

"She says she does not want to be confirmed," Gertel responded.

Father Lee frowned. "I'm afraid it is because you are attending the Mennonite church here too much. You are not setting a good example. I'm sorry, but I will not be able to serve communion to you anymore if you do not stop attending the Mennonite services."

Gertel did not give him the satisfaction of an answer, but she thought, *Fine. If you won't give me communion, I won't come anymore.*

Next the bishop himself paid her a visit. In an understanding, gentle way, he asked why she was not attending services at St. Andrew's anymore. She told him of Father Lee's dictum.

"I'm sorry you have had this misunderstanding. Certainly we will serve communion to our members, even if they attend services elsewhere occasionally. I hope you will reconsider. We really need you in the church," he pleaded. "We miss your strong singing voice. When you are not there, the singing sounds flat."

By this time Gertel knew what she wanted to do. "I am planning to join the Mennonite church," she told the bishop.

But she had not yet told Ernest.

44

Selia's Children

Before Gertel had a chance to talk with Ernest about her desire to join the Mennonite church, she was surprised with a unique opportunity that came from her friend, Miss Lil. On her many trips to town to purchase stamps, Gertel often stopped at Miss Lil's house to relax and unburden her heart. Miss Lil, an elderly mother figure, often had good advice to offer.

"You know Selia?" asked Miss Lil one day while the two women enjoyed a cup of tea together on the verandah of her little house.

Gertel nodded. Selia was a single mom who lived on Miss Lil's street.

"Well, she wants to go to the States to work."

Gertel frowned. "What about her children? She has small children, doesn't she?"

"Yes, she has three. Two boys and a baby girl. She asked me if I knew of anyone who would take care of her children so she can go. I thought of you."

"Me?" asked Gertel, taken aback.

"I knew you loved children, and you don't have any little ones anymore. And you have big girls to help."

Gertel thought swiftly. It would be nice to have some little people around again. And she knew the girls would love it. "I think I'd like that," she ventured.

Accordingly, a few days later, Selia herself appeared at the house. "Miss Lil said you would take my children," she began.

"What are their ages?" Gertel asked.

"The baby, Tresia, is only five months old. Then there is Anthony, who is six, and Dwayne is four. They are good children, but I can't take them with me to the States. I will send you money to care for them."

Gertel agreed to take the three children, but when Selia brought them the next week, there were four.

"Karen was already staying with her auntie, but she was not happy there. I think they beat her," explained Selia, pushing a shy two-year-old toward Gertel. "Maybe you could take her too?"

Gertel's heart went out to the forlorn-looking children. The two boys stood there uncertainly, each clutching a valise and studying her with frightened eyes. Karen, whose dark hair hung in tangled strings, kept her eyes on the ground. Only the baby looked happy.

"Michael," Gertel called, "come and take these little boys into your bedroom and show them where they will sleep. Sandra, you take Karen into your room and show her some books. The baby can sleep with me." She lifted the bright-eyed girlie from her mother's arms and cuddled her. How good it felt to have a little one in her arms again!

Anthony and Paul were close to the same age, and they soon became good friends. Dwayne tagged along with the bigger boys, and the girls quarreled over whose turn it was to care for little Tresia. It took Karen longer to adjust. She had obviously been abused, and she cringed whenever anyone touched her. It took time to comb out her long, thick, beautiful hair every morning, but the girls did it patiently, and she soon learned to trust them.

Sweet and obedient, the foster children caused no trouble and quickly became part of the family. The little house nearly burst at the seams with five girls in one tiny bedroom and seven boys in the other. Ernest built an extension onto the back of the house, and Gertel moved her kitchen into it. The addition included a small bedroom for Alvan; sometimes some of the younger boys bunked with him.

When Gertel sat in church with Tresia on her lap and Karen beside her, she felt as though they were her own. Selia regularly sent money from the States, so the arrangement worked out well.

By this time the little Mennonite congregation near Red Creek had grown to include a Friesen family from Spanish Lookout, a Miller family who built a house close to the Overholts, a Troyer family who farmed in the valley south of town, and numerous people from the village. The girls delighted in the youth group that met for Bible studies, singing, and recreation. They spent a lot of time with the other girls, either at Red Creek or at their own house. Gertel always tried to make her girls' friends feel at home, and they loved to come to the Wagner house. They knew they would always find a welcome there and lots of good food.

The association with people from a different culture brought new customs, especially new foods, into their lives. Mary Overholt took the girls under her wing and taught them to preserve food in jars. In June, when the mangos ripened, she would buy a large quantity, and the girls would join in the job of peeling, cooking, straining, filling jars, and processing the sauce. Preserving food was a new concept for the Belizeans. "We have so much fruit all the time, why would we want to put it in bottles?" Gertel marveled.

"But we don't have mangos all year," the girls pointed out. "And you could can tomatoes when they are cheap and use them in soups and stews the rest of the year."

She had to admit they had a point.

The girls learned to make cakes, cookies, bars, and puddings.

"Too much sweet stuff," Ernest complained. They didn't typically eat many sweets.

While the girls made noodles or rolled pie dough, Mary would listen to their concerns and guide their thinking into good paths. She served as a mentor to them, encouraging them greatly.

The girls didn't always like some of the new taste sensations. The Friesens fed them something called *pluma moos,* which consisted of stewed prunes, apricots, and raisins in a thickened sauce. The girls had been taught that it was impolite to say they didn't like something, so they swallowed fast and got it down.

The Americans didn't always excel at cooking the local food. One night the girls' hostess fed them beans that were still hard. They could hardly chew them. Then, over their protests, she generously sent the leftover beans home with them. The girls ungraciously fed them to the dog, but even he wouldn't eat them.

"Your mom can still cook better than they can," Ernest concluded with satisfaction.

Ernest took pride in his girls, but he did get impatient with their "endless giggling and carrying on," as he called it. After a night with the youth, the girls would be in their bedroom, talking it all over as girls do. Then Pa would bang on the wall. *Thump-thump-thump.* "Time to get to sleep," he'd growl.

They would try to keep their whispers to a low murmur. Next they would hear Pa prowling out into the kitchen and—snap!—everything would go dark. He had flipped the breaker. They knew then that they had better settle down.

He kept them in line too. When they left for a night out, he would look them over. Sometimes he'd say, "Glenda, that dress is too thin. Go put on another slip." Or, "Rosie, you know what the church standards are. That dress is too short." Although not a Mennonite, he expected them to be good ones.

Grandma Liza became more and more feeble. Gertel spent a lot of time caring for her—tempting her to eat, changing her bedding, and bathing her. Grandma always enjoyed hearing the children sing and watching them play. Eventually her body wore out, and she died peacefully in her sleep at the age of ninety-three. Gertel sorely missed her. Grandma Liza had been more of a mother to her than her own mother, and Gertel needed to spend some time working through her grief.

45

Change of Church

One day Miss Lil quizzed Gertel about the Mennonite church. "I hear they have very orderly church services," she commented.

Gertel nodded. "Yes. They do not let the children run in and out and make a commotion. They sing in four-part harmony that sounds like angel choirs. They preach the whole Bible, and they live it too. I really enjoy their services. They have a good school too. They make the children obey, and the teachers help them to understand their lessons. In the government school, a lot of the teachers just teach for their salary, and if the children get it, they get it; and if they don't, too bad. They don't care.

"I plan to join the Mennonite church myself," she added after a long pause.

"Well, do it then, if that's what you want," encouraged her friend.

By now all of her girls had become members of Cayo Christian Fellowship, the Mennonite church. They had been baptized upon the confession of their faith. Even though she had been baptized as a baby and confirmed in the Anglican Church, Gertel knew she would have to be baptized as a believer to become a member there.

After praying much for courage, she approached Ernest about her decision.

As she served him his supper one evening, she ventured carefully, "Ernest, I would like to be baptized and join the Mennonite church."

He continued to spoon food into his mouth while nodding his head. "Go ahead," he said between bites. "Maybe someday I'll follow you."

Gertel's knees felt weak with relief. What if he would? Oh, she hoped that would happen.

Her father, as she had expected, reacted much differently. "What do you want to change churches for? They're all the same anyway," he stormed angrily.

She let him talk. She knew he had to blow off steam. To her the name of the church did not matter so much, but she believed that the Christian life meant trusting God and serving Him, and to do so she needed to find fellowship with those who had the same desires. Her father remained upset with her for quite some time, but she refused to let him dominate her in this matter.

She knew she needed to make new dresses according to the pattern they wore in her chosen church, but she hesitated to ask Ernest for the money. She didn't have to. After several weeks, he offered to take her shopping for dress material. "You always wear blue," he observed. "Let's get some different colors." He chose a gray, a pink, and a green piece. He attended services with her occasionally, although he continued to walk to St. Andrew's most Sunday mornings.

The instruction class reminded her of the confirmation class she had attended as a child, except that this class covered the doctrines of the

Gertel Wagner on the day of her baptism.

Ernest Wagner

church more thoroughly and also introduced her to the seven ordinances. She appreciated the way the teaching emphasized living the whole Gospel.

She was baptized in the new church building that had been built beside the Overholts' house. She enjoyed the monthly sewing circles where the ladies met to cut quilt patches or knot blankets, but her main focus was still her home.

The Wagners enrolled their younger boys in the school held in the basement of the church. The boys liked going to school so close to home, but they had a hard time getting used to the new curriculum. "I'll have to go back nearly a whole grade," moaned Ernest, Jr., now called Ernie. He had a hard time accepting this setback, because he had been an excellent student. When the time came for him to take the public school exam, he had to attend the Catholic school in Esperanza for a few weeks to prepare since their own school was not registered yet. He passed the examination with flying colors, however, and wanted to go on to high school.

Ernest's work had been sporadic lately, so the Wagners had little money. "We can't afford to send you to school," they told their son regretfully. Anna, too, who loved to read and study, had been unable to go to high school. She determined that someday, when she had saved enough money, she would go. Ernie had to be content with the same goal.

Ernest tried to interest his namesake in following his footsteps. Not only did Ernest supervise a contracting crew, he also drew blueprints. If someone needed a house plan, Ernest would ask how big he wanted it, what material he wanted to use, where he wanted the rooms and the windows, and other particulars. Many evenings he sat at the table, large sheets of paper spread in front of him, a sharp pencil in his hand, and a ruler within reach. He smoked one cigarette after another while the ashtray in front of him filled up with stubs. Gertel watched, fascinated, as he drew dots and lines and noted numbers. It looked complicated to her. He would figure out the entire material list right down to the last nail. When he handed someone a materials list, it always included just enough with little left over. None of his boys, however, inherited his interest in building.

Selia's support money did not suffice to send her children to the private school, so they continued to attend the village school. Karen went off to school in her new uniform to join her brothers, and only little Tresia was left at home. Sometimes when the others had gone to work and she and Gertel were the only ones in the house, it felt too quiet.

Sandra was combing Karen's long hair one evening soon after she started school, when all at once she exclaimed, "What's this?" She picked something from Karen's hair and held it up between her thumb and forefinger.

Gertel came to look. "Lice," she pronounced. "She has lice."

"Oh, no. What are we going to do? I'll get them too," wailed Sandra in despair.

"Very likely," said her mother, unruffled. "But we know what to do with those pests." She went for her jar of Vicks. Without mercy she rubbed the sticky, pungent stuff all over poor Karen's head while the child wailed and squirmed. The smell made tears in her eyes even without the crying. Then Gertel wrapped her head in a towel and told her to leave it on all night.

It took a long time the next morning to comb all the dead lice out of her long tresses. "You girls never had such long hair," commented Gertel as she ran the fine-toothed comb repeatedly through lock after lock. Lice were a common scourge, and she had learned long ago that Vicks killed them all.

46

Spreading Wings

The Overholts' chicken-butchering business across the road, now known as Homestead Acres, had expanded to the point where they were hiring extra help. The three older Wagner girls began working there several days a week, which helped with the grocery bills at home, as well as providing them with a little spending money for themselves.

Even Robert worked at Homestead Acres. His job was cutting off the chickens' heads. Then he learned to bag parts. The other workers placed a pile of chicken feet at his left hand and a pile of necks at his right. He could put two chicken feet and one neck into a bag and send it along the line. He did get confused sometimes, though. If someone happened to switch the location of the piles, he could not figure out what to do. Still, he enjoyed the job for the most part. It pleased him to be earning money like all the rest.

When Sandra and Glenda were eighteen and nineteen, some kind friends of the Americans at Red Creek offered to sponsor them to go to Calvary Bible School in Arkansas for two months. At first Gertel did not want to hear of it. She had never been farther from home than Belize City, and she didn't see why anyone would want to go all the way to a different country. They would be out of her reach, and she wouldn't be able to keep track of them.

The girls kept pressuring her, and some of the church sisters encouraged her to loosen the apron strings and let them go. She knew they were growing up and would leave the nest sometime, but she wasn't ready for this yet. At last, however, she gave her consent.

After a whirl of getting passports and visas, sewing dresses, and gathering supplies, the girls were off, traveling in a crowded van up through

Mexico and into the States.

The house seemed empty without the girls. Anna worked at the chicken plant, and Rosie and Gertel managed to keep meals made and the clothes washed. Everyone tried to keep an eye on Robert, but they didn't always know what he was up to.

Grandpa Morris had a horse in which he took great pride. He kept the horse in the Wagners' pasture at night, but he often used it during the day to carry firewood or bags of corn. He expected one of the grandchildren to bring the horse when he needed it and to come and lead it back to their place at night. The Wagners had a horse of their own that they rode, and they liked to ride Grandpa's horse too, but he would not let them. "This is not a lady's horse," he had told them sternly. "I don't want you girls riding my horse, nor little boys either—nor Rob, especially." He did not trust Robert. Often Robert led Grandpa's horse back and forth, and he occasionally rode the horse when no one was looking.

One evening just after dark, Robert stumbled up the steps, his hand over his eye and blood dripping through his fingers. When they had cleaned him up, they saw he had a cut over his eye. He kept repeating, "I washn't ridin' hosh, I washn't ridin' hosh." From his denial they concluded that he *had* been riding the horse and had somehow fallen off—although since nobody had seen him, they never did find out exactly what had happened. Gertel realized again that Robert would always be a little boy in a man's body and would always need her protection.

William and Alvan had left home and established homes of their own. Ernie now had a day job, and the three little boys attended school. Ernest got so lonely for his girls away at Bible school in the States that he actually cried a few times. The two months seemed long, and Gertel did not breathe easily until they had arrived safely at home again.

The girls felt glad to be eating at their mom's generous table again.

"We nearly starved at Bible school," they said.

"We ate soup, soup, and more soup."

"And celery! *Raw* celery! Yuck!"

"And they made this cold macaroni salad, which wasn't too bad, but it was full of celery."

"We gave our salad to the boys across the table. They were always hungry too."

"And then we had to fast on Wednesdays." The girls held their stomachs in remembrance of the agony.

"I wish I could have been there. I'd have cooked them up plenty of rice and beans and fried chicken," Gertel declared.

"Well, eat up now," invited their dad. "You don't need to go hungry here."

Yet their time in the States also held pleasant memories. They had learned valuable lessons and made lots of new friends. In later years they made many more trips to the States.

Anna used some of her money from chicken butchering to order a correspondence course. In the evenings she hunkered over her books, determined to get an education.

Gertel's older girls were beginning to attract the attention of boys. The four of them, however, presented a defensive front to these advances. They had too much fun as a group of girls to want boys in their lives. The presence of Ernest also deterred admirers. There sat old Pa under the house, working with his tools, and glowering at idlers like a watch dog.

One young man, bolder than the rest, came around whenever Sandra was washing under the house. Jimmy would loiter under the trees across the road and watch her. She hated it. Sometimes she just left the laundry and took refuge in her room. To add insult to injury, Glenda teased her about Jimmy.

One time the girls were having a confrontation on the front steps. "Ha! I saw Jimmy watching you this morning. He's your boyfriend," taunted Glenda.

Sandra bristled. "He is *not* my boyfriend. I can't stand him."

"You just say that. I think you like it when he comes around. Maybe you will marry him someday. Ha-ha! Mrs. Jimmy . . ."

"You stop that!" shouted Sandra, nearly in tears. She pushed at Glenda.

Gertel came to the door. "You girls stop this fighting over nothing. It isn't right. You are Christians. You should be able to get along."

Later she told Sandra in private, "Glenda is just trying to provoke you. When you get mad, she has her fun. If you wouldn't get so upset, it wouldn't be fun for her to tease you, and she would quit."

Sandra decided to try something. The next time Glenda teased her about Jimmy, she answered, "Yeah, he is kinda cute, isn't he? I think maybe I like him a little."

Surprised, Glenda didn't say anything more. Was Sandra really falling for the fellow? The thought worried her for a while. She didn't want Sandra to marry Jimmy.

Eventually Jimmy gave up and left Sandra alone. But then a boy from town tried to be friendly with Glenda, and it was her turn to take the teasing from the other girls. Since this boy was not a Christian, she chose not to return his attention.

The Wagners continued to cast their bread upon the waters by opening their home to friends and strangers alike. On one occasion, though, even Ernest thought their hospitality had gone too far.

Early one Christmas morning, three young British soldiers from the military base near the river a few miles away stopped at the house. The boys had been in town partying the night before and were on their way back to the base, happy and boisterous after a few too many beers. Gertel offered them food, but they assured her they weren't hungry.

Before long two of them got up and left. They had a curfew, they said, and they feared they wouldn't make it. The third man didn't move. He sat on the couch beside Rob, who had brought a hymnal for him to look through. As he paged through the songbook, the soldier became nostalgic. "Ah, we used to sing these songs when I was a lad in England," he mused. Rob offered to sing for him, and he listened politely to Rob's droning. After a while his head lolled back against the back of the couch, and he fell asleep.

"Put him on our bed," Gertel told the boys. They carried him in and dropped him there, just as he was.

Later in the afternoon he stumbled out of the bedroom. He sat down again and began talking about the customs of his homeland. He almost cried about some of the memories. Then he began eyeing the girls. He said that one of their Christmas customs was to get a Christmas kiss from all the girls. At that, the four girls disappeared into their room. They couldn't help peeking through the crack, though, as he kept looking in their direction. The boys had thoroughly tired of him by this time and wished they could get rid of him. Gertel tried offering him food, but he said he was not hungry. They knew he'd never make it back to his base before dark. Finally he left and the girls could come out of hiding.

"You wouldn't have had to give him our bed," Ernest grumbled. The sheet had been badly soiled by the soldier's dirty boots and uniform. The next day they saw the three soldiers running past the house. They were carrying huge rucksacks, sweat dripping from their red faces— their penalty for coming in late.

47

Sickness

One morning Ernest dropped into his chair, propped his elbows on the table, and leaned his head against his hands with a groan. "I don't feel good," he mumbled.

Gertel looked up, alarmed. "What's wrong?" she asked.

He clutched his head. "I don't know. My head feels thick, and I'm a little dizzy. I don't think I want anything to eat."

"Maybe you should stay home."

He shook his head. "Naw. I'll go to work. Maybe I'll feel better once I get going." He picked up his hat and lunch box and descended the stairs, though not with his usual energy.

Gertel fed the children, saw the girls off to the chicken plant and the little boys and Karen off to school, opened the door for the post office, combed and dressed Tresia, washed a bucket of clothes, and then went over to sweep her mother's house. All the time a niggling worry about Ernest gnawed at the back of her mind.

About midday the worry turned into a real concern. A car pulled up in front of the house, and she knew something was wrong when she saw Ernest in the passenger seat. She met him at the door.

"I need to change my clothes," he explained briefly. "I feel bad. I'm going to the hospital. I wonder if it's high blood pressure."

He must be feeling poorly if he comes home from work to go to the hospital!

Daniel and Marietta Miller had come from the States and moved into one of the mission houses next to the chicken plant. She and Gertel had become good friends, so Marietta now willingly agreed to take care of Tresia so Gertel could go along.

The doctor confirmed Ernest's suspicion with a diagnosis of high blood pressure. He insisted that Ernest stay in the hospital for a few days. All their attempts to get his blood pressure down to an acceptable level with medication failed.

"You're going to have to stop smoking, Mr. Wagner, or we will not be able to get your blood pressure down," the doctor warned him.

To Gertel's surprise and relief, Ernest agreed. He had stopped drinking years ago but had always smoked. Now he quit.

"I want to get back to work," he said impatiently.

"You should not go back to work yet," the doctor warned. "Your blood pressure is going down, but there is still grave danger of a stroke. You will have to rest for a while."

Ernest frowned. "How soon can I go home?" he growled.

"I think we can let you go tomorrow, but you can't go to work."

At home Ernest fidgeted on the couch. "We are building a silo in Belmopan," he told Gertel. "I should really be there to supervise." He stared moodily out the window.

"Nesto! You have to listen to the doctor. You don't want to have a stroke. You are nearly fifty years old, you know."

"I'm only forty-nine," he contradicted, running his hands through his graying hair. "I'm used to working. I can't stand sitting around."

The very next morning he got up early and dressed for work. When Gertel protested, he said, "I have to go. I won't work. I'll just supervise."

"But you know what the doctor said. You might have a stroke."

"I said I won't work," he repeated, irritated. "I'll just supervise." With that, he left for work.

She knew she couldn't stop him. She would have to let him go and leave him in God's hands. She prayed for Ernest as she went about her work. Above all, she prayed that he would accept the Lord as his Savior. He was not ready to die.

That evening Ernest returned with a triumphant grin. "It was all right. It didn't hurt me to go to work," he declared.

He went to work the next day and the next. She thought he looked more tired and pale every night, but she said nothing.

The following morning while Ernest was dressing for work, he admitted, "I'm not feeling so well today."

"Then stay home," she urged.

"I have to go. They are doing a big pour of concrete today, and the other fellows don't know how to do it. I need to be there to supervise. I won't do any work."

Gertel went to the kitchen and fixed a cup of tea for her husband. She stood at the stove and fried eggs while he sipped his tea. All of a sudden she heard his spoon clatter onto the table. She gave the eggs another stir. "What's wrong?" she asked over her shoulder. "Are you all right?"

"No," was all he said.

"You'd better stay home," she repeated, turning to look at him. He sat slumped awkwardly to one side, his face twisted grotesquely.

She rushed to his side, shouting, "Sandra, call the mission! We need to get Pa to the hospital!"

Later, in the hospital room, the doctor sat down with Gertel to explain what had happened. "He had a stroke," he said. "We have given him medication to prevent more damage, but we cannot undo what has already happened. As you can see, half of his face is paralyzed. It might improve with time and it might not. We don't know yet how it has affected his legs. They do not seem to be paralyzed, and hopefully he will be able to walk. Time will tell."

Gertel sat alone with her thoughts after the doctor left. Ernest couldn't seem to talk. He made noises, but they were not words. Only his agonized blue eyes told her that he had understood what the doctor said. She held his hand while her thoughts raced. What were they going to do now? The future seemed like a black void in front of her. *God is in control.* The thought washed over her like a calming wave. She prayed, committing the uncertain future into His hands. She knew that He had always been faithful in the past, and He would show them the way through this dark time as well. She needed to trust and not be afraid, as her little son had done on the dark night when he went out to get water for his fearful older siblings.

After several days Ernest was released from the hospital. "There's nothing more we can do for him here," they were told. "Time will heal, but he will never be able to work in construction again."

Ernest refused to give up the idea of going back to work someday, but the immediate problem was his twisted face. He tried to talk, but because the muscles on one side of his face failed to move, the words came out twisted as well. The family soon learned to decipher what he was trying to communicate.

"Will his face ever get better?" wondered Miss Elsa, their neighbor, concern and sympathy lining her forehead.

"The doctors say not. The damage is permanent," said Gertel forlornly.

"I know someone who might be able to help," she offered. "She's an old woman who uses herbs from the bush. Would you like to try it?"

Gertel looked at Ernest, her eyes questioning. He nodded.

"It won't hurt to try," she said, opening her hands wide, ready to try anything that might help. She remembered how her mother had gotten help for her tumor from a bush doctor like this.

"I'll take you there tomorrow," promised Miss Elsa.

The next day they followed her far into the bush to a small thatched house. An old woman with a dark brown, wrinkled face welcomed them inside. She studied Ernest's face with her sharp eyes. Then she nodded, hobbled out the back door, and disappeared into the bush. She returned some time later with a basket of leaves and bits of bark and roots.

"What is his name?" she asked, poking more wood into her fire.

"Ernest," Gertel told her. Ernest still couldn't talk well enough to be understood by strangers.

The woman nodded wordlessly and dropped the leaves into a kettle that was boiling on the hearth. Her lips moved noiselessly and rapidly as if she were praying.

Gertel watched her uneasily. Was she praying, or was she using some kind of enchantment? She knew the herbs would likely do their healing work, but she didn't want any dark powers to be involved. "Lord, keep your hand in this," she prayed. "If it helps Ernest, let all the glory be yours."

When the boiled leaves had cooled, the old woman spread them over Ernest's face and bound them on with bandages.

"Keep them on his face till the night time," she said, breaking her long silence. She plucked a handful of leaves from her basket and put them into a bag. "Make a tea of these, add a little salt, and have him drink it often," she instructed, handing it to Gertel. She tied a small bundle of bark and roots with string and said, "Steep these and bathe him with it. Do all these things for nine days, and come back tomorrow so I can work on his face."

For nine days they made the trek to the old woman's house. Each day she cooked the brew in her pot and put it on his face. They also made several trips to the hospital to check his blood pressure and get more medicine.

"Is it helping?" Miss Elsa wondered.

"A little," Gertel answered weakly. "His face seems to be straightening out, but you can still hardly understand him."

Miss Elsa's eyes brightened. "I know! You have to try nutmeg," she exclaimed.

"Nutmeg?"

"I just remembered. Put nutmeg under his tongue. That will cure his heavy tongue. It worked for my uncle!"

It wouldn't hurt to try, thought Gertel again. They added nutmeg to the daily regimen, and it actually seemed to help. He was taking so many kinds of medication, though, that it was hard to tell which one helped. Gertel thanked God for each small improvement.

His speech improved but never returned to normal, and the man who had been quiet all his life became even more silent. He could walk, although with a slower and more shuffling gait than before. He might have been able to go back to work except that at times, without warning, he would black out and drop to the ground. No one seemed to know why. He did not have seizures; he would simply go blank for a few seconds. Someone—usually Gertel—had to help him up again, and in a few minutes he felt all right. Ernest, always a big man, had gotten quite heavy with the passing of time. It took a great deal of effort for Gertel to get him up off the ground and support him until he could find a seat where he could recover.

In addition to high blood pressure, it was discovered that he had also developed diabetes. One of his doctors thought his fainting spells were probably caused by too much medication, so over the next months they made numerous trips to the doctor to try to regulate his doses.

He would never be able to work at construction again. His right hand was weak and unsteady. Always an active man, Ernest began to get depressed with his lack of ability.

"I don't know how we're going to make it," he told Gertel." How will we live if I can't work?"

"Don't worry," she told him, speaking with more confidence than she felt. "We'll make it. God will provide. The girls are working at the butcher plant, and only the little boys are in school. Maybe I should go to work at the plant too."

Ernest shook his head glumly. "I didn't want you to work. Maybe there's something I can do with just my hands."

Gertel brightened. "That's a good idea! I think there might be something you could do. We'll just have to think for a bit."

Ernest nodded and said, "I already thought of sharpening saws. It's a job not too many people do."

Ernest's idea worked. He soon had a small business sharpening hand-saws and skill saw blades. He could work at it under the house, and it brought in a little cash. Before the saw could be sharpened, the teeth had to be set. His hands were not strong enough to operate the little press that set the teeth, so someone else had to do that for him. Alvan and Glenda learned how to crimp every other tooth one way and then sight along the saw to see if they were lined up. If Alvan and Glenda were not available, Gertel had to do it for him.

Gertel's days became busier than ever with Ernest at home. Normally she would leave the post office door closed until she had finished her morning chores. But Ernest, ever his affable, hospitable self, would hail the neighbors passing by. They would say, "Is the post office open? Is there any mail for me?"

He would return, "Just go on up. It's open anytime. Just ask Gertel for your mail."

When that happened, Gertel had to drop whatever she was doing and go take care of them.

After his stroke, Ernest acted more irritable. He expected his wife to come help him whenever he called. Many times she prayed for forbearance to rein in her impatience with these interruptions.

More travelers than ever stopped to visit with Ernest, and then he would call for her to feed them. She didn't know where they would get the money for so much food, but she had learned that God always supplied when she freely gave.

48

Losing the Children

Anthony, Dwayne, and Karen attended the small Catholic school in Esperanza. One day the teacher paid Gertel a visit with a complaint about Anthony.

"Anthony is often not in school," he reported. "He and some other boys go down to the river and fool around."

Gertel had heard rumors of this playing hooky and had scolded Anthony about it, but apparently her scolding hadn't had much effect. "Thank you for telling me," she answered. "My husband can't walk very well, but I will tell my son Alvan about it. We'll try to see that Anthony is in school."

"Good," nodded the teacher, shaking hands with her. "The absences are hurting his grades."

When Alvan stopped in after work that evening, Gertel told him about the problem.

"Guess I'll go look for him someday when he is at the river," he said.

A few days later Alvan stopped at the school. He peered into Anthony's classroom. "Is Anthony here?" he asked.

The teacher shook his head. "He didn't come to school today."

"He'll be here soon," promised Alvan with a determined set to his jaw.

Alvan made his way to the swimming hole. He approached stealthily. Anthony was just climbing out of the water when Alvan arrived. His eyes widened, and he turned to dive back into the water, but Alvan was too quick. He grabbed the little culprit and smacked him hard. "Why aren't you in school?" he demanded. "You get back there right now."

Anthony's eyes snapped, but he kept his head down as he grabbed his clothes and hurried down the trail ahead of Alvan, who watched him and nodded in satisfaction. This wouldn't happen again.

For a week or two all went well. Anthony showed up for school every day, and that crisis seemed to be over. Then one morning as Gertel was sorting the mail, she noticed a letter addressed to herself.

"From the States," she muttered. "Wonder who . . . Ah, it's from Selia."

She slit the envelope with a hairpin, unfolded the letter, and began scanning quickly. She slowed down and re-read it. "Oh, no!" she exclaimed.

"What's wrong?" asked Sandra, coming to peer over her shoulder.

"Someone must have told Selia that I let Alvan lash Anthony," Gertel groaned. "But I'm sure they didn't tell her why."

"Well, what does she say?" Sandra prodded.

"She says I am not to keep the children any longer. I have to give them to her sister who lives in Belize City," Gertel replied numbly.

"But she can't do that!" Sandra exclaimed. "They've been here for five years. This is their home."

"I know," said Gertel. Her eyes filled with tears. "I'm so attached to them! After five years they seem like my own." Then she blinked and wiped her eyes. "The children are coming," she said. "We can't let them see us crying."

Karen tripped into the living room and began chattering about school. Her black eyes sparkled, and her long, black ponytail swung as she described the skipping game they had played. Gertel nodded, but didn't really hear what the child was saying. Finally she cleared her throat and pulled Karen against her side.

"I got a letter from your mom today."

Karen looked puzzled, but waited to hear the news.

"She says you must go live with your aunt in Belize City."

The light of joy left Karen's face. "What?" she cried. "No! I don't want to go to Belize City. I want to stay here with you! You won't make us go, will you?" She threw her arms around Gertel, sobbing violently.

Gertel held the little girl close. She shook her head. What could she do? "Karen, your mom says you have to go," she said gently. "I can't do anything about it." Her heart ached, but she realized she had no legal guardianship of these children, and she would have to let them go. Karen jerked away, dashed into the bedroom, and locked the door. Gertel wished she could do the same.

It was one of the saddest days of her life when she took the children to Belize City. She found the aunt's house, located in a poor neighborhood with decrepit houses and cluttered yards. She did not have the heart to go inside. She simply left them with the aunt who appeared at the door. The two boys seemed sober and stoical about the change, but Karen clung to Gertel and sobbed brokenheartedly. Tresia wailed in sympathy with her big sister. Gertel rode away, willing herself not to look back. "God, watch over the children," she prayed, wiping away her own tears.

A cloud of gloom hung over the Wagner household, which was much too quiet now. Paul missed Anthony, his companion, and the big girls missed caring for the little girls. Even Ernest was quieter than usual, and nobody wanted to sing in the evenings.

In church the next Sunday, as Gertel sat alone on the bench with no little Karen on one side and Tresia on the other, the tears flowed again. It was as if she had buried four of her children. She felt that she could never again care for someone else's children. It just hurt too much to let them go.

A few months later she met Sophie at the market. Sophie had seen the children in Belize City. She clicked her tongue and said indignantly, "You should just see Karen and Tresia now. They go to school with their hair uncombed and their clothes all wrinkled." She leaned closer and whispered, "They say they want to come back, all of them. Don't you think you could get them back?"

Gertel raised her eyebrows and put her hands on her hips. "Nuh-uh. Their mother took them away, and I'm not taking them back. She said her sister could take care of them."

Sophie shrugged. "She'd probably reconsider if she knew how the children felt."

Gertel shook her head. "I don't think I can ever take another child. It's too hard to let them go after they've been a part of your life for five years."

Her father came by again with another demand. "Mom is sick. You need to come and take care of her. There is nobody else right now and I can't do it."

Gertel's life became a round of constant caretaking, helping Ernest get going in the mornings, then running to her mom's to get her up and bathed and fed, then running back to cook for both households. Sometimes Ernest called for her to set saw teeth for him or move something in his work area. She needed to put her mother to bed in the evenings and keep both houses clean. On top of that she had the work of the post office, including getting stamps and mailing letters. Weariness dogged her days as she tried to be all things to everyone who depended on her. Every morning she prayed for strength for the day, and every evening when she fell into bed, she thanked the Lord for helping her.

As Ernest became more independent, Gertel decided to join the girls at the chicken plant, working part time. Standing on her feet for hours produced some strain, but the actual work was not hard, and the extra dollars it brought provided a welcome boost to the family income. When Ernest had told her that he didn't want her to work, he hadn't counted on being unable to work himself.

With the help of the younger boys and Glenda, Ernest put an indoor bathroom into a corner of one of the bedrooms. That relieved Gertel of a lot of work in caring for his needs and provided a convenience to the entire family. They now had running water in the kitchen as well. No more carrying buckets up from the pump down the road.

Robert still posed his unique challenges. Gertel had followed the doctor's advice and taught him to listen to her. If she asked him to go rake the yard, he did it. He did not have the same respect for his younger brothers and sisters, who sometimes tried to give him orders.

"Rob, go and get the hammer for me, will you?" called Michael one day.

Robert bristled. "What you think? I de *man,*" he declared, standing up straight and glaring at Michael. He meant, "I am older than you, and I don't have to take orders from you."

He enjoyed going to church, where he would sit paging endlessly through his Bible, helping to sing and shaking hands enthusiastically with everyone afterward. He liked to carry his Bible out onto the little verandah in front of the post office door and preach. In loud tones he would declaim phrases like "Jesus, the Savior," "Word of God," and "Don't drink or dance," as he waved his Bible and turned the pages. Sometimes he would sing, swaying and clapping to his own rhythms. He still worked at the chicken plant, cutting off heads and bagging parts. Gertel no longer sent him to the store to buy groceries, since there were too many dishonest people around who would try to talk him out of his money. He had become an adult in body, but she still had to keep track of him, just like a small child.

49

Spanish Teacher

Harold and Orpha Kratzer and their family, originally from Pennsylvania, now owned the butcher plant. Their daughters, Ellen and Melody, became friends of the girls and often came over to play volleyball, along with their brothers. The Wagner girls had stitched together a row of woven plastic onion bags for a net. One night Ken, one of the Kratzer boys, brought over a package. "It's a present for the family," he said. The package contained a new volleyball net.

Unknown to nineteen-year-old Rosie, Ken had long admired her. After some time had passed, Ken and Rosie began dating. Rosie would spend hours in the kitchen baking cupcakes, cookies, or pies to serve Ken when he came to see her. Ernest complained about all the sweet stuff she made. He thought it unnecessary.

Gertel wondered if her youngest daughter would be the first to get married. Sandra had been asked to date, but she had always turned down the requests. She traveled to the States as often as she could, and she enjoyed her life of freedom. The other girls preferred the company of their crowd of girlfriends and the youth activities of the church. The house often rang with the voices of young women cooking, baking, sewing new dresses, singing together, or simply enjoying each other's company. Their involvements added to Gertel's duties, but she relished the social life it provided for her. She usually sat down and visited with the girls and, of course, tried to feed them. Anna had persevered at her correspondence courses and was now teaching school at Red Creek. Ernie, who had dreamed of being a doctor, had tried to do correspondence, but found it too difficult to study and hold down a job at the same time. He was working at the Belize Trade School, a school for delinquent boys run by another church group.

Finances always seemed tight in those days. Paul had finished his primary school exams. Partly due to the superior teaching he had received, and partly due to the God-given gift of a good brain, he had scored the highest in the whole country. Consequently, he earned scholarships to go on and was now attending Sacred Heart College in San Ignacio. Even though his fees were paid, he incurred other costs related to his continuing education. Both Benjie and Michael had been glad to be done with school and were now working at the chicken plant too.

That chicken plant had become a lifesaver for the Wagners. Gertel continued to work there two days a week. Ernest suffered another slight stroke and spent some time in the hospital. After that he used a cane to steady himself when he walked. His blood pressure medications and continuing need for medical monitoring ate up a lot of money.

Ernest could no longer walk into town to attend St. Andrew's, so Alvan sometimes took his dad along to the Baptist church he attended. At other times Ernest would walk down the road with Gertel to the Mennonite church. He had always supported her decision to join there. If she forgot to put her veil on in the morning, he would remind her. Grateful for his support, she wished he could find peace with God for himself. Any attempt to speak to him about the need of his soul brought that blank, closed look over his face and a stubborn set to his jaw. "I'm not changing churches," he would say shortly.

"It's not about changing churches," she would try to explain. "It's about having your sins forgiven and surrendering your life to Christ."

He would walk away. She knew only the Holy Spirit could penetrate his hard heart. All her children who had chosen to follow Christ joined their mother in praying for the salvation of the father they loved and respected.

More and more Spanish-speaking people had begun attending the Mennonite church. One Sunday after the service, Harold Kratzer, the pastor, approached Gertel. "You speak Spanish, don't you?"

Gertel nodded.

"We have been wishing we could have a Spanish Sunday school class for these Spanish-speaking people. Do you think you could teach a class in Spanish?"

Gertel blanched. She felt panic well up in her. She stammered, "Well, I can speak it, yes, but not so well—and I can read it, but I have never tried to write it. I am not a teacher. I've never taught a class of anything. I didn't even finish primary school. I don't know . . ."

"I think you could do it," the pastor encouraged. "We would surely appreciate it. We don't have any other member right now who knows the language well enough to teach."

"I . . . I don't even have a Spanish Bible," she floundered, seeking a way out of this new challenge.

"We'll get you one," he promised. "I'll bring you one tomorrow. Here is an English Sunday school book. Just teach the same lesson, only do it in Spanish. We'll be praying for you." His encouraging smile was lost on Gertel.

She walked home in a daze, her thoughts spinning. "Now what have I gotten myself into? How am I going to do this thing? I never went past Standard Five. I can't teach."

At dinner Gertel ate in silence, her mind preoccupied with the daunting assignment.

Ernest looked at her sharply. "What's bothering you?" he asked.

"They want me to teach a Spanish Sunday school class!" she blurted, hoping for sympathy.

Ernest shrugged. "And that's hard?"

"Yes, it's hard. I don't know if I can do it."

He raised his eyebrows in challenge. "You have faith, right?"

Gertel swallowed and looked down. She did have faith in God. Maybe he had a point. Maybe this was a time to apply it. If God gave her a job to do, surely He would enable her to do it. He had always helped her before with anything she faced.

In the following weeks, she spent many hours poring over her Spanish Bible, preparing for her teaching assignment. She was rewarded with an eager response from the grateful class. In time, some of those Spanish-speaking people were converted and became members of the church.

She breathed a sigh of relief a year later when the new list of Sunday school teachers was announced. God had helped her, but she would be glad to turn the responsibility over to someone else.

Then Brother Harold announced the upcoming marriage of Alberto and Sofia, a Hispanic couple who had been in her class. Now they were to be united in Christian marriage. Gertel rejoiced to hear the news. She felt a motherly satisfaction about it. She did not realize until after church that she would be involved in the affair.

"I would like to perform the ceremony in Spanish," Brother Harold told her. "Could you translate it for me?"

Gertel gulped. Another challenge! "I could try," she ventured.

"Good. I'll give you the book, and you can translate the vows and then read them onto a cassette so I can hear how it should sound."

Gertel nodded, but all the while she was thinking again, "What have I gotten myself into now?"

Gertel pored over the wedding vows, translating everything with the help of a Spanish-English dictionary. She sometimes found herself floundering for words. She needed to use formal language, nothing like the street language she used with her friends.

Finally she reached the end. In reading it over, she shook her head. It just didn't sound right. She had attended a number of Spanish weddings, and this didn't ring true for some reason. She glanced at the clock, which informed her that it was time to go to work at the chicken plant. She would take it along and get a coworker who knew Spanish to look at it.

Marisol read it over. "It sounds all right to me," she said, handing the paper back to Gertel.

Gertel still didn't feel satisfied. The next time she went into town to buy stamps, she visited a justice of the peace, the man who regularly performed wedding ceremonies in Spanish, using vows somewhat different from those she had translated from the Mennonite *Minister's Manual.* "Can you tell me if this translation is correct?" she asked, handing him her paper.

He read it over silently, made a few corrections, and handed it back. "That should do it," he said with a smile.

Gertel thanked him and took the paper. Outside the building she unfolded it and looked it over carefully. She frowned. It still didn't seem quite right. On the walk home she racked her brain to think of someone who could fix the wording. She needed someone proficient in both English and Spanish. Then she thought of Marcos, a Salvadoran university student who sometimes stopped by to post letters. He knew English well enough to study in that language, but Spanish was his first language. She would ask him.

Marcos helped her gladly. He sat down at her table and set to work. After ten minutes, he handed the edited script back to her. She read it aloud slowly.

"That's it!" she exulted. "Now it sounds right. Thank you so much! Now I can make the cassette tape."

A week later Gertel sat in the audience and listened to Brother Harold read her translated vows. He did well, except—she hid a smile behind her hand—he never could roll his *r*'s correctly. Otherwise, the ceremony seemed perfect, and Gertel felt a glow of satisfaction for her part in making it possible. She felt thankful that the Lord could take a simple country woman who didn't have much education and had never traveled far from home, and use her in His kingdom work.

50

Jenita

On a Monday morning after the others had gone off to work and school, Miss Julia, a lady from the other end of the village, appeared at the house with a baby girl in her arms.

"Miss Waggy," she said. "You want this baby?"

"What?" exclaimed Gertel. "Who is giving away a baby?" She leaned closer to peer at the rather thin baby with a mere film of dusty fuzz on her little black head.

"Her mother can't take care of her. She says she wants to give her away. Will you take her?"

Gertel thought of Selia's children and her resolution to never take another child. "I don't really want her, but I might be able to find someone who does," she ventured.

Ernest shuffled over to stand beside her. He clucked at the baby and chucked her under the chin. The baby rewarded him with a luminous smile. "Take it," he said.

Still smiling, the baby looked up at Gertel with bright black eyes. Gertel's heart lurched; she could never resist a baby's eyes. She smiled back and gently pinched the baby's cheeks.

Miss Julia spoke urgently. "Rose, her mom, is just a young girl herself, and she boards in my upstairs. She doesn't take care of the baby. I worry about her. Sometimes the baby just cries and cries. The other day the baby was crying, and then all of a sudden everything was quiet. I yelled up the stairs, 'Rose, if you kill that baby, I'll report you to the police.'

"Rose, she say, 'No, I no do nothing to her.' But my grandchildren, they tell me that sometimes when the baby cries, Rose puts a pillow over her head to stop her. I'm afraid she's going to suffocate the child someday.

She says she wants to give the baby away so she can go to work. The poor little thing is only four months old. I wish you would take her."

"We'll talk about it when the girls come home," Gertel promised.

When the girls came home for lunch, she told them about the baby.

Excited and unanimous, they declared their verdict: "Oh, Ma, let's take her."

"Your Pa isn't working," Gertel protested. "We can't afford to keep a baby and buy milk."

"We could all help take care of her."

"We'll use our wages to buy milk for her."

"Paul is big now. We haven't had a baby around here for a long time."

"The poor little thing. You have to take her, Ma, before her mother kills her."

As soon as school had dismissed for the day, Anna said, "I'm going to go look for that baby." Gertel went along.

Miss Julia met them with the baby in her arms. "Her mother isn't home yet," she explained. "I took the baby away from her because I was afraid she would do something to her. I would be relieved if you would take her. She tried to give the baby away twice before, but then she always went and took her back again. I told her, 'You have to give the baby away for real this time,' and she agreed."

Doubts filled Gertel's mind. Would this Rose do the same to them as Selia had? She must not let that happen. She prayed silently for wisdom.

Finally she said, "We will go home. If Rose wants to give the baby to us, we will wait at our house until she brings her there."

After dark there was a timid "halloo" at the door. A very young, slender girl stood there juggling the baby, a bag of clothes, a can of powdered milk, and a bottle.

Gertel spoke sternly to her. "Are you sure you want to give this baby away?"

"Yes, ma'am," muttered the timid girl, not looking her in the face.

"Why?"

"The father doesn't help, and I have to work. I can't take care of her."

She shifted the baby in her arms.

"You'd better be sure. If I take this little one, you are not going to come around later and take her back. If I take her, it will be for keeps, you understand? It won't work if you are going to change your mind."

"Oh no, ma'am. I won't do that. You can have her. I can't take care of her."

"Did you bring the birth papers?" asked Gertel.

Rose nodded and handed the baby to Sandra, who held out her arms. She fumbled in her bag and handed over some folded papers. She set the bag of clothes and the can of powdered milk on a nearby chair and turned to leave. She didn't even give her baby a farewell kiss.

No one spoke after she left. Glenda picked up the bag of clothes, opened it, and sniffed. She wrinkled her nose. "Whew! We can't put these clothes on the baby until we wash them."

"The baby doesn't smell so good herself," remarked Sandra. "I'm going to give her a bath."

"I think I can find some old baby things to put on her for tonight until we can get her clothes washed." Gertel went into her bedroom to look. She kept a box of diapers and sleepers on hand for the times she babysat for someone.

"What's the baby's name?" wondered Benjie.

Ernest unfolded the birth papers. "It's Shanti Natasha," he read.

"Humph!" snorted Gertel, returning with a handful of clothing. "I don't like that name. If she is going to be ours, we'll give her a nice name."

From the bathroom they could hear Sandra speaking quietly to the baby over the sound of running water. Baby shrieks of distress soon followed. Gertel hurried to the open bathroom door. "What happened? What are you doing to that poor baby?"

Sandra chuckled as she lifted the dripping, squalling infant from the bathwater and wrapped her in a towel. "I don't think she's used to being bathed. She doesn't like it." She rubbed the little body gently.

"Poor baby," Gertel clucked, handing Sandra the clothes. "I'll fix her bottle while you get her dressed."

Gertel held the baby while she sucked eagerly at the bottle. Within minutes she had filled her diaper noisily.

"She has diarrhea," concluded Gertel. "We'll have to change her often and keep feeding her."

"I'll take her to bed with me," Sandra offered.

Gertel shrugged. *Why not?* At fifty-two years of age, she didn't look forward to getting up with a baby every night. Sandra, twenty-five, could well have been married with babies of her own by now. *Let her do it,* Gertel thought.

The whole household slept lightly that night, like new parents. Gertel awoke around 5:00. She hadn't heard a squeak out of that baby all night. Silence reigned in the house. All at once a stab of fear shot through her. Had Sandra, unused to sleeping with a baby, rolled onto the infant during the night?

She jumped out of bed and hurried to the girls' room. Just as she reached the door, she heard the baby whimper and then give a healthy cry. She sagged with relief. "Did she sleep all night?" she asked Sandra.

"She woke up once, and I changed her and fed her some more. Then she rolled over and went back to sleep."

"I can see that she is used to taking care of herself," Gertel commented. "Nobody fussed over her in all her life."

The family all fell in love with the baby girl from the start. Even twelve-year-old Paul, who had never shown any interest in babies, tried to make her smile. Their church friends also crowded around to admire her. Some of the girls offered to help find her a good name. They gave various suggestions, and the family finally settled on Jenita Darlene. They planned to take the birth papers to the city, get the name changed, and secure legal guardianship of her. Gertel stopped working at the chicken plant so there would be one constant caregiver at home for Jenita.

In the meantime, the horrible diarrhea continued. It seemed the milk ran straight through her. She no sooner had downed a bottle than she filled her diaper. She would soon be crying a hunger call. The girls, who at first vied for the chance to feed her, began to dread the job, because it always meant changing a smelly diaper.

"We have to take her to the doctor," Gertel decided.

The doctor told them the baby was suffering from malnutrition, and they should just continue to feed her. They did, but still she did not grow. She only became thinner and thinner. Something had to be done.

Other people gave suggestions. "Give her lime . . . give her ginger tea . . . give her papaya."

"Try rice cereal," suggested one young mother. They tried, but it didn't work. Everything she ate went straight through.

Gertel felt so helpless. The baby was starving in front of her eyes, her little belly looked swollen, her arms and legs had shrunken to sticks, and her eyes seemed enormous in her small, pinched face.

A Salvadoran man, passing through on his way back home, saw the baby. "What's wrong with her?" he asked. "She don't look too good." They told him they had tried lots of things, and nothing was working.

One day when Gertel bathed Jenita, the diarrhea ran right into the bath water. She cried tears of helplessness as she wrapped the child in a towel. "Lord," she prayed in desperation, "you brought this baby to me. If it is your will that I raise her, show me what to do for her. Surely you didn't mean for her to die."

Then, in the silence, she distinctly heard a voice saying, *Give her cornstarch.* Startled, she looked around, but no one was there.

She got up and heated water, stirring in some cornstarch to thicken it, and then she added the milk powder. When it had cooled sufficiently, she fed Jenita six ounces of the mix. She held her breath—no diarrhea! After several feedings of the cornstarch mix, Jenita's bowel movements became thicker and less frequent. "Thank you, Lord!" Gertel exclaimed fervently.

From that day, Jenita began to gain weight and became a happy, sociable child. Michael and Benjie liked to toss her in the air or lay her belly-down on their outstretched hands and swoop her around the room in airplane rides.

"Don't you drop that baby," Gertel would warn. Jenita loved all the attention. The big girls liked to dress her up and carry her with them to some of their social gatherings, where she charmed everyone.

The man from El Salvador came back and couldn't believe it was the same baby. "I thought she would die," he admitted. "I wonder if she would like to eat some of my vegetables. I grow vegetables," he explained. "I'll bring you some when they are ready."

A few weeks later he returned with a basket of tomatoes, peppers, and radishes. They gave her a piece of tomato, and she smacked it down with delight, the red juice oozing out at the corners of her mouth. They tried some ground-up peppers next, and she ate them too. But when she tasted a radish, she grimaced and dribbled it out onto her bib. "That's the first food I've ever seen her refuse," laughed Gertel.

Jenita grew and thrived. She learned to walk and then to talk. The big girls brought her gifts and treats when they returned from their trips to the States. She learned to expect them. "What you bring me this time?" she would ask. They made her more dresses than she needed. The boys bought soda and sweets for her, and Ernest wouldn't let anyone whip her. More than once, when she had disobeyed and Gertel threatened to spank her, she would run to Pa for refuge. "She's had a hard life," he would say. "We need to be patient with her."

"But we have to teach her," Gertel would protest. She worried that they were spoiling the little girl. Sometimes she did punish Jenita, but too often the child got her own way.

51

Not My Mommy

One day when Jenita was about two and a half years old, Gertel was selecting a head of cabbage at the market stand when the vendor startled her with a question.

"Miss Waggie, you know that baby's mom come back?" asked the vendor furtively. "She say she come to get her baby. Be careful. She might come to your house," he warned.

Gertel felt her insides pinch in fright, but she tried to stay outwardly calm. "Okay. I'll see her if she comes. Thanks for telling me."

At home, the first person she encountered was Ernie, who had come home for the weekend. "Did Rose come around here?" she asked him.

He looked at her, puzzled. "No."

She told him what she had heard at the market.

He scowled and his eyes sparked. "Let her try. She'll go down those steps faster than she came up," he threatened.

For a few weeks the whole family remained on guard, watching for Rose and making sure Jenita was not left alone in the yard. When she didn't show up, they relaxed again.

About a month later, however, Gertel received a letter in the mail from Rose.

> *My father says I should come get my baby because the place for a baby is with the mother.*

Gertel sat down immediately and wrote a reply.

> *Please send me your father's address. I will explain to him why we have the little girl and what agreement we made.*

They waited in vain for an answer. Instead, Rose herself appeared at their door. "I want my baby back," she stated flatly.

Gertel fixed a stern eye on her. "Fine," she said. "If you are willing to pay me support money for all the years I have been caring for her, you can have her." She paused to let that soak in, and then she added, "Remember, we are training her to love and obey God. If you take her away and fail to raise her in the fear of God, God will hold you responsible for her eternal soul."

Rose appeared flustered and uncertain. Finally she dropped her eyes, turned slowly, and went down the steps. Gertel breathed a prayer of thanks.

When Gertel told Miss Julia about it, Miss Julia sputtered, "I told Rose, 'Look, you leave that child right where she is. You see her? She is healthy and happy, and she fits right in with their family. You know you can't take good care of her. Leave her where she is.'

"And Rose, she said, 'No, no. I won't take her away. I don't have a home. I don't have a husband. I can't give her the things she needs. I can't mind her. I have to work.' I don't know why she came and told you she wants her now."

"She probably feels guilty about giving her away," Gertel surmised. "And when she sees how pretty and happy the girl is, she wishes she had her."

"I'm glad you stood up to her." Miss Julia nodded her head emphatically. "Jenita is much better off here. You know the night she brought that little girl to you, she told me, 'If Miss Waggie wouldn't have taken that baby, I would've left her by the side of the road.' And now she thinks she can have her back again. Huh-uh."

Gertel's heart still ached for Selia's four children. She knew they had been shuttled from the aunt to another friend, and then to a third place since they left her house. Once or twice, when she had seen the children, the girls had cried, reached for her, and begged to come home with her. She determined more than ever not to let Jenita go.

Rose stayed in the area. Although she seemed to have given up her campaign to get her daughter back, she still showed up from time to time to visit her. One time she scooped up Jenita, carried her to the edge of the balcony railing, and threatened to throw her over. Jenita stiffened and screamed in terror.

Ernie came to her rescue. He snatched Jenita from Rose's arms and growled at her, "If you know what's good for you, you'll leave."

Rose backed away, her eyes wide with fear. Then she turned and ran down the steps.

Rose stayed away after that, but a deep fear of her had been planted in Jenita's heart. Whenever they passed the house where Rose lived, she would cling to Gertel or whoever was with her. If she saw Rose pass on the road, she would run and hide in her bedroom or behind the sofa.

"Don't worry," Gertel would assure her. "No one is going to take you away. You are safe here."

At church, if anyone asked her where her mom was, she would point to Gertel. "That's my mommy," she would say.

Sometimes neighbor children would tease her. "Rose is your mom," they would taunt.

She would deny it hotly. "Rose is not my mommy. God gave me to this family. I am a Wagner." She never called Rose her mother. To her, she had become part of the Wagner family.

· ·

Many changes were taking place, both in Gertel's country and in her family. In 1981 Belize had declared its independence from England. A new flag fluttered from the flagpoles, its coat of arms depicting a white man and a black man flanking a mahogany tree. "God Save the Queen" had become obsolete, replaced by a new national anthem. These changes, however, did little to affect Gertel in her little brown house by the side of the road.

The paving of the road that ran past the house and the busses that replaced truck travel both added convenience to Gertel's life. No longer did she need to walk into town for her stamps. Poles and lines bringing round-the-clock electric power meant that the family could read or study any evening.

The arrival of grandchildren constituted another new and delightful change. Both William and Alvan brought their growing families to visit. The grandchildren always found a welcome at Grandpa's house. Ernest loved to watch the children play. Sometimes if their noise bothered him, he would poke at them with his cane and threaten to beat them. They loved their grandpa but learned to stay out of reach of his cane if he seemed annoyed. Gertel enjoyed feeding them and watching them play without having full responsibility of them. Since Jenita's brothers and sisters were all much older than she, she grew up with the grandchildren for playmates.

Robert, of course, still lived at home. "This is the one son who will never leave me," Gertel joked. He had grown into a big, strong fellow, and she appreciated his strength when she had to move heavy furniture or help Ernest after a fall.

52

The Nest Empties

Gertel marveled at how the lives of her grown daughters differed from her own early years. Her three oldest girls, still single, were now all older than Gertel had been when she got married. Tall Sandra reminded Gertel of her grandmother in the way she walked and held herself. Glenda, the shortest of the girls, most resembled her mother.

The American girls who came to teach at the little school at Red Creek felt nervous about staying alone. They begged Sandra and Glenda to come and stay with them, so the two girls moved their belongings out of their small bedroom and into the teachers' trailer in the Kratzers' yard. They still came home to eat supper in the evening and to help their mom on Saturdays, but they worked and slept at Homestead Acres, the chicken-butchering business.

Their first trip to the States had given Sandra and Glenda travel fever, and nearly every year one or both of them were packing their bags for another trip. They had made many friends in the States. Periodically a married friend would call and ask if she could buy a plane ticket for one of the girls to come help her with her family for a month or two, and away they would go. "Humph! When I was young I never went anywhere," Gertel would say. Even now, she had no great desire to leave the comfort of her home. As the children grew bigger, the little house seemed to shrink. Gertel didn't mind. She was happiest when there was a full table for her to feed.

Anna, once a chubby child and now a slender young woman, neared the realization of her ambition to become a nurse. She had completed her high school correspondence course and taught school for several years. She began working at Loma Luz, a new hospital that had been built by the Seventh Day Adventists, less than a mile from their home. Reports of her experiences injected a medical note into the discussions around the table.

Rosie, the youngest but tallest of the four, taught at Red Creek Mennonite School, where Jenita attended. She threw her abundant energy into the job and spread her papers and art projects all over the table in the evenings. Since she and Ken Kratzer were dating, he often frequented Gertel's table. He had endeared himself to her by his revolutionary ideas about who should do the dishes. One of the first times he and his sisters ate at their house, Gertel got up as usual after the meal and said, "Well, you young folks go ahead now and play volleyball."

"Aren't you going to help with the dishes?" Ken asked the girls.

"No," Rosie explained. "Guests don't do the dishes. The cook does the dishes."

Indignant, Ken went on. "The cook has done all that work to make the food. She shouldn't have to clean it all up."

But Gertel confirmed the tradition. "I cook and I do the dishes. That is the way it is in Belize."

"Well, that is one Belizean custom that could be changed," Ken contended. Continuing in a sing-song tone, he said, "All the fine compliments and all the good wishes cannot replace help with the dishes."

After that, Gertel contented herself with sitting back and letting the young people do the dishes. If they forgot, someone was sure to recite the little rhyme Ken had taught them.

Ernie was still working at the boys' school and hoping to get a visa to go to the States and study. Michael had found his niche driving a bus on the new highway, and Benjie eagerly awaited the day when he could get behind the wheel of a big truck.

Gertel had thought she was busy when all the children were small. Now she felt like a traffic controller in an airport. Keeping track of all their jobs and schedules, fielding all the varied reports and opinions, and trying to be all things to all men taxed her brain. "When they were little, all I had to do was feed them and keep them in clean clothes," she complained to Ernest. "Now I am supposed to be judge, counselor, nurse, teacher, pastor, bookkeeper, and travel agent, as well as chief cook and bottle washer." He just smiled and nodded. She could do it, he knew.

In September of 1984, Rosie married Ken Kratzer.

She is about the same age as I was when I got married, thought Gertel, sitting on the front bench at the ceremony. "I wonder if she will have as many children as I did. And I suppose they will come in all colors, with a white father and a black mother." How thrilled she felt to see them establishing a Christian home.

The new couple moved into the house beside the church that had been vacated by Ken's brother and family. Ken now owned the chicken business and the two houses that flanked it. That made one more vacancy in Gertel's

At the wedding of Ken and Rosie Kratzer: Aunt Myrtle (Gertel's sister), Granny and Grandpa Morris (Gertel's parents).

house, although Rosie was not far away. Rosie's sisters moved into the apartment under her house. They still spent most of their free waking hours in their mother's kitchen.

A year later, Ken and Rosie's first child was born. Rosie's prenatal appointments had taken place at the new Loma Luz Hospital, but the foreign doctor there did not yet have his papers to practice in Belize. He told her he could not deliver the baby at the hospital, but he would come to the house if she wanted to have the baby at home. The night Sterling arrived, Gertel anxiously waited with them for the doctor. He barely made it in time. "Have you ever delivered a baby?" he asked Gertel when he had finished his work and was getting ready to leave.

"No way," she asserted. "I bore eleven children, but I never helped anyone else."

"Well, you almost had a chance tonight."

I'm glad he made it in time, she thought. *I'm no doctor and I don't want to be.*

Paul, her baby, graduated from high school with honors. He told his parents that it hardly felt as though he had gone to school for four years; studying came so easily to him that the time flew. Scholarships were available to him to go on to sixth form, a sort of junior college, and from there to University.

"You should go," urged his father. "The money is there for you. Take the opportunity to get an education. Most of your brothers didn't have this chance."

"I am tired of going to school," countered Paul. "I think I'd like to work for a year and then go back to school."

His dad shook his head. "If you work for a year, you will never go back," he predicted.

But Paul had his way. Homestead Acres had grown into a large enterprise. Ken offered Paul a job in the office, where they were transferring all the accounts to computer. In order to do the job, Paul enrolled in computer courses in town. He completed the course, but he never went for the exam which would have certified him as a qualified computer technician. "I don't really like office work," he complained to his mom. "I don't want to spend the rest of my life sitting behind a desk dressed up in a shirt and tie."

"Well, you're working in an office now," she pointed out.

"Yeah, but I'm getting tired of it. Anything that goes wrong, it's my fault. I have to fix everyone else's problems. I'll stay there and help Ken for a while, but I don't think I'll always stay there."

"What do you want to do?" she asked.

He grinned. "What I really like to do," he drawled, watching her for her reaction, "is fix cars."

She threw up her hands. "Fix cars! All your education and you want to fix cars?"

He shrugged. "I like to work with my hands. I've been helping Ken's brother Dave in the mechanic shop sometimes, and I enjoy it. It's fascinating to figure out what's wrong and then get my hands dirty to fix it."

"Well, I guess you have to do what you like to do," she said resignedly.

Ernie finally got his break. The people he was working for helped him to get a student visa, and he left for the States. He planned to complete high school and then decide what he wanted to do from there. When she said goodbye, Gertel felt in her heart that he would probably never return to Belize.

· ·

In the next two years, Rosie had two more baby boys. Glenda and Sandra took turns helping her, and Gertel enjoyed the babies. It reminded her so much of her own busy years when the children were small. "Only I didn't have a washing machine, an indoor bathroom, and sisters to help me," she reminded Rosie.

Like her mother, even with her arms full of babies, Rosie was always looking for ways to cast her bread upon the waters. When a young girl asked Rosie to care for her infant daughter, she agreed. The arrangement began as temporary one, but then the mother died and Felicia stayed.

"As if you didn't have enough babies already," her mother scolded.

"But I have no little girls," explained Rosie.

Before Felicia turned two, Ken and Rosie had another little boy of their own whom they named Jonathan.

Sandra was now working in the office at the plant when she wasn't in the States, so Glenda stayed busy getting up early to wash, bake, and clean for Rosie, then go to work at the plant. Gertel would have liked to help her daughter more, but she was already trying to take care of two households and two semi-invalids, her mother never being in very good health. She contented herself with cooking up pots of chicken and *bollos* and sending them over for her daughter's family.

53

Generations

"Ma, we are going to the States. Why don't you come along?" Rosie suggested one day when her mom stopped in.

"Me? Go to the States?" Gertel's hands flew to her chest. "Why would I want to go to the States?"

"We want to go to Emmaline's wedding, and you could see where Sandra has been staying for the last couple months, and then we could take you to see your sister Myrtle."

"Well . . ." Gertel hedged. "I haven't seen Myrtle for years."

"We plan to fly," Rosie went on. "And we can't handle all these children by ourselves. You can come along and help."

"But who will stay with Pa? And I don't have a passport." Gertel raised her objections.

"Ken will help you get a passport," Rosie promised.

"Gladys and I will come and stay with Pa," offered Paul. He had pursued his dream of working with engines and now had his own business as a heavy-duty mechanic. He and Gladys lived a few miles away.

"Aren't you scared to get on one of those airplanes?" asked Miss Lil when Gertel told her she was going to the States.

Gertel shook her head. "No. I have traveled in boats and trucks and busses. This won't be any different. You just get on and go where it takes you."

"But you are just hanging up there in the air. What if it drops?"

"God knows where I am, and He will take care of me. If He wants me to die in a plane, that is up to Him. I don't worry."

Armed with her new passport, a new suitcase, several new dresses, and a multiple-entry, indefinite visa, Gertel walked across the pavement at the Belize City airport and climbed the stairs into the big jet. As she settled into her seat between Rosie's children, she told herself again that it was no different from sitting in a bus.

She enjoyed her time in the States. The countryside in summertime reminded her of home. Yes, the trees were different, but the grass was green and the flowers were beautiful. She attended some large churches where Rosie introduced her to her acquaintances, but most of the people did not greet her. It seemed there were so many people there that they didn't have time for visiting.

Along with Sandra, they went shopping in several large stores, but she did not have money to spend, so she did not buy much. Rosie mentioned with a smile that her mother seemed like a child, always asking, "When are we going to go home?" She worried about Ernest and Robert and the post office. Visiting with Sandra and Myrtle and seeing many American highlights caused the weeks to pass swiftly, and Gertel was soon on her way home. She didn't know if she would ever go again. She had not become a fan of the States. Home felt more comfortable.

Orlando Matute, a Hispanic man from Georgeville a few miles down the highway, had joined the church and begun to pay attention to

At Matt and Glenda Matute's wedding. A jovial Ernest with his sister, Grandpa and Granny Morris, and Granny's brother in the center.

Glenda. At first she resisted, but in time she came to appreciate him. In 1992 there was another family wedding. As was the custom, Matt, as he was called, paid for the wedding; but Granny Morris donated a turkey and wanted Glenda to dress for the wedding in her house so she could see her. Gertel and Rosie cooked some chicken, and others helped with the rest of the food. Ernest was feeling fairly well, so he participated in the wedding. Matt and Glenda settled down in his home in Georgeville.

Later that same year, Anna left her home and church and married a Belizean-born U.S. Marine, who took her to the States. There she completed her training to become a registered nurse.

"She was the one who said she would never leave me," Gertel grieved. But she committed her daughter into God's hands and allowed her to make her own decisions.

Rosie came over one day, with Felicia, now five, and Johnny, age four. In her arms she carried a light-skinned baby girl. "See my new baby?" she said with a big grin.

"What?" exclaimed Gertel. "You found yourself another baby girl?"

"I sure did."

Gertel gathered the baby into her arms and wrapped a blanket securely around her while Rosie settled herself on the couch and began her story. "You know that old granny I like to visit down beyond the bend? Well, every time I went there lately, I would see this baby lying in a hammock. She was always soaking wet and dirty and sometimes shivering. I could hardly stand it. She belongs to the granny's daughter, but the girl pays no attention to her. Last time I went there, I told them that if I find the baby like that again, I'm going to take her home with me. I was just there this morning, and the baby was wailing pitifully. I couldn't stand it. I picked up the baby and said, 'I'm taking this baby home with me.' The old granny just said, 'Good. Take her.' I told her that if the mom wants her, she can come get her."

"I don't know if you need another baby . . ." Gertel began doubtfully. "But I can see you couldn't leave her there."

The mother never did come for her baby. Eventually she signed the papers to make Denise a part of Ken's family.

When Glenda's first child was born, she felt lonely for female companionship. Sandra was visiting Anna in Hawaii, where Anna's husband was stationed, and Jenita still attended school. "You just come on over here," Gertel told her. "I'll take care of you."

For a few weeks Glenda recuperated in her old home while her mom cooked for her and fussed over the baby girl, whom they had named Monica.

Then Gertel's mother became seriously ill. Gertel went with her parents to the hospital. They waited a long time for the doctor to admit her and get her settled into a bed. She felt very weak and complained of a stomachache. Gertel stayed as long as she could, but she needed to get home, check on Robert and Ernest, and prepare the chicken for the next day. She didn't know where she should be. She hated to leave, but her mother said, "Go home. You can get me some more clothes and a clean towel. Go do your chicken and then you can come back for the night."

Ken took Gertel home. She cut up and seasoned her chicken, then started to walk up to her mom's house to get the clothes she wanted. Before she had gone far, Ernest called her back. "They phoned from the hospital," he said. "Your mother has passed away."

Gertel deeply regretted not being there. *Why didn't I stay?* she agonized. But she couldn't change it now. She remembered how her mother had laid her head against her shoulder while they waited for the doctor to come. Had she known it wouldn't be long? *So it goes,* she thought. *One generation passes away . . .*

After the funeral, Gertel's father did not want to stay alone. He begged to move in with them. Although she had been taking care of her parents for years, Gertel felt reluctant to have her dad come. He had long ago forgiven Ernest for coming from Belize City, but both of the men were fractious, and she did not think it would be a good idea to have the two of them under one roof. Her dad, however, accustomed to manipulating her, insisted.

Finally Ernest had a suggestion for him. "Get one of those little houses they build over at Spanish Lookout and move it here. Sandra can take care of you."

A one-room house was moved onto a spot just behind theirs, and Grandpa moved into it.

During the next months Gertel grew closer to her father than she had ever been. He had mellowed and seemed to appreciate her kindness to him. She found that many of her old resentments had faded, and she forgave him for his ill treatment of her. He often sat and visited congenially with her and Ernest in the evenings.

Sandra, now in her upper thirties, assumed responsibility for Grandpa, washing, cleaning, and cooking in the little house. "If I'm going to take care of Grandpa, I want my own space," she said after a few weeks of this. "I have money saved. Pa, could you build a couple more rooms onto Grandpa's cabin, and then I could live there?" Sandra had rejected the overtures of an English soldier and even a man from church. She decided she would never get married, but she did want to have her own house.

Working at his own speed, and with the help of the boys, Ernest added a bathroom and two bedrooms to the little house. Sandra paid for the supplies.

Less than a year after her mother passed away, Gertel's father also died at the age of ninety-four. Active to the end, he had been valiantly

Gertel with her brother Charles and sisters Marlene and Myrtle, celebrating their father's 93rd birthday.

trying to chop out the stump of a big avocado tree in the yard. He got so weak that he collapsed, and they took him to the hospital. To Gertel's distress, he did the same thing as her mom. She had been with him all afternoon, and then he urged her to go home. "Go," he said impatiently. "It's almost dark."

"I'll wait until Sandra comes. She said she'd come sit with you for a while."

"She'll soon come. Just go on home."

She walked out into the lobby and saw that Sandra was coming up the walk. She went back in and told her dad she was going now. He looked at her and nodded. But before she had reached home, he died.

The little house in the backyard became Sandra's. She had a place to spread out and display all the little knickknacks and pictures she had accumulated over the years. Sandra's house became a gathering place for the single girls who served at the mission, and she lived close enough to help her mom anytime.

At Christmastime the clan gathered in Ken and Rosie's yard at Homestead Acres. The tables were spread with offerings of *bollos,* chicken, tortillas, rice and beans, barbecued pork, potato salad, and Gertel's famous light cake, a Belizean specialty. As she and Ernest watched the children squeal and scramble in a candy toss, Gertel reflected on the cycle of birth and death. In the year since her dad had died, both Rosie and Glenda had birthed baby girls, and Gertel's sister Marlene had died in an accident. *One generation passes away and another comes. For those left, life simply goes on,* she thought.

54

The Burdens Mount

N ow over sixty-five years old, Gertel still cooked for a big family. She often made lunches for Rosie's children and cooked up big pots of food for the children and grandchildren who liked to stop in after school and work.

Ernest again spent some time in the hospital with another stroke. Anxious days and nights passed until he was finally allowed to come home. *More bills to pay,* she mused. *More work too.*

If she thought she had been busy before, it was nothing compared to her present routine. Caring for Ernest became her priority. A bed patient now, he could not walk or dress himself. His arms and legs had become weak and unsteady, although not completely paralyzed. Gertel fed him his meals, bathed him in bed, and massaged his useless limbs. Turning him over, helping him to sit up, and changing the sheets left her with a constant backache. Her husband's helplessness and pain made him more irritable, and he expected her to be at his beck and call. He resented when she had to run to take care of post office customers or help Jenita with her homework. Sandra helped as much as she could, but she was working at the Homestead Acres office. Both Rosie and Glenda kept busy with their own households. Gertel did not have the energy of youth, and the demands placed upon her sapped her strength. More than once she escaped to the bathroom to have a good cry.

The hospital bills worried her too. Ernest took so many expensive medications that she didn't know how they would ever get on top. If they had been hard-pressed before, now it was worse. She was too old to go back to work, which wasn't a possibility anyway since she had to take care of her husband.

Three sisters (L to R): Glenda, Rosie, Sandra.

"Why? Why, Lord?" she prayed. "Why does life have to be so hard?" She recalled the many times over the years that she had cared for her ailing mother. Now it was her husband. "Why am I always the one who has to take care of everyone?" Then she felt the stab of conscience. Who was she to question God's designs? "Forgive me, Lord," she sobbed. "You have always helped me in the past, and I know you will give me the strength and courage to go on. Help me to do what I have to do every day, to be patient with Ernest, and to trust you to supply our needs."

They faced more than one crisis in those days. One morning Ernest started to have hiccups. "You swallowed too fast," Gertel scolded.

The hiccups did not stop. For an hour, then two hours—*hic, hic, hic,* on and on and on. Ernest began to get annoyed. He swallowed several glasses of water without taking a breath; he beat on his chest; he held his breath until he was red in the face; but nothing worked. The hiccups did not let up all day. When he tried to eat, he almost choked when a hiccup interrupted the food on its way down his throat. He was becoming frantic. That night he never slept a wink, and neither did Gertel. One time after a particularly hard round of hiccups, he could scarcely get his breath. By morning they were both exhausted. She called Ken to come and take him to the hospital.

"Is Pa going to die?" asked Jenita, in tears, as they helped him into the truck.

Gertel had never heard of anyone dying of hiccups, but she had never seen a case of hiccups like this. The doctors at Loma Luz tried having him breathe into a paper bag; then they had him swallow crushed ice; then they hooked up an IV and administered one or two drugs that were supposed to help. All the procedures failed, and they were at a loss what to do. The constant irritation had worn Ernest out.

"We'll have to send him to Belize City," said the doctor. "Maybe they can figure out what to do there."

Ernest's stubborn streak surfaced. "I'm not going to the city. Just let me die right here," he insisted, convinced he would die of hiccups.

Finally a doctor suggested another drug they could try, and this time the hiccups stopped.

Knowing her husband was not ready to die, Gertel thanked God his life had been spared.

When Glenda gave birth to a little boy, Gertel insisted she come and stay with them. "I can't help you way over there in Georgeville. If you are here, I can at least cook for you and watch after the girls."

One day after a strenuous struggle to get Ernest bathed and the sheets changed, she lowered her aching old back into a chair and closed her eyes. How much longer could she do this? If only Ernest could stand up on his feet. She determined to ask the Lord for this one special favor. "Please, Lord," she prayed. "I don't care if he can't walk or if I have to help him eat, but please, if he could only stand up by himself, it would make it so much easier. Then he could get out of bed and sit in a chair, and I wouldn't have to lift him. I just can't do this anymore." She got up and wiped her flushed face with a cold washcloth and went back to work.

A few days later Ernest called her. "Bring the walker," he ordered.

Wondering, she brought the walker he had used sometimes before. "I want to try to walk," he said with determination.

She helped him to sit up and positioned the walker in front of him. With her help, he slowly raised himself to his feet and stood there unsteadily.

Then, with white knuckles gripping the handles, he pushed the walker ahead an inch or two and shuffled his feet. Slowly, ever so slowly, he inched across the bedroom to the door.

Gertel, almost holding her breath in amazement, hovered at his elbow. He was actually walking! "Thank you, Lord!" she exulted. "You answered my prayer just when I needed it."

When Sandra came home from a trip, she saw how her mother was wearing herself out trying to meet the invalid's demands. "Ma, I think he could be helping himself more," she said.

A few nights later she had a confrontation with her dad. Gertel was talking on the telephone. Ernest called her from the bedroom. She ignored his summons because the caller was reporting the details of an accident that had involved her aunt. Ernest continued to call for her. His calls became urgent and angry. "Come here. Right now. Come quick," he shouted, banging his cane on the floor.

Sandra hurried to the bedroom door. "What do you want?" she asked, annoyed at his demands.

"I need Ma. Tell her to come."

"She's on the phone. What do you need?"

"I need water to brush my teeth."

Sandra lost her patience. "Get up and get your own water. You can use your walker to walk to the bathroom. You don't need Ma to do everything for you."

As she walked away, he whined, "Nobody thinks about *me!*" but he did get up and make his way to the bathroom and brush his teeth. After that he tried to be a bit more independent.

The Baptist minister from Alvan's church came to visit him. After covering the peripheral topics of weather and politics, the minister asked him point-blank, "Ernest, have you ever accepted Jesus as your personal Savior?"

Caught off guard, Ernest shook his head.

"It is of utmost importance that you do," the minister admonished kindly. "You can't get to heaven just on good works. You need to ask

Jesus to save you."

"I'm a member of the Anglican Church," Ernest responded. "I don't want to switch churches."

The pastor shook his head. "No. I'm not talking about changing your church. You need to accept Jesus as your Savior. Make Him the Lord of your life. It is the blood of Christ that saves you, not the church."

Ernest brushed him off. "I'm not interested in changing churches," he repeated. He drew his closed look over his face and would discuss the issue no further.

Gertel, listening from the kitchen, sighed. She'd become a Christian under the influence of a Nazarene evangelist while she was a member of the Anglican Church, and she had remained an Anglican for many years after that. Why did Ernest remain hung up on the idea that it was all about church membership?

"Please soften his rebellious heart," she prayed as she had so often.

55

Gertel Wagner, JP

Gertel was sorting the mail one day when she spotted an official-looking envelope addressed to her. "Now what?" she wondered. Could it be that Rose was still trying to claim Jenita after all these years?

She scanned the short missive quickly. It asked her to appear at the San Ignacio Hotel on April 9 at 10:00 a.m. to be appointed as justice of the peace.

Gertel's hands dropped and her eyes widened. "What now!" she exclaimed.

"What's wrong?" asked Sandra, coming from the kitchen.

Gertel waved the letter. "They want to make me a justice of the peace."

"You? What? Why?" sputtered Sandra.

"I don't know why!" Gertel sank into a nearby chair and shook her head. "Except that my dad was a JP for many years. But he's gone now. I wonder if this is his doing. He always did push me into doing things I didn't want to do, and he's still at it, even after his death. I sure didn't ask for this. This is something else!"

In spite of her initial misgivings, Gertel talked the matter over with the family and her pastor, and she finally decided to accept the position. She knew that many of her neighbors needed papers signed, and it would be a help if they could do it close to home. Accordingly, she presented herself at the San Ignacio Hotel on April 9. Along with several other citizens, she signed her name and received a book of laws outlining her responsibilities as a justice of the peace.

At home, she rattled off her duties to her assembled family: "I can sign applications for passports, work permits, and social security cards; I can sign land transfers and titles, I can perform marriages . . ."

Glenda hooted. "Perform marriages! Can't you see Ma doing that?"

The whole family laughed heartily at the picture of their comfortable, gray-haired mother officiating at a wedding.

Gertel shook her head vehemently. "I won't marry anyone. No way. I will sign papers for people, but I won't marry anyone or send anyone to jail. Somebody else can do that."

"How much do you get paid to do all this?" asked Benjie.

"Nothing. I am not allowed to charge for my services. It says here that if the government finds out I have charged someone, they will fine me. The job of a JP is a public service. I only did it so I can help people out. If people from here need something signed, I can save them a trip into town."

Over the next years, Gertel did sign passport applications, social security applications, land transfers, and burial certificates. Often people tried to pay her, and for all the time it took her to explain that her services were free, she could just as well have let them pay. However, she stuck to the law. She also stuck to her resolution to never perform a marriage ceremony.

. . . .

When Jenita was ready to go to high school, Ernie and Anna offered to pay her way. "Send her to Belize City," advised Ernie. "There is a good high school there. She could board with some of Pa's family."

Gertel watched Jenita's excited preparations with mixed feelings. Her last fledgling would soon leave the nest. She remembered how William had left home at this age and had never really been a permanent part of the family thereafter. She did wish for Jenita to have the chance to get an education. She knew how long Anna had had to struggle to become a nurse. Jenita had become a Christian, but she was so very young, and there would be many temptations in the city. She wondered if they were doing the right thing to send her away.

As the time drew closer for her to leave, Jenita seemed to be less and less enthusiastic about going.

"Why aren't you packing?" Gertel asked her.

Jenita hung her head. "I don't think I want to go after all," she said in a low voice.

"Oh! Why not?"

"I just don't want to." And she stalked out of the house.

Gertel couldn't figure out what troubled the girl. She had always been headstrong, but something didn't make sense.

Sandra thought she knew. "I think it's Loren."

Loren's grandmother was a member of their church and lived nearby. Loren often spent time at his grandmother's place and attended church with her, though he made no profession of Christianity.

A boy! Gertel had never faced this problem with her other girls at this age. She hardly knew how to handle it.

Gertel confronted Jenita. She admitted it. "Loren says if I go to Belize City, I will forget him. He doesn't want me to go."

"But you are far too young for a boyfriend, and you do want to go to high school, don't you?"

"Yeah, I do," Jenita admitted. "Couldn't I just bus back and forth every day?"

Gertel frowned. "No way! That won't work. It's two hours to Belize City. You can't ride home two hours, do your homework, and then get up early to go again." She shook her head. "You have to choose. Either you stay here and don't do high school, or you move to Belize City and do high school. You can't do both."

Jenita clamped her lips together and left the room. Gertel watched her go. In her heart she knew already what Jenita would choose. The girl had usually gotten her own way.

Gertel was right; Jenita stayed home. Four years later, after a stormy courtship, and against the wishes of her family, she married Loren. She was eighteen years old.

56

Lessons in Trust

As the twentieth century drew to a close, Gertel passed her days quietly and without event. When Ernest was in a good mood, she liked to sit beside him, embroidering or reading a book. Even if he didn't talk much, at least he provided company for her besides Robert. Sometimes she would speak of all the experiences they had lived through together.

At times the house again filled with the laughter of children as the grandchildren added up. William, Alvan, and Michael came regularly with their families to eat from their mother's bottomless pots. "I used to feed strangers all the time, and now I feed my grandchildren," she joked.

Nearly every day one or the other of her daughters would be on the phone. "Ma, what shall I do? Denise stuck a bean up her nose," or, "Ma, Monica has hives. What do you do for hives?" And Gertel would help them out if she could.

Glenda's little Regina acted like a tomboy. "Ma, she comes in dirty half a dozen times a day!" Glenda wailed. "And she tears her clothes up . . ."

"Ha!" Gertel responded with a smug smile. "Do you remember the time you came home from school and you had ripped the skirt half off the waistband of your uniform and tried to pin it together with safety pins?"

They both laughed at the memory.

"Like mother, like daughter," quoted Gertel wisely. "You are just getting back all I had to put up with when you were little."

If one of the mothers was sick, Gertel would say, "Come on over here and I'll take care of you." They would come, bags and babies, and she would minister to them physically and spiritually.

Sandra returned from one of her trips to the States with Anna's son Joshua in tow. Anna was working and had agreed to let Sandra take her two-year-old son back to Belize with her. He lived with Sandra in her house but spent lots of time with his grandparents over the next year.

Ernest's health was deteriorating. He would place his hand over his heart, breathe heavily and say, "It hurts." Gertel would try to arrange pillows to make him more comfortable, but sometimes the pain kept him awake at night.

One night his groaning woke her. "What's wrong, Nesto?" she asked, worried.

He cried out and groaned again. Alarmed, she put a hand on his head. It was burning hot and she could feel his pulse beating violently.

"Pain," he gasped. "Help me!"

She looked around frantically. Robert was the only other person in the house.

"Just hold on, Nesto—I'll call for help," she promised. She ran to the phone and dialed Michael's number. He lived the closest.

"Michael's catching chickens tonight," his wife explained. "What's wrong?"

"Pa is in pain. He needs to get to the hospital. I'll call Alvan."

"No, Alvan is not here," his wife, Joanna, answered.

What am I going to do? thought Gertel. Tears rolled down her face as she tried to plan the next step.

"What's wrong?" asked Joanna. "What is that noise?"

"It's Pa! I have to get him to the hospital."

Gertel knew Paul had to get up early to go to work, but she decided to call him anyway. He came gladly. Together with Ken and his teenage son, they got the suffering man loaded into the truck and transported to Loma Luz Hospital.

Gertel watched, cried, and prayed as the emergency staff worked over Ernest. Her thoughts raged in turmoil. *What will we do now? If he has to stay in the hospital, it is going to cost money, and we don't have any. We already owe them five hundred dollars from the last time he had to be here. And what if he dies? He isn't ready to die. Oh, Lord,* she pleaded, *please give him another chance. And what will become of me if he dies?* She wept tears of helplessness.

"Lord," she cried out. "You just have to help me. I know you will provide for all my needs. I just have to trust you. Help me to wait on you."

As she had suspected, it was his heart. "He's had a heart attack. He needs to stay here in case he has another one. Will someone be able to stay with him?" the doctor asked her.

Over the next few days Gertel scarcely left her husband's side. Restless, he suffered from chest pains. She wet his lips, fed him what food he would take, sang to him, and kept an anxious eye on the monitors that were blinking and beeping beside him. Ernest's sister came from Belmopan, and the children took short shifts staying with him. Gertel became so weary she hardly knew whether she was standing on her feet or on her head. "You need to get some rest, or you'll end up here in another bed," a nurse told her.

One night Alvan persuaded her to go home and get a good sleep in her own bed. "We'll get the nurses to give you some sleeping pills," he suggested, knowing that she would be too worried to sleep much.

"I don't want sleeping pills," she insisted, and reluctantly went home. She was afraid Ernest would die when she wasn't there, just like both of her parents had.

At home she found a full mailbag waiting to be put on the bus, Robert wanting her to cook him some good chicken, and a pile of dirty clothes under the house begging to be washed. How would she keep on?

Again, hot tears pricked her eyelids. "Why, Lord? Why do you ask so much of me?" she sobbed. Then she gulped and repented. "Lord, you have promised that you will help us to bear our burdens. Give me the strength to go on."

Later that evening Anna called from the States. "How is Pa?" she wondered.

"He's not so good. He can hardly sleep. Somebody has to be with him all the time."

"Ma, how are you holding up?"

"I'm all right. Just tired to death. But I'm afraid your dad won't live much longer, and he isn't saved. That weighs on me the most."

"I'm going to come," said Anna decisively. "I'm a nurse. I'll help you take care of him."

"But your children, your job . . ." Anna's husband had left her, and she now had two children to support. She had repented of her hasty marriage and reconciled with her parents.

"I'll just quit my job and bring the children. I'll stay as long as you need me and as long as you'll have me."

Gertel felt herself go limp with relief. "I'd be so glad if you could come, and you can stay however long you want. This is always home for you."

"Give me a few days to get things in order, and then I'll be there."

"Thank you, Lord," Gertel breathed as she hung up the receiver. "You sent the help just when I needed it."

After a long hospital stay, Ernest came home and settled into the hospital bed they installed for him at home. On good days they would help him into a wheelchair so he could sit out on the verandah and watch the world go by. He needed help with everything and often complained of pain. He hardly spoke anymore except to call for help, but they knew he understood all they said to him.

Anna and her two small children moved into Sandra's house, and she insisted that her mother let her take the night shift in nursing. Sandra, who didn't like nursing, said she would rather do the cooking and housekeeping for all of them.

Gertel worried primarily, however, about the need of her husband's soul. He stubbornly refused to listen to any of the people who tried to help him. He didn't listen to the Mennonite minister when he came to visit, or to the Seventh Day Adventist pastor, or to the Holdemans, or to the Baptist preacher. He always insisted, "I don't want to be jumping from church to church." They all tried to tell him it wasn't about church membership, but about receiving Christ as his Savior. Gertel, knowing it would do no good to talk, kept praying and trying to serve him as best she could.

57

The Eleventh Hour

As the year 2002 crawled by, it became evident that Ernest did not have long to live. He had constant pain, and his blood pressure could not be controlled with medication. He could barely speak coherently anymore. Often he called out for help. He would cry for his mother and his sister to help him. Both had been dead for a long time.

"Help me. Let me go," he pleaded with Gertel numerous times.

"I'm not holding you. You can go," she would tell him.

"I think he's worried about what will happen to me if he dies," she told Anna. "I tell him, 'God will take care of me.' I used to worry about what I would do without him, but I know that God will provide. He always has. I just wish your dad could turn to the Lord before he dies. Maybe that is what is holding him here."

Several days later Anna stepped out of the bedroom, her eyes misty. "Ma, I think you should try to talk to him. I think he might listen to you now."

Ernest was tossing restlessly. "Help me, oh, help me!" he pleaded.

She sat down beside him and took his hand. "Ernest, nobody can help you. The only one who can help you is God."

He focused his eyes on her. She had never been so aware of their blue intensity before. "Help me," he repeated, gripping her hand.

She shook her head. "I can't help you. I am trying, but only God can forgive your sins and give you peace."

Her voice grew stern. "Ernest, I am sorry to say this, but you are too stubborn and rebellious. You need to humble yourself and call on God for help."

His restless tossing stilled. His eyes softened as they locked with hers.

"Are you ready to ask God to help you?"

There was a pause, and then the grizzled head nodded.

"Will you turn your life over to Him and ask Him to forgive your sins?"

He nodded again.

There in the darkened bedroom, Gertel prayed the sinner's prayer with her husband of fifty years. He confessed his sins and asked her forgiveness.

She looked into his blue eyes again. "I forgive you for anything you have done to me over the years. There is nothing between us anymore. You are free to go anytime you want. Don't worry about me. God will provide for me. I can let you go in peace now, knowing that you will be with God."

Tears welled up in his eyes. He nodded gratefully. Then he closed his eyes and fell into a peaceful sleep.

The next couple months seemed like a foretaste of heaven for Gertel. She felt as if she were standing at the portal with Ernest. Peaceful now, he did not cry out for help anymore, neither did he demand her attention. That old stubborn pride of his had been broken by the Lamb of God. Her heart filled with gratitude that he had found peace at last. All the memories of his irritable demands on her during his long illness seemed to recede, and she thought of him only as he was now.

He would lie quietly on the bed, his hand often over his heart, but he did not complain. He spoke gently to her and the grandchildren when they tiptoed into the room to greet him. He closed his eyes and listened when they sang to him. Even turning him over in bed was easier, it seemed, because he was relaxed and at peace. Gertel scarcely wanted to leave his side.

Late one night as she sat with him, he motioned for her to turn down the foot end of the bed. She did so. Then he motioned for her to lower the head end. She did that too. "All right?" she asked.

He nodded. He was lying flat on the bed. She noticed that he was sweating. He placed his hand in the familiar position over his heart.

His body shuddered as though in a spasm. She saw him look straight up as though looking through the ceiling. She gently took his hand and placed it down by his side. He did not resist. He turned and looked at her, then closed his eyes and lay quiet.

She continued to hold his hand. *Good,* she thought. *He has gone to sleep.* She sat there for some time in the semi-darkness. Ernest never moved. A glance at the small alarm clock told her it was past midnight. Anna was planning to come and take over at midnight, but Nesto was sleeping so peacefully, she wouldn't bother calling Anna. She needed her sleep too. Gertel dozed in her chair.

"Did Pa call?" Anna appeared at her side. "I thought I heard him call. Oh, he's sleeping." She bent over the still form on the bed.

"Ma," she said softly, "he's gone." Just that peacefully, his spirit had departed.

All of the children came home for their father's funeral. The body was taken to the morgue for a day or two until Ernie could fly home from the States. The morning of the funeral, the boys erected a big tent in the yard, and neighbors and friends came to the wake to pay their last respects to the quiet man who had scattered so many crumbs along the way. The lines of people kept filing by. Gertel was amazed at all the people who stopped to tell her, "I was in need and Ernest helped me . . ." She knew he had been generous, but she never dreamed of all the people his life had touched.

The funeral was held in the big Baptist church in San Ignacio, and the pastor from her church had part in the service. Ernest's body was buried in the community cemetery. Rosie and the other girls took care of arranging the sandwiches for the wake, and the church ladies helped serve the crowd. After the funeral, the family gathered for a chicken barbecue. Gertel felt thankful to have all her children and grandchildren gathered around her at this time. She knew she would miss Ernest, but she rejoiced that his suffering had ended. How her heart thrilled to know that he had repented of his sins and turned to Jesus. She had faith that she would see him again someday. They had been married for fifty years, and Ernest had been unwell for half of them. She couldn't imagine a life without him, but the God who had been with her up until now would still be near—and life would go on.

The Wagner sons after their father's funeral. **Back (L to R):** Alvan, William, Robert, Ernest, Jr. **Front (L to R):** Paul, Michael, Benjie (Andrew).

58

Traveling

Gertel felt lonely after Ernest died. Her married children came often to visit and share a meal with her, but the hours in between dragged. She busied herself in helping the girls by making the school lunches for their children and babysitting for them. She thanked God for Robert's presence. Cooking and washing for him gave her a reason for living. She felt secure with him sleeping in the next bedroom. Sandra lived in her own house just a few feet from her back steps, but she was often gone, helping Rosie or Glenda.

Gertel worried about the unpaid hospital bills and where she was going to get money for groceries. Just when she thought she was at the end of her rope, the deacon would come along with a gift from the church, or one of her children would bring a sack of beans or flour.

A year after Ernest died, Ken and Rosie and their eight children moved to the States. Ken's father had died, and his mother asked him to come home and take over the farm and business. Gertel hated to see them go, but this was another of those things she couldn't control. She allowed the current to sweep her on. By now she knew that life brings many changes with their accompanying joys and sorrows. Sandra went with Ken and Rosie to help them get settled in their new home, and silence settled over the brown house. It still housed the Esperanza Post Office, and she enjoyed sharing a cup of tea and having a chat with the neighbors who stopped by to pick up their mail. She embroidered elaborate designs on sheets to create bedspreads.

Less than a year after they moved, Ken and Rosie returned to Belize to take care of some business, and before they left again, Rosie proposed, "Ma, why don't you come along up with us? We'll buy your ticket. You need to come see where we live."

Gertel had no excuse to not go, and so she flew to the States a second time. Due to weather complications, they spent the night in the Miami airport. Gertel awoke stiff and lightheaded after a night on a hard bench.

She enjoyed seeing Rosie's big farmhouse, her huge garden, and the nicely-fenced fields of Pennsylvania. Rosie's four boys had become young men now, and her girls were growing up.

For some reason, Gertel couldn't shake her tiredness and stiffness, and her lack of appetite kept her from enjoying all the good food served to her. One morning she complained about feeling cold. Ken and Rosie couldn't figure out why she was cold in the midsummer heat. "I guess you're just a Belizean and are used to being hot," concluded Rosie, bringing her a sweater. Still she shivered. She lay on the couch, covered with blankets, but she couldn't get warm. "You must be sick," decided Rosie. A few hours later Gertel started to feel hot and was soon throwing off the layers of blankets. That night she had a fever that left her feeling weak the next day. Her "flu" seemed to be over, however, and in the evening she went along to a social event with Rosie. The next day she was shivering again.

"This acts like malaria," said Ken. "You probably had it before you came. You should be in Belize where you could get treatment for it." After another round of chills and then fever, they were fairly certain she had malaria, but Ken knew it would be difficult to get it diagnosed and treated in the States. So, her visit got cut short, and they sent her home.

Gratefully she climbed the stairs to her own house at the end of the long trip. The stairs seemed especially high to her, and she felt faint by the time she stood in her own living room. Next thing she knew she had passed out on the floor and Sandra and Glenda were hovering anxiously over her. With proper medication, she got over the illness, but she declared she would never go to the States again.

Two years later when Ernie called from Oklahoma inviting her to his wedding, the children felt sure she would want to go.

Gertel shook her head. "No way. I'm not going. Sandra can go and take pictures."

In 2007, Gertel changed her mind about traveling and flew with Sandra to the States. They spent some time with Ken and Rosie in Pennsylvania and then traveled by bus to Arkansas to see their old friends Daniel and Marietta Miller. After a long bus ride of two days and nights, through mountains that reminded Gertel of the Pine Ridge back home, the driver told them, "This is as close as I'm going to Harrison. You'll have to get off here." Harrison, their destination, was still thirty miles away.

Gertel and Sandra almost panicked. Now what were they to do? They were in the middle of who-knows-where, and they had no way to contact the Millers. Gertel wished fervently that she had stayed at home in her own small, safe country where friendly people would help anyone in trouble. The driver, seeing their distress, relented and drove them to the nearest Walmart, where he left them in front of the store. "That's the best I can do," he told them.

While they were standing there, bewildered and frightened, a kind lady took pity on them and offered to drive them to Hillcrest Home, a Mennonite-run nursing home in Harrison. They thanked God for the angel He sent to deliver them. From there, they were able to call Marietta to come get them. There were nice people in the States after all.

They went with the Millers to Tennessee for a Belize reunion and there visited with many people who had served in Esperanza. *Such a huge country, the United States,* Gertel thought, awed and intimidated by the sheer distances they had to travel. One day's bus ride would take a person from one end to the other of her country!

Another bus ride took them to Oklahoma for Ernie's graduation from the Oklahoma Panhandle State University with a bachelor's degree in psychology. He was forty-four years old when he finally attained his goal. Gertel was introduced to his wife along with their two girls and infant son.

Anna, who lived not far away in Kansas, was happy to have them in her home for a while. Here the land spread around them flat and open, with few trees. Gertel marveled at the tumbleweeds piled up along the fences like balls of tangled wire.

"The U.S. sure is a big country," she told Anna.

"You're not even halfway across it," replied Anna with a chuckle. "I used to live in California, and that is clear out on the West Coast."

Gertel shook her head. "Well, Belize is small, but it used to take us almost as long to travel a hundred miles as it takes to go a thousand now. And then if you fly . . ." Her voice trailed off as she thought about how the world was moving too fast for her.

Finally they headed all the way back to Pennsylvania for Rosie's oldest son Sterling's wedding. How the years had flown. She remembered the night she almost had to usher him into the world. Why, that was only yesterday!

At last the time came for Gertel to head back to her quiet house near the jungle. She smiled at the thought. She would feel at home there.

Gertel experiences cold weather in Pennsylvania in 2007.

59

He Always Comes Through

In 2008, William was diagnosed with Hodgkin's disease. He went to Mexico for chemotherapy treatments, but to no avail. Less than a year later, her oldest son died.

Sorrowfully, Gertel filled in the second line of the "Deaths" column in her Bible.

His death was harder on Gertel than Ernest's had been. William was only fifty-five. "Why couldn't it have been me?" she mourned. "There is something unnatural about a child dying before the parent. One generation should pass away first," she brooded. She relived the moment when she had held her firstborn in her arms and recalled how he had left home, a puny adolescent, to go to school in Belize City. Now he was gone and she was still here. She found it hard to trust God's purposes in this.

After William's death, Gertel seemed to lose interest in living. She didn't even feel like cooking anymore. She sat, silent and grieving, on the couch while Sandra cooked. She allowed others do the work for her. She felt too tired. She wanted to go home to heaven.

Rosie lured her mother to Pennsylvania again to celebrate her eightieth birthday. Gertel kept fussing about Robert at home. "I'm afraid he is missing me," she repeated often. Ken and Rosie thought maybe Ma was missing Robert more than he missed her. They took her out to Anna's place in Kansas. The girls had planned that she stay there with Anna for as long as she wanted, but she was so homesick that after a short visit, she flew home again.

When Sandra planned to go to Rosie's again, Paul offered to move his family into Sandra's house in her mother's backyard. "That way Sandra can come and go when she wants, and we will be here for you," he said. "When Gladys and I are at work, the children can be with you." Paul, Jr., Precious, and little Melva ate lunch at Grandma's and came over after school. They felt equally at home in both houses.

Slowly Gertel began to take an interest in living again. Her grandchildren cheered her, and she felt her faith in God growing again. He gave her hope for the future—a future of living her twilight years to the best of her ability.

When the postal service consolidated its small, rural offices into one centralized location in town, Gertel lost her last source of income. "Take the phone too," she told the boys. "I'm tired of its constant jingling. Sandra has a cell phone. If somebody wants to talk to me, they can call on that."

One day an unfamiliar woman appeared at her door. Gertel explained that the post office was no longer open.

"I don't need a post office," the woman said. "My mother is in the hospital in Belmopan, and I need to take her clothes, but I have no money for the bus. I thought maybe you could help . . ." Her voice trailed off as she looked hopefully at Gertel.

"How much do you need?" Gertel wondered sympathetically.

"The bus passage is $3.00."

"Let me see what I have." Gertel went into her bedroom and peered into her change purse. She poured the coins out into her hand. "Oh, dear, I only have $2.75." She returned to the front room. "This is all I have. Will it help?" she asked, handing the change to the stranger.

"This is good. Thank you!" said the lady, her eyes lighting up. "I'll find the other shilling[28] somewhere. Thank you," she repeated as she hurried back down the steps.

Gertel walked to the kitchen. She lifted the lid on her flour bucket. Almost empty. She peeked into the rice bucket. Only a cupful left. Where was she going to get money for groceries? Then, remembering

---

[28] Because of the British influence in Belize, a quarter (25 cents) is always called a shilling.

the many other times she had been in need, she reminded herself, "The Lord will provide."

The next day Paul stopped by with a card from Rosie. A piece of paper fluttered to the floor. "A check!" she exclaimed, examining it. "Enough to keep us going for three weeks. 'Freely ye have received, freely give,'" she quoted. "You see, when you share with others, it comes back to you," she told Paul, who just stood there shaking his head, marveling at her faith. "Now take me to the store," she ordered. "I need to buy rice."

Similar scenes had transpired over the years when Gertel shared what she had with those less fortunate. First it had been her grandmother who taught her to cook for the stranger. Then her husband had cultivated the habit of helping those in need. Sharing her resources had become such a way of life to her that she continued to cast her bread upon the waters even when she had only crumbs to share. And she never went hungry. God always gave back to her, providing for her needs and even filling her cup until it overflowed.

As they climbed into the car to go to the store, Gertel gave her son a pointed look with a satisfied gleam in her eyes. "Back in those years when your pa was sick and I was so tired and the hospital bills came rolling in, I would wake up every morning and ask God for grace and strength to get through another day," she reflected. "And He always gave me what I needed. I still ask Him for help every day, and you know what? He always comes through."

Epilogue

Today the grandchildren like to visit the little brown house. They climb the stairs, greet their grandma, and then head straight for the kitchen to see what's in the pot. They know there is always good food at Granny's house.

I sit with Gertel and several of her grandchildren, listening to her reminisce about the old days. "When I was young," she begins, "we just ate good, wholesome food, and we worked hard to raise it, and we weren't sick. Now you have all this junk food and all kinds of fancy health foods, and everybody is sick. I get so hungry for things like sweat rice. I guess you don't even know what sweat rice is, do you?" She arches her brows and looks around the circle of children. They shake their heads.

"What is sweat rice, Granny?"

She squints her eyes half shut and folds her hands in her lap. "Well, we grew our own rice, you know. When it was time to harvest it, we took a machete, grabbed hold of as many stalks as we could hold in one hand, cut them off at the bottom, and laid them on a tarp to beat out later. There were always some heads that dropped off. We'd gather those up and throw them in a drum. When the drum was full, we built a fire, put just a little bit of water in the bottom of the drum with the rice, and set it to steam. As it heated, or 'sweated,' the kernels would pop open a bit. After that we spread that rice out in the sun to dry, and then we pounded it in the mortar. That was hard work."

She lifts her arms above her head, her hands clasped around an imaginary mortar, and brings them down to show how they used to beat the hulls off the rice. "Then we would cook that rice just like you cook ordinary rice, and we'd add some fresh okra and maybe a strip of the dried, smoked pork we had hanging above the fire hearth. My, that was good. I wish I could taste some sweat rice again, but nobody makes it now.

"And when we harvested the sugar cane . . . now that was *hard* work, chopping down those tough stalks of cane. We took it to a neighbor man who had a press that squeezed out the juice. Then he'd boil that juice down into syrup. While it was cooking, we'd take dry pumpkins from the field—those hard-shelled ones, you know, and bore holes into them and throw them into the cooking juice. My, that was a sweet treat when it was done."

Granny Gertel also administers what they call "advices."

"When I was young," she says, wagging her finger at them, "children were not allowed to speak unless spoken to. Nowadays the children are so rude. They interrupt their parents and even sass them. Be sure you have respect for your elders. And you see how your uncles dress? You would never see your grandpa without a shirt. I scold the boys, but they say I am just old-fashioned. Well, I guess I am old-fashioned, but I have an old-fashioned God, and there was a lot less crime in the world

The grandchildren love to be with Granny Gertel and listen to her stories and "advices."

when I was young. Why, we used to walk about in the city after dark. You wouldn't want to walk about in Belize City after dark these days. And always cook for the stranger," she adds. "You never know when it will come back to you."

Miss Gertie, as everyone calls her now, looks at her surroundings with contentment. She still lives in the house that Ernest built more than fifty years ago. She points out that the original siding has never needed replacement, and when the boys replaced the roof a few years ago, the rafters underneath were still sound. "He built well," she says fondly of her husband.

Out in the kitchen Sandra is seasoning chicken, sorting rice, and grating cabbage. For so many years Miss Gertie worked and served her family and friends, and now that they are taking care of her, she can't get used to it. Still, she is grateful for their help. Her eyes get tired when she reads too long, and her fingers don't want to hold the needle steady enough to embroider.

We walk out onto the small concrete porch that has replaced the old wooden one. She stands with her hands clasped behind her back like a trussed iguana, watching the traffic whiz by. *Be-e-e-ep!* A big truck blares its air horn as it roars past. She waves. "That's Benjie. Both he and Michael drive rigs, sometimes all the way to the States and back."

She frowns at the old pickup truck and the piles of car parts that decorate the front yard below the porch. Sighing, she says, "I used to have flowers out here. I loved flowers. But now nothing will grow. For years Paul changed oil and did his mechanic work right here, and now the ground is poisoned."

Robert is still with her. She is grateful that the Lord gave her Robert. He is always there. He goes everywhere she goes. He rides along to church, where he still pages through his Bible and helps to sing. He putters around the yard, moving things and cleaning up leaves and casting suspicious glances at any newcomers. He lies in the hammock under the house and sings and talks to himself in his own language. He still comes when she calls, and listens to her. Even though he is limited, she feels safer knowing Robert is in the house at night.

Sandra lives with her when she is not visiting Rosie or Anna in the States. She keeps house for her mother and Robert, and she makes meals for Paul's children.

Gertel's youngest grandchild, Paul's little Melva Gertel, likes to climb the stairs to Granny's house, her white rabbit slung over one chubby shoulder. She takes the rabbit into Granny's bedroom and shakes powder over him. She then adds a dab of perfume while the rabbit wriggles in protest. "Isn't she something else?" Gertel says with a fond shake of her head.

Even though her house is often empty and her days are long, Miss Gertie is still casting her bread upon the waters. She always extends a welcome and shares her food. No matter who enters her house, each one comes away feeling cheered by the smile of an elderly lady, as well as being challenged by her faith.

About the Author

From the time she learned to read books, Elizabeth Cressman Wagler wanted to write books. Now, sixty years later, she has authored ten books and many short stories that have appeared in print.

Born and raised in southern Ontario, Elizabeth taught school for several years; then she and her husband Glen moved west. They helped to plant churches in British Columbia and Saskatchewan while raising a family of six children.

The Waglers have fond memories of spending ten years in a Maya Indian village in Belize. Here they made close friends and adapted to a new culture. After leaving Belize, they retired to a rural area in Manitoba where Elizabeth enjoys making quilts and interacting with their twenty-one grandchildren.

Elizabeth enjoys hearing from her readers and can be contacted at glelwagler@hotmail.com or written to in care of Christian Aid Ministries, P.O. Box 360, Berlin, Ohio 44610.

Christian Aid Ministries

C hristian Aid Ministries was founded in 1981 as a nonprofit, tax-exempt 501(c)(3) organization. Its primary purpose is to provide a trustworthy and efficient channel for Amish, Mennonite, and other conservative Anabaptist groups and individuals to minister to physical and spiritual needs around the world. This is in response to the command to ". . . do good unto all men, especially unto them who are of the household of faith" (Galatians 6:10).

Each year, CAM supporters provide approximately 15 million pounds of food, clothing, medicines, seeds, Bibles, Bible story books, and other Christian literature for needy people. Most of the aid goes to orphans and Christian families. Supporters' funds also help to clean up and rebuild for natural disaster victims, put up Gospel billboards in the U.S., support several church-planting efforts, operate two medical clinics, and provide resources for needy families to make their own living. CAM's main purposes for providing aid are to help and encourage God's people and bring the Gospel to a lost and dying world.

CAM has staff, warehouses, and distribution networks in Romania, Moldova, Ukraine, Haiti, Nicaragua, Liberia, Israel, and Kenya. Aside from management, supervisory personnel, and bookkeeping operations, volunteers do most of the work at CAM locations. Each year, volunteers at our warehouses, field bases, Disaster Response Services projects, and other locations donate over 200,000 hours of work.

CAM's ultimate purpose is to glorify God and help enlarge His kingdom. ". . . whatsoever ye do, do all to the glory of God" (1 Corinthians 10:31).

The Way to God and Peace

We live in a world contaminated by sin. Sin is anything that goes against God's holy standards. When we do not follow the guidelines that God our Creator gave us, we are guilty of sin. Sin separates us from God, the source of life.

Since the time when the first man and woman, Adam and Eve, sinned in the Garden of Eden, sin has been universal. The Bible says that we all have "sinned and come short of the glory of God" (Romans 3:23). It also says that the natural consequence for that sin is eternal death, or punishment in an eternal hell: "Then when lust hath conceived, it bringeth forth sin: and sin, when it is finished, bringeth forth death" (James 1:15).

But we do not have to suffer eternal death in hell. God provided forgiveness for our sins through the death of His only Son, Jesus Christ. Because Jesus was perfect and without sin, He could die in our place. "For God so loved the world that he gave his only begotten Son, that whosoever believeth in him should not perish, but have everlasting life" (John 3:16).

A sacrifice is something given to benefit someone else. It costs the giver greatly. Jesus was God's sacrifice. Jesus' death takes away the penalty of sin for everyone who accepts this sacrifice and truly repents of their sins. To repent of sins means to be truly sorry for and turn away from the things we have done that have violated God's standards (Acts 2:38; 3:19).

Jesus died, but He did not remain dead. After three days, God's Spirit miraculously raised Him to life again. God's Spirit does something similar in us. When we receive Jesus as our sacrifice and repent of our sins, our hearts are changed. We become spiritually alive! We develop new desires and attitudes (2 Corinthians 5:17). We begin to make choices that please God (1 John 3:9). If we do fail and commit sins, we can ask God for forgiveness. "If we confess our sins, he is faithful and just to forgive us our sins, and to cleanse us from all unrighteousness" (1 John 1:9).

Once our hearts have been changed, we want to continue growing spiritually. We will be happy to let Jesus be the Master of our lives and will want to become more like Him. To do this, we must meditate on God's Word and commune with God in prayer. We will testify to others of this change by being baptized and sharing the good news of God's victory over sin and death. Fellowship with a faithful group of believers will strengthen our walk with God (1 John 1:7).